JOHN DIEFENBAKER: A FREEDOM FIGHTER

John Diefenbaker's critics say he was a paranoid, antiquated, madman. Progressive Conservative Party powerbrokers looked down on the Prairie populist even though he won three elections.

Folklore created by his opponents in the media, across the aisle, and even in the White House, led to the myth that Diefenbaker caved to American pressure to cancel the technically superior Avro Arrow fighter jet. Then he was pilloried for criticizing the American administration during the Cuban missile crisis. Some of Diefenbaker's own cabinet ministers called him a danger to national security.

Yet, the evidence reveals that Diefenbaker's decisions as prime minister were wise, prescient, and have endured. He was often out of step with Canadian elites but was rarely disconnected from the people or on the wrong side of history.

Diefenbaker instinctively took the side of the underdog. He fought for Canadian values. He advanced the cause of liberty and freedom by opposing all forms of discrimination and by resisting government overreach into the lives of everyday Canadians. The record shows that Diefenbaker sided with Indigenous Canadians more so than any prime minister. He also overcame early setbacks to pursue his vision of a Canada without systemic discrimination or hyphenated identities.

In this meticulous, evidence-based, and compelling sweep of John Diefenbaker's life and legacy, bestselling author Bob Plamondon reveals that Canada's thirteenth prime minister is underrated by historians and deserves to be followed and recognized as one of our greatest leaders.

John Diefenbaker was Canada's freedom fighter.

ABOUT THE AUTHOR

Bob Plamondon is the author of five critically acclaimed books about Canada and its history: *The Shawinigan Fox: How Jean Chrétien Defied the Elites and Reshaped Canada, The Truth about Trudeau, Blue Thunder: The Truth about Conservatives from Macdonald to Harper, Full Circle: Death and Resurrection in Canadian Conservative Politics,* and *Hay West: A Story of Canadians Helping Canadians.* A *Globe and Mail* bestselling author and frequent columnist, Bob has been associated with three Canadian universities and has enjoyed a career in public policy, finance, and governance.

www.bobplamondon.com

FOR A BETTER CANADA

Published by The Aristotle Foundation for Public Policy.

ISBN (hardcover): 978-1-7775432-9-7
ISBN (softcover): 978-1-0692545-0-4
ISBN (audiobook): 978-1-0692545-2-8
ISBN (e-book): 978-1-0692545-1-1

Book design and cover design by Milan Szabo.
Cover image: Library and Archives Canada
Photos in book: JFK Archives, University of Saskatchewan, Tourism Saskatchewan

Printed in Canada.
Book distribution by Sandhill Book Marketing.
www.sandhillbooks.com

FREEDOM FIGHTER

JOHN DIEFENBAKER'S BATTLE FOR CANADIAN LIBERTIES AND INDEPENDENCE

BOB PLAMONDON

FOREWORD BY THE RIGHT HONOURABLE JEAN CHRÉTIEN

"I am a Canadian, a free Canadian, free to speak without fear, free to worship God in my own way, free to stand for what I think right, free to oppose what I believe wrong, free to choose those who shall govern my country. This heritage of freedom I pledge to uphold for myself, and all mankind."

"Some say to me: 'History—What's it mean? What are you concerned about the past for?' And my answer is a simple one—he who does not know the past can never understand the present, and he certainly can do nothing for the future."

The Right Honourable John G. Diefenbaker, P.C.
The 13th Prime Minister of Canada

FREEDOM FIGHTER

CONTENTS

THE FINAL ACT

FOREWORD BY THE RIGHT HONOURABLE JEAN CHRÉTIEN

I was a political opponent of John Diefenbaker but never an enemy. Though we had our differences, we shared much in common, particularly our optimism about Canada.

We were both small-town lawyers with a deep connection to ordinary Canadians. That may be why we were often underestimated and certainly not highly regarded by those on Bay Street or within establishment circles. Neither of us subscribed to groupthink. At our core, we were common-sense politicians who trusted the judgment of the people.

Although Diefenbaker was a Conservative and I am a Liberal, the record shows he ran deficits while I ran surpluses. As party leaders, we both won three elections. His two minority governments and one majority gave him nearly six years in the prime minister's chair, while my three majority governments gave me a decade in office.

I was first elected in 1963, so I never witnessed Diefenbaker as prime minister. However, I came to know him during our 16 years together in the House of Commons, until his passing in 1979.

He was a great performer in Parliament and a fierce competitor, unafraid to strike his opponents below the belt. His dramatic courtroom style, honed in western Canada, and his outsider sensibilities could be as irritating as they were effective. He knew how to land a punch.

Diefenbaker was a man of strong convictions, and we had sharp disagreements on many issues. His attachment to tradition and the Commonwealth led him to resist adopting a Canadian flag. He predicted that Canadians would never accept the new flag, but I'm glad we persisted as a government and established a symbol that continues to inspire pride.

Despite our differences, I often spoke with Diefenbaker about Canada on the floor of the House of Commons. We shared political stories and the occasional joke, which we both enjoyed.

John Diefenbaker was undeniably a proud and passionate Canadian. He devoted his life to public service and inspired others to do the same. I hope his memory will continue to encourage others to serve their country, which is why I am happy his story is being told.

– Jean Chrétien, Ottawa, December 2024

PREFACE

John George Diefenbaker was eight or nine years old when he told his mother he would become the prime minister of Canada. He had an inauspicious start, losing five municipal, provincial, and federal elections between 1925 and 1938. In 1940, he was elected the federal Member of Parliament for Lake Centre, Sask., by 280 votes. Two years later, he unsuccessfully sought the leadership of the Progressive Conservative Party. He tried again when the leadership came open in 1948. In neither contest was Diefenbaker taken seriously.

When he announced his candidacy for leadership the next time the position was up for grabs in 1956, the power brokers in the party orchestrated a "Stop Diefenbaker" campaign. The premier of Ontario, Leslie Frost, remarked, "Sometimes I really do think he's crazy." Party organizer Eddie Goodman responded, "Why only sometimes?"

But the party's grassroots members wanted to give the prairie populist a shot. Those close to the retiring Conservative leader were heard to say, "If Diefenbaker wants it, let the crazy son of a bitch have it. People want John Diefenbaker, and there is no use kicking against the pricks." They thought he would be a provisional leader. "Diefenbaker has been around for a long time, so let him have it. The Grits will win the next election anyway." Unlike the top Tory brass, the Liberals were rooting for Diefenbaker to win the leadership, someone they regarded as indecisive, temperamental, and a lone wolf who had passed his peak.

On his third attempt, Diefenbaker decisively won the leadership on the first ballot. Despite this show of dominance, he remained an outsider to the elites in the party. Dalton Camp, a future party president, thought Diefenbaker was nothing if not persistent: "No Canadian politician before him ever rose so steadily through a succession of humiliations."

In his first national election as leader in 1957, Diefenbaker defied all expectations and won a minority government with 112 out of 265 seats, 21 short of a majority, which nine months later he converted into a massive majority, holding 208 seats or 78 percent of the seats in Parliament. That 1958 landslide remains the most dominant feat in Canadian federal politics. Diefenbaker held power with a narrow minority government in 1962 and was defeated in 1963. He held the Liberals to a minority government in 1965 and remained leader of the Progressive Conservative Party until September 9, 1967.

Before Diefenbaker took the helm, Conservatives had managed three victories over the previous 15 elections, one under a coalition of Conservative and Liberal members during the First World War brought together to implement conscription. Ending a 22-year drought and returning the Tories to power with three consecutive wins should have made Diefenbaker a hero in his party. But his leadership did not end well.

For much of the past 50 years, history has been unkind to John Diefenbaker. The predominant narrative came from author Peter C. Newman's book *Renegade in Power: The Diefenbaker Years.* To Newman, "Diefenbaker gave the people a leadership cult, without the leadership... he had not the least inkling of what he wanted to do when he achieved high office... a self-charmed politician (who) foundered because he couldn't help believing his own legend."

A more balanced assessment of Diefenbaker was authored in 1995 by academic Denis Smith. In *Rogue Tory,* Diefenbaker is shown to be complex but not without purpose or accomplishment. Still, Smith wrote Diefenbaker had given Canada a "decade of continuous convulsion... a man who was out of time and place in late twentieth-century Ottawa."

In 2014, columnist and Carleton University professor Andrew Cohen railed at the renaming of a government building in Diefenbaker's honour, claiming, "More than a half-century after his defeat in 1963, historians find him a failed prime minister—a blowhard, fantasist and paranoiac." Historian Jack Granatstein observed that Diefenbaker was "venomous, self-serving and notoriously unreliable."

A 2023 book by journalist John Ibbitson, *The Duel: Diefenbaker, Pearson, and the Making of Modern Canada,* concluded that Diefenbaker had been underrated and had set in motion many of the achievements credited to his successor, Lester B. Pearson. Ibbitson also observed that Diefenbaker's conduct was baffling, replete with suspicion and vendettas.

Among the storylines repeated over the past five decades was that Diefenbaker had caved to American pressure to cancel the technically superior Avro Arrow fighter jet. He was pilloried for not immediately falling in line with U.S. President John F. Kennedy during the Cuban missile crisis. Diefenbaker's ministers called him a danger to national security after he hesitated to accept American-controlled nuclear weapons on Canadian soil at the height of the Cold War. It was Diefenbaker, we are led to believe, who led a profligate administration that caused the Canadian dollar to implode and who recklessly terminated the governor of the Bank of Canada. Of Diefenbaker's proudest achievements, the Canadian Bill of Rights, his critics scoff that it was not worth the paper it was written on.

Unsurprisingly, when *Maclean's* ranked Canadian prime ministers in 2016, Diefenbaker ranked 11th out of 13 long-serving prime ministers. A 2003 panel of 28 eminent Canadians assembled by the Institute for Research on Public Policy to rank our prime ministers over the previous 50 years placed Diefenbaker only ahead of Joe Clark, John Turner, and Kim Campbell. These three placeholder prime ministers served a combined 484 days in office, while Diefenbaker served in the role for 2,129 days.

Diefenbaker deserves a fresh look, not just for his accomplishments and failures but for what his legacy teaches us about Canada. This book concludes that Diefenbaker was ahead of his time and stood for timeless principles. While under constant attack, his decisions and the causes he championed that earned him ridicule within his party and the business establishment have mostly been proven wise and prescient. He was often out of step with his party and the elites but was rarely disconnected from the Canadian people.

Beyond the battles he confronted from within his ranks and the parties opposite, Diefenbaker faced a hostile media that openly signalled its intent to defeat his government. Then, there was the most blatant electoral interference ever undertaken by a foreign government in Canadian history. Many historians and political observers have called Diefenbaker paranoid, but the evidence is overwhelming that President Kennedy overtly and covertly plotted his defeat using all means at his disposal.

The principles and values that guided Diefenbaker are as instructive to Canada today as they were 100 years ago when he first ran for elected office. Diefenbaker took the side of the underdog and sought to improve the lives of the impoverished. He fought for Canadian independence to counter the power of American interests and influence. He advanced the cause of liberty and freedom of individuals. He opposed all forms of discrimination and resisted government overreach into the lives of everyday Canadians. He was not impressed by corporate interests, and he established institutions that strengthened the nation and protected the well-being of the common person. The record shows that Diefenbaker was on the side of Indigenous Canadians more so than any prime minister.

Diefenbaker was a nation-builder more than he was the leader of a political party or the head of cabinet. He came to Parliament with a vision and a purpose borne of a youth characterized by poverty and hardship forged over a life marked by the discrimination that came with having a Germanic surname. His innate sense of justice was sustained by a legal career of defending the wrongly accused, the scapegoated or those facing excessive punishment. He endured in politics and overcame a succession of defeats because he believed he had a destiny to fulfill.

He understood the ordinary man and put equality above all else. His political blind spot was Quebec, and he failed to understand the anxieties felt by those who believed the French language was under threat in North America. While it was common to refer to French Canadians and English Canadians, Diefenbaker believed there were only Canadians. He opposed any form of hyphenated Canadian identity.

Diefenbaker was not without contradictions, but his intent was always evident. And he had a command of language as evidenced by this quote that defines his legacy:

> I am a Canadian, a free Canadian, free to speak without fear, free to worship God in my own way, free to stand for what I think right, free to oppose what I believe wrong, free to choose those who shall govern my country. This heritage of freedom I pledge to uphold for myself and all mankind.

Diefenbaker was Canada's ultimate freedom fighter, seeking liberty and equality for all Canadians. His vision was for an independent Canada built on its traditions, free of discrimination, resolved to do what was just in its time.

– Bob Plamondon, Ottawa, January 2025

THE EARLY YEARS

- 1 -

A MAN OF DESTINY

From my earliest boyhood, I was given to romanticization of the future in which I would be able to do something for my country.

Prairie legend John George Diefenbaker was born on September 18, 1895, in Neustadt, a small Ontario village about 170 kilometres northwest of Toronto. In the summer of 1903, the family moved west and settled in Saskatoon after living in several remote communities. Diefenbaker's father, William, shortened the original family name to sound less German. Nonetheless, John Diefenbaker wore his heritage on his heart and sleeve, taking pride in being the only prime minister with a surname of neither English nor French origin. He colourfully referred to his ancestors as an odd lot of "dispossessed Scottish Highlanders and discontented Palatine Germans."[1]

In the first of his three-volume autobiography (released in consecutive years beginning in 1975), Diefenbaker described his parents as "New Testament people." His father was a teacher in a one-room schoolhouse where Diefenbaker recalls posters on the walls warning of the dangers of consuming alcohol and tobacco. The warning had the intended impact, as Diefenbaker rarely consumed either over the course of his life. Also, the shepherd's compassion was evident: When hunting with his dad, he would later admit that neither son nor father could pull the trigger when a deer was in sight. Gophers were another matter. A decent man to the end, the inscription on William Diefenbaker's tombstone in Saskatoon, Saskatchewan, reads, "He found happiness for himself in bringing happiness to others."

"I was eight or nine years old," Diefenbaker wrote in his memoirs, "when I said to my mother, 'Someday I am going to be prime minister.'"[2] While she preferred that her son become a minister of the gospel, Mary Florence Diefenbaker took her son's ambition seriously. And it was not just ambition and ego that drove him forward. "From my earliest boyhood, I was given to romanticization of the future in which I would be able to do something for my country."[3] Not surprisingly, his childhood heroes were politicians: Conservative Sir John A. Macdonald and Liberal Sir Wilfrid Laurier.

According to his secondary school teachers, Diefenbaker was not a model student. He admitted to being irritating: "I spent more time than necessary seeking clarification of theories enunciated in class. I was reluctant to accept unchallenged what I was told and always wanted to follow propositions through to their logical conclusion."[4] Accepting at face value the views of those in authority did not change over his lifetime.

Diefenbaker was 15 years old when he first encountered a federal politician. He often told the story of selling newspapers at the Saskatoon train station when Prime Minister Wilfrid Laurier breezed through: "I sold him a newspaper. He gave me a quarter—no better way to establish an instant rapport with a newsboy. We chatted about Canada. I had the odd feeling that I was in the presence of greatness. That afternoon, when he laid the cornerstone (at the University of Saskatchewan), he included in his remarks a reference to his conversation with a Saskatoon newsboy, which, he observed, had ended with my saying, 'Sorry Prime Minister, I can't waste any more time on you. I've got work to do.'"

Diefenbaker ran a robust newspaper-selling business in his teens and employed a handful of underlings. He was leading distributor for the *Winnipeg Telegram* and The *Calgary Eye-Opener* and became an honorary member of the *Newsboys' Association of America*. Diefenbaker was also a political animal during his teen years. "Elections gave rise to bitter controversy, even between normally friendly neighbours," he recalled. "But those meetings provided unrivalled public entertainment. I never missed one. The fact that I was too young to understand all of the issues in no way diminished my enthusiasm as I viewed the proceedings from my front-row seat."[5]

Despite his father's Liberal inclinations and admiration of Sir Wilfrid Laurier, Diefenbaker was only sixteen when he first identified as a Conservative:

> The [1911] election had a profound influence on me and perhaps, more than anything else, made me a Conservative. I attended all the meetings in Saskatoon... we cleaved to our British heritage in defiance of American manifest destiny and Grit continentalism. The result was a tremendous revelation of Canadian determination to be Canadian. This impressed me greatly.[6]

There was sadness in his household that Sir Wilfrid Laurier lost the 1911 election, which was fought over the issue of free trade with the United States. Diefenbaker's father regarded Laurier as a nation-builder and statesman. However, Diefenbaker would not support a leader or party who he thought would throw Canada deeper into the American vortex. Inspired by his idol, Sir John A. Macdonald, who revered Canada's connection with the monarchy and the parliamentary system, Diefenbaker believed reciprocity would lead to an economic union between Canada and the United States, followed by political absorption. The statement by U.S. Speaker of the House of Representatives, Champ Clark, in 1911 that he hoped to see the American flag fly over every square foot of the British North American Colonies clear to the North Pole served as an ominous and enduring warning to the young Diefenbaker.

When questioned in 1925 about his family's Liberal connections and his admiration of Laurier while a teen, Diefenbaker replied, "Well, as I get older, I see the indiscretions of my youth." In 1969, when no longer the leader of his party, he reflected on his choice of political party that he had made at such a young age: "I chose it because of certain basic principles... the Empire relationship of the time, the monarchy, and the preservation of an independent Canada. None of these things I thought the Liberal party could support."

In 1912, he became leader of the University of Saskatchewan student Conservative party and Leader of the Opposition in a mock Parliament. The university magazine's summary of the event prophesized that Diefenbaker would hold the actual role by 1955.[7] This prediction was off by only one year.

In his youth, Diefenbaker was a nervous and reluctant public speaker, which he overcame with training, practice, and persistence. He learned the art of salesmanship in the summer of 1915, setting records by selling a series of Christian books in small towns across Saskatchewan under the title *The Chosen Word*. The books covered Bible lessons, a layman's law book, and an introduction to the First World War. The ambitious and hard-working Diefenbaker travelled the province by bicycle to earn his 40 percent commission. One setback was getting arrested in Hankley, Saskatchewan, for selling goods without a license. His bicycle was confiscated but returned when his employer furnished the certification. He was also detained in Outlook, Saskatchewan, on suspicion of vagrancy. These incidents may have contributed to Diefenbaker's suspicions of authority figures impinging on individual liberty without proper cause.

Most of his customers were farmers, the backbone of the Saskatchewan economy and way of life. Diefenbaker believed that farmers were exploited and abused by commodity brokers and the moneyed establishment who never broke a sweat. When the grain was delivered, the grading agent would declare it damp or inferior, leaving the farmer with little choice but to accept the verdict and a lower price for the harvest. He concluded that while there were many grain elevators, there was no competition.

> I have never forgotten this exploitation of the Western farmer, the pioneer, by the great grain interests.... While the lords of opulence lived in Winnipeg, the farmers were subjected to practices that soured their thinking and seared their souls.... I would be about thirteen, old enough to be expected to do a man's work. I got up (at a meeting of farmers) and said, 'This thing is wrong. Someday, I'm going to do my part to put an end to this.'[8]

Later in his political career, he established programs to support farmers and advocated that executives convicted of combining to restrain trade should be jailed rather than fined.[9]

Always attuned to injustice, Diefenbaker never hesitated to challenge his teachers and professors, but he also came to their defence when authorities treated them harshly. During his post-secondary studies at the University of Saskatchewan, he protested the firing of four professors and spoke of publicly burning his diplomas to demonstrate his contempt that they were dismissed simply for expressing views on the university president that were not appreciated.[10] His political science instructors inspired him, and he remembered what they told him about human nature: that people could never be made good by legislation and that the law is what the community ordains it should be.

Diefenbaker followed in his father's footsteps and, while attending university, taught summer school for grades one to five. One misfortune was that Diefenbaker was in the schoolyard with a rifle, shooting gophers, when the school inspector made a surprise visit. "Gopher shooting wasn't on the curriculum that year and that was the last time I had a license to teach school."[11] Later in life, Diefenbaker retold the story for humour and to better relate to his audience.

In March 1916, before finishing his academic studies at the age of 20, Diefenbaker enrolled in the military, receiving a commission on May 16 as a lieutenant in the Infantry of the Active Militia. Later that summer, he completed his studies and began writing law articles in the Saskatoon office of Russell Hartney. He resumed his military career on August 25, 1916 and volunteered for overseas service. He was sent to Winnipeg for officer training but was dismayed that commissions were handed out based on political and personal friendships. After being deployed, Diefenbaker got his first sight of Europe. While in London, he frequently visited the British Parliament and saw then-prime minister Lloyd George in action, taking note of his emotions, gestures, and the glare of his eyes.[12]

The reality of his circumstances was never far from Diefenbaker's mind. He could hear the echoes of artillery bombing from his camp, and his commanders would warn: "Do you realize that sixty-five percent of you will be pushing up daisies within three months?" His fellow officers and friends would be by Diefenbaker's side one day and appear on the casualty list a few days later. Nonetheless, Lt Diefenbaker wrote that he enjoyed army life even when it meant digging trenches during training. It was there that he was struck with a heavy entrenching tool and suffered a deep gash. He said he resisted informing his superiors, fearing it would delay his call to go to the front lines with his friends. But in the ensuing days, he was bleeding from the mouth and was hospitalized. As he was declared unfit for further duty, Diefenbaker's injury led to him being sent home just five months after he arrived in Europe.

Diefenbaker and some of his biographers are at odds over the nature and extent of the medical condition that ended his military service. Peter C. Newman wrote that the details of his military service were obscure. Biographer Denis Smith dug into the military records and noted that Diefenbaker's diary contradicts the contention that he suffered a momentous physical injury during a training exercise. After the date Diefenbaker claims to have suffered the blow, there was a mixture of social events and military activities on his calendar, all of which occurred before being hospitalized and discharged. To Smith, "It was [Diefenbaker's] first great test as a man and, according to all conventional standards of the time, he had failed."[13]

If he had embellished his injury, it was odd that once back in Canada, Diefenbaker secured a doctor's certificate attesting to his fitness to serve so he could reapply for military service. His application was rejected. It remains unresolved whether the cause of his return to Canada was of a psychosomatic origin or a physical injury.

- 2 -

AN EARLY CALLING: THE PRACTICE OF LAW

No man who sought my services would, through his poverty, suffer in prison of grave injustice.

Diefenbaker was precocious and ambitious—as already noted, informing his mother of high ambitions for the highest office in the land while still a lad. Similarly, only a few years later, at the age of 12, he decided to become a lawyer. "[I was] impressed by the lives of those who, in the practice of law, stood for the liberties of the individual and the assurance that no one, however poor, should be denied justice." John Diefenbaker's journey into the legal world was not merely a professional pursuit but a passionate odyssey filled with trials, triumphs, and unwavering dedication to clients who had suffered under a legal system he believed was stacked against them. His passion for politics also meshed well with an interest in the law.

Diefenbaker appreciated that the practice of law was more art than science and already connected it in his mind and spirit to the longstanding development of the law in England over the centuries. "Canadian law, like English law, is a living thing... a reflection of a free people in the civil conduct of its business... and the greatest single guarantee of individual liberty for Canadians," he observed years later.[1] To that end, his earliest formal training for his dual career in politics and law was a public speaking course taken after hours in high school. "I always had an ambition to be able to speak in public, but my diffidence and nervousness were hard to overcome," Diefenbaker remembered.[2]

The topics he chose for his five-minute speeches were great figures of history. He chose the 18th-century philosopher and British parliamentarian Edmund Burke, the 19th-century British prime minister Benjamin Disraeli, and the expatriate Scot and first Canadian prime minister, Sir John A. Macdonald. Diefenbaker was bathed in the presumptions and assumptions of 19th and early

20th century British classical liberalism, writing and speaking of the various touchstones of English-inspired landmarks of freedom, such as the Magna Carta (1215), The Petition of Right (1628), and the Habeas Corpus Act (1679).

Protecting ordinary people from the abuse and arbitrary use of power by figures of authority deeply resonated with Diefenbaker. The Magna Carta provided access to swift and impartial justice with particular protections for the church and barons from illegal imprisonment. The Petition of Right stipulated no taxation without the consent of Parliament, no imprisonment without cause, no quartering of soldiers on subjects, and no martial law in peacetime. The Habeas Corpus Act was passed to prevent unlawful or arbitrary imprisonment.

During his high school years, Diefenbaker sat in the back of the High Court in Saskatchewan, noting the speaking styles and strategies of various litigators.[3] When it was his opportunity to "perform" in the courtroom—as he did with flair—he noted how his early research led him to become a composite of the most effective litigators he had observed. Enthralled though young John was with the law, his parents were not advocates of his chosen profession. Instead, they cautioned their son that law and justice were not synonymous, as the poor were often denied a fair shake in the system. "Instead of discouraging me, these observations aroused in me a determination that when I became a lawyer, no man who sought my services would, through his poverty, suffer in prison of grave injustice," he wrote in his memoirs.[4]

A good example of his early commitment to battling for those with no voice or who might have been wrongly convicted comes from his position on capital punishment. Though not a popular opinion at the time, Diefenbaker opposed the death penalty and felt compelled to defend anyone accused of a capital crime where the hangman's noose awaited those convicted. His view was that the death penalty was antiquated because it carried the risk of being imposed on the innocent. "However difficult the case, I would make myself available to act for the accused in a capital case if my services were requested." While prime minister, his cabinet carefully reviewed each case, and the number of executions was never more than three in any year, fewer than in previous governments. This was despite the fact that nearly 100 death sentences were handed down between 1957 and 1963, the years when Diefenbaker was prime minister.[5] The last execution in Canada took place in 1962.

In the 1910s, becoming a practising lawyer required modest academic and apprenticeship training. Diefenbaker took a few legal courses at undergraduate and graduate schools, five months at law school, and articled for less than a year. When he sat for the bar exam in 1919 in Saskatchewan, he ranked seventh among 39 candidates.[6] Diefenbaker maintained his standing in the legal profession until he became leader of the Progressive Conservative Party in December 1956.

Because he wanted time on his feet in the courtroom, Diefenbaker started an independent law practice rather than serve as a junior lawyer in an established firm where, at best, he would sit in the second chair. In 1919, he hung up his shingle emblazoned with the words "Walk In" in Wakaw, Saskatchewan, 90 kilometres northeast of Saskatoon, then and now a tiny hamlet, a place he wryly noted had more murderers than drunks.[7]

Diefenbaker identified with the underdog in legal matters. Not mainly motivated by money, he had no blue-chip clients in his roster. He developed a flair for the dramatic and was known to be persuasive with penetrating eyes and a penchant for swinging his courtroom robes while making his arguments. With wildly gesticulating arms and hands, he was a showman with a commanding presence. If he had a legal role model, it was Abraham Lincoln, a small-town lawyer with a grand vision for justice who identified with the oppressed. Diefenbaker found himself in the middle of numerous high-profile murder cases as his law practice gained attention. Many were considered unwinnable, which only enhanced his reputation as someone who was not afraid to take on a challenge or the establishment.

He had not been in practice long when a father and son from the nearby town of Cudworth came to his office after being charged with the attempted murder of their neighbour. The argument for the defence was that they thought they heard a coyote near a corral of ducks and took a shot. Their last shots hit their neighbour in the face and shoulder, removing part of an ear and causing blindness in one eye. Save for the well-known animus between the shooters and the victim, and that others had heard threats of violence, the story of an accidental shooting might have been believed. Diefenbaker did not expect the jury would accept his client's contention that it was an unintentional shooting and had been angling for a conviction under a lesser charge, but the jury returned a verdict of not guilty. Jurors later said they were swayed by the sincerity of the defence counsel's arguments and determined that since it was his first case, they would give him the win.

In another high-profile case, R. v. Harms, a tawdry love triangle ended in murder. John Harms had been charged, convicted and sentenced to death.[8]

When Diefenbaker picked up the file on an appeal, there was no dispute on the facts, but he argued the circumstances of the crime suggested that it was not murder but manslaughter. The date was set for Harms' execution, and the appeal came days before the final event. The critical question was whether Harms had been provoked into the shooting since the man he shot was the common-law husband of the woman with whom Harms was having an affair. Harms was also intoxicated at the time. Diefenbaker was not sympathetic to his client: "(My client) was a womanizer, an adulterer, and anathema to most of the people of the town where he lived," wrote Diefenbaker. However, he managed to reduce the conviction to manslaughter, with the ensuing sentence lowered to 15 years.[9] Between sobs, Harms expressed his gratitude to Diefenbaker. "It's not that I was afraid to die, but in dying that way."[10] It was the first time in 25 years that a death sentence had been quashed.

If the lawyer was often on the side of the average person no matter their faults or even guilt, with his Germanic surname, Diefenbaker also identified with the discrimination faced by minorities and was thus often in their corner. When school board trustees Rémi Éthier and Léger Boutin of the Éthier School District in Saskatchewan were found guilty of violating the law prohibiting French instruction in public schools, Diefenbaker took the high-profile case on appeal in 1922 to defend the trustees from government prosecution.[11] He won, albeit on a technicality, when the judge ruled that trustees could not be held accountable for the conduct of individual teachers. Diefenbaker instinctively dismissed warnings that taking on such cases—in this circumstance when the French minority had little public sympathy on much of the prairies—would harm whatever political career might lie ahead. This never entered Diefenbaker's calculations. If he were to later succeed in politics, it was not because he had courted the powerful, wealthy or the dominant class.

Diefenbaker occasionally acted as a crown prosecutor when requested but sarcastically said he did a "lousy job at it" owing to the many convictions he secured. He moved from Wakaw to Prince Albert, where he took on the case of a 17-year-old who had been convicted of the murder of his father. The youth contended his mother had committed the crime and had convinced her son to offer a confession. The jury found him guilty and gave him the death sentence after 17 hours of deliberation. Diefenbaker made a pleading to the minister of justice for mercy as experts reported his client to have the mental capacity of a 12-year-old. Diefenbaker had the death sentence commuted to life in prison.

While the justice system is designed to be blind, that did not mean it applied equally to the wealthy or the poor; the sharp from the dull. Nadia Bajer, abandoned by her husband, lived a destitute life. When not cleaning homes, she would sleep with her customers for a dollar or less. She gave birth to a child who died after being dropped. She told no one at the time, hoping it would not be noticed she was no longer pregnant. After a police investigation was launched, she took them to where she buried the child, and a doctor concluded the child died of suffocation. The murder trial began and ended on October 9, 1930. Diefenbaker's defence highlighted the horrific conditions and the abandonment his client faced, and the shame that caused her to bury her child. That was an insufficient defence, so he poked holes in the expert testimony and raised reasonable doubt on the cause of death, for which the jury determined she was not guilty. She was instead convicted of concealment of a childbirth. It was a case of Diefenbaker being sympathetic to someone whose life circumstances had dealt them a bad hand. Even the judge took sympathy on the woman and suspended her sentence.

After being elected to federal Parliament in 1940, Diefenbaker continued to practise law, notably selecting cases where he could represent the "little man" who might be a convenient scapegoat for powerful interests. This was the circumstance of a 22-year-old railway telegraph operator, Jack Atherton, charged with manslaughter following a fatal train crash near Valemount, British Columbia, in 1950. Botched instructions were given to the train conductors, leading to a tragic collision that took the lives of 21 people, mostly Canadian soldiers. Sixty others were injured. The railway and the minister of transport pointed to the lowly telegraph operator as the culprit. Atherton had gone to Diefenbaker's wife, Edna, who was then in feeble health, to ask her husband, who was 10 years a Parliamentarian, to take the case. Diefenbaker thought the blame had been passed down the line and that the railway company had some culpability.

Atherton claimed he had delivered the instructions thoroughly and faithfully to the train conductors, but the transmission must have been cut off. Diefenbaker raised the prospect that communications could have been impacted by seagulls dropping fish on the transmission line and that snow had garbled the lines. He then went after a high-ranking railway official: "I suppose the reason you put these soldiers in wooden steel cars on either end was that no matter what they might have subsequently found in Korea, they'd always be able to say, 'Well, we had it worse than that in Canada.'"[12] To that, a Crown counsel, who had been a colonel in the military, interjected, "I want to make it clear that in this case, we're not concerned about the death of a few privates going to Korea." Diefenbaker jumped on this transgression, repeating the testimony and declaring, "Oh, colonel!" Diefenbaker summed up his case this way: "No small men shall be made goats by the strong and powerful in this country."[13] The jury, which included war veterans, was not impressed with the apparent disregard the colonel had for his troops. Diefenbaker secured an acquittal on all charges.

The financial records of Diefenbaker's law practices reveal that most of his work was civil rather than criminal and that he had an exceptionally high income relative to his peers. His papers revealed he bought a new Buick sedan in April 1936 and took at least one European vacation to France and Germany. His net income was almost double that of successful Saskatchewan lawyers.[14] That helped him to establish a rule that he never charged Métis or Status Indians who sought his advice or representation. "I was distressed by their conditions, the unbelievable poverty and the injustice done them," he remarked. One case he carried to the Court of Appeal involved a Status Indian charged with hunting on a game preserve. Diefenbaker contended that the relevant treaty had been routinely broken without recourse. While unsuccessful in the case, Diefenbaker took note and insisted that should he ever be in a position of authority, treaties with Indians would be respected.

The case of Grey Owl was not about Indian rights and treaties, but it did involve one of Canada's most notable self-proclaimed Indigenous figures, which put Diefenbaker in the position of defending a man he knew was a fake and a phony. After moving from England to Canada as a young man, Grey Owl, born Archie Belaney, became a notable woodsman, trapper, author, and raconteur. He was also a respected conservationist who exposed the destruction of Canada's natural habitat, drawing attention to the declining stock of Canada's national symbol, the beaver, which had been hunted to near extinction. Diefenbaker labelled Grey Owl remarkable but not always admirable: "A genius; no doubt a charlatan, a poseur, and a faker." Diefenbaker never believed the claim that Grey Owl was of Indian blood. When Grey Owl died in 1938, his will left half his estate to his daughter and half to a woman with whom he was not long married. It was discovered that he was also married to Angele Eguana, an Indian woman from Ontario's Temagami region. Eguana had taught him Indian ways and bore him a family. Grey Owl deserted her in 1925, thirteen years before his death. While Diefenbaker acted for the more recent wife, he persuaded her to share the estate with Eguana to achieve a more just outcome.

Diefenbaker was instinctively compassionate to those imprisoned. That 70 percent of those incarcerated became recidivists, he concluded, was a stain on society. When in Parliament, he remembered a case where he represented a son who had murdered his father and was given a life sentence. He knew the man had acted in an isolated incident and was at no risk of reoffending or harming society. His conduct in prison had been exemplary. Diefenbaker approached the minister of justice and future prime minister, Louis St. Laurent: "He shouldn't be there. He should be out on ticket of leave. He wants to join the army," Diefenbaker said.[15] The young man was released and then deployed for military service.

In the crucible of the courtroom, Diefenbaker honed his skills as a formidable advocate, adept at weaving a compelling narrative that resonated with the collective conscience of the jury. His legal prowess transcended the confines of the courtroom, earning him a reputation as a champion of the oppressed and a fearless defender of civil liberties.

- 3 -

UNFULFILLED AMBITIONS

It was more in sorrow than anger that I now concluded my political ambitions would never be realized.

John G. Diefenbaker was 25 when he won his first election as a town councillor for Wakaw, Saskatchewan, population 400, by a dozen votes. A long electoral drought followed this early win: Diefenbaker would lose the next five elections he contested at the municipal, provincial and federal levels. His primary obstacle in the elections he lost was that he ran as a Conservative in a province that, at the time, overwhelmingly voted Liberal. As Diefenbaker would remark, "The only protection Conservatives in Saskatchewan enjoyed in those early days was afforded by the game laws."[1]

Diefenbaker understood why the Liberals had such a stronghold in his home province. Liberal organizers told the influx of immigrants that they represented the party of freedom and liberty, while Conservatives stood for tyranny and autocrats. Indeed, the Union government of 1917, led by Conservative Robert Borden, deprived naturalized Canadians of many fundamental rights, including suspending habeas corpus, invoking censorship, banning strikes and stripping the vote. The government also interned thousands of enemy aliens. Diefenbaker aligned with the Unionists in that election but condemned the discriminatory legislation. The Liberal Party also had an incumbency advantage, holding power from when the province was established in 1905. Liberal patronage achieved machine-like efficiency where nearly all public works jobs were screened for party affiliation.

Liberal organizers approached Diefenbaker on numerous occasions to run as a candidate. They even elected him as the riding secretary of the Wakaw Liberal Association when he was out of town. Diefenbaker declined the appointment.

In the 1925 federal election, Diefenbaker ran for the Tories in Prince Albert, Saskatchewan. He finished third with fewer than half the votes of the Liberal candidate. Conservatives won the most seats nationally in that election but were prevented from forming a government because of a fleeting coalition between Mackenzie King's Liberals and Thomas Crerar's Progressive Party.

During that campaign, Diefenbaker, who turned 30 that year, felt at home as a Conservative, believing, as Edmund Burke counselled, that it was a party with a disposition to preserve and an ability to improve. The Conservative party embraced the Monarchy and the Commonwealth and resisted American incursion into Canadian political affairs. This attachment to Great Britain and a wariness of the American colossus—well-established in Canada at the time of Confederation and by some Americans who fled their country after the revolution to come to Canada as United Empire Loyalists—was a sentiment shared by Diefenbaker. During this campaign, however, what was most notable was his opposition to what we today call "identity politics." In contrast to ethnicity-pandering, Diefenbaker adopted the mantra that he stood for *One Canada*, which meant the end of hyphenated citizens, such as German-Canadians. He later went so far as to oppose a question in the Canadian census that identified a respondent's ethnic background, saying in a cabinet meeting that it was "hard to see how the bonds of unity and the development of the concept of one nation would be furthered by the perpetuation of a system which emphasized the racial origin of the groups that made up the population."[2]

When labelled a "hun" in the 1925 campaign, a derogatory term for Germans, Diefenbaker recoiled. To an overflow audience in Prince Albert, he shot back:

> They call me a hun! Probably the opposing candidates do not, but their minions most certainly do. The only crimes they can pin upon me are those of youth and German ancestry. My great-grandfather left Germany to seek liberty. My grandfather and father were born in Canada.... my grandmother and my grandmother on my mother's side spoke no English; being Scottish, they spoke Gaelic. If there is no hope for me to be Canadian, then who is there hope for?[3]

With no desire to repudiate his ancestry, Diefenbaker told his audiences that over his political career, it would have been much easier had he lived with his mother's maiden name, Campbell-Bannerman, rather than Diefenbaker.

Unapologetic yet realistic, he told his wife, "My name will prevent me from becoming prime minister."[4]

Despite his youth and inexperience, Diefenbaker thought for himself and did not obey his party's hierarchy in 1925. When his leader, the Conservative Opposition Leader Arthur Meighen, threatened to repeal the favourable Crow's Nest Past freight rates, a subsidy to the benefit of Western grain farmers, Diefenbaker knew it was political poison in Saskatchewan. In response, Meighen made it clear he was unhappy with Diefenbaker's tendency to speak his mind and counselled him accordingly: "Young man, you have all the ideas of the Western farmer, but you haven't got the national picture."

Meighen also opposed expanding the Hudson Bay Railway in Manitoba that would have given western grain farmers access to Europe. Diefenbaker countered his leader's commitments and told Prince Albert electors that if he were successful, he would resign his seat if rails were not laid within two years of his election. When confronted with the inconsistency by his Liberal opponent, Diefenbaker replied that he would represent his views and those of his constituents in Parliament. He earned less than one-quarter of the votes in an election where no Conservative in Saskatchewan won a seat that year.

The 1925 election gave the Conservatives 116 seats to 101 for the Liberals, led by Mackenzie King. It was a minority Parliament, and King attempted to hold power with the support of Progressive, Labour and Independent MPs. When King lost a vote of confidence on June 25, 1926, he went to Governor General Julian Byng to request an election be called. Byng refused and asked Meighen to form a government instead. That government lasted three days before losing a confidence vote. In this circumstance, Byng had little choice but to agree that an election was necessary, held on September 14, 1926.

Diefenbaker believed Meighen had erred in attempting to form a government and should have accepted King's challenge to hold an election rather than put the matter in the hands of the Governor General in what is known as the King-Byng affair. Meighen squandered his advantage by letting the Governor General's decision not to follow the advice of Prime Minister Mackenzie King to call an election become the decisive election issue.

In the 1926 campaign, Diefenbaker was again a candidate in the riding of Prince Albert, but this time, his opponent on the ballot was Liberal Leader Mackenzie King, who chose to run in Saskatchewan to bolster a federal Liberal presence in the West. Liberal campaign officials took out ads in the local *Ukrainian Voice* stating that the Conservative party's position was to deprive all naturalized Canadians of their right to vote. In public meetings, Liberal organizers charged that deportations would be the Conservatives' next step.

As outrageous as the claims were, they became credible when one eastern Tory supporter claimed King had gone to Prince Albert to run because "he doesn't like the smell of native-born Canadians. He prefers the stench of garlic stinking continentals, Eskimos, Bohunks, and Indians." A Tory candidate from Ontario sneered—Tory being a party moniker that Diefenbaker rarely used as it harkened to an era when powerbrokers controlled the party— "King is running in a riding among the Doukhobors, up near the North Pole where they don't know how to mark their ballots." The taunts of eastern Tories were offensive to Prince Albert electors, and Diefenbaker paid the price. The tally was 65 percent of the vote for King, who had promised the local voters a national park, and 35 percent for Diefenbaker, who carried the burden of racism in his party. Whatever respect Diefenbaker had for the eastern establishment figures in his party was extinguished by their bigotry.

Diefenbaker supported Hugh Guthrie in the 1927 federal leadership contest, a onetime Liberal who had aligned with Conservative Prime Minister Robert Borden in the 1917 election as a Union candidate. Guthrie stayed loyal to the Tories, but it did not help his cause one decade later in his leadership run when he addressed delegates at a 1927 meeting in Winnipeg choosing their next leader by welcoming them to the "greatest Liberal convention in history."

After flaming out federally, Diefenbaker shifted to provincial politics with an ambitious attempt to revive the fledgling Tory cause in Saskatchewan. Though the Conservative party gained ground in popular support in the provincial election of 1929, it won no seats. Failing to win in three elections only intensified Diefenbaker's ambition. In 1933, when the Prince Albert mayoral contest was headed for acclamation, Diefenbaker entered the race at the last moment with a campaign promise to secure funding from the federal government for public works and to reduce the city's debt. With only one week to campaign, he surprisingly came within 48 votes of beating his opponent, Harold John Fraser.

Not initially a supporter of Prime Minister R.B. Bennett (who was in office between 1930 and 1935), Diefenbaker came to admire the Tory leader's willingness to represent the "common man" during the Great Depression. He also admired Bennett's independent streak and willingness to defy "the self-appointed eastern bosses of the party" while leading a government that did not "sit on its hands," which earned Diefenbaker's respect. Policy-wise, "not sitting" included how the Bennett government established the Bank of Canada and the Canadian Broadcasting Corporation and passed the Farmers' Creditors Arrangement legislation that saved tens of thousands of farmers from bankruptcy.

If Diefenbaker had run in 1930 under Bennett, he would likely have won a seat. Diefenbaker was offered the Tory nomination in Prince Albert but declined due to poor health. A lesser-known Conservative candidate, Dr. W.D. Cowan, was victorious in Diefenbaker's home constituency. Diefenbaker chose not to run in the 1935 federal election but took note of the devastation caused to Conservative party prospects by the defection of a leading cabinet minister, Henry Herbert Stevens, who established the Reconstruction Party. Stevens took almost nine percent of the vote, most drawn at the expense of Conservatives.

Just before the 1935 federal election, Prime Minister Bennett offered Diefenbaker an appointment to the Court of King's Bench as a district court judge. But Diefenbaker preferred to be an advocate rather than an adjudicator in court. It would also have stifled his political ambitions, so he declined the offer.

Bennett thought Diefenbaker had leadership potential. He offered encouragement, but it was delivered in an odd way. Bennett asked Diefenbaker if he had yet sent him a wedding gift. The question came eight years after his 1929 marriage. To his surprise, a cheque for $2,500 from Bennett marked as a "wedding gift" was sent to Diefenbaker's Prince Albert home (worth about $55,000 in 2024).[5] Bennett was wealthy, and the gift was less likely related to Diefenbaker's nuptial and more of an investment in his protégé's political future.

Diefenbaker was fascinated at the time by the populist and demagogue Senator Huey Long of Louisiana, who had begun his career in law fighting for the underdog and then advocated for progressive policies that became part of Franklin Roosevelt's "New Deal." Diefenbaker wrote to Long in 1935 to encourage him to "make the lot of the underprivileged a better and happier one." Diefenbaker explored his version of a progressive agenda in a speech entitled "Capitalism Controlled."[6]

Just before the leadership convention that replaced R.B. Bennett in 1938 with Robert Manion, Diefenbaker was unhappy about how the party had treated its leader, who had warned convention delegates, "Unless the party is united in the leader... the Conservative party will pass out of existence." Diefenbaker took note of Bennett's remarks and kept a copy of the speech in his papers for future reference with this passage highlighted:

> Every time you publicly criticize anyone in your party you do a great harm to your party and every time you publicly criticize the leader of your party you add fuel to the fires of opposition that must always burn against him... I ask you—why assist the enemy?

When Diefenbaker was approached to stand for the leadership of the Saskatchewan Conservative Party, he understood the importance of loyalty. Before accepting the leadership Diefenbaker made one precondition: "I would sooner stay at my profession as I know what a sacrifice it will be on my part. I'm prepared to take a try at it, but only if the party would unite behind me."

On October 28, 1936, a string of men were nominated from the convention floor for the provincial party's leadership, but only one rose to accept—John Diefenbaker. Of the new leader, the *Regina Leader-Post* remarked, "He carries his 40 years lightly, is dark, slim and erect, and thunders forth his convictions and ideas in resonant tones of purposeful youth."

Diefenbaker was determined to bring his provincial party closer to the middle of the political spectrum or even lean slightly towards the progressive. His election platform was criticized by those who considered themselves "True Blue Tories."[7] He advocated policies that were no more radical, even if ineffective, than those advocated by R.B. Bennett during the Great Depression. But he inherited a Saskatchewan Conservative party with limited depth, a shambles of an organization, and no money.

For the 1938 election, Diefenbaker made a personal loan to the party to cover election deposits for 22 Tory candidates. He was distressed to encounter Alberta-born Ernest Manning, the Social Credit party's chief organizer and prime architect of conservative vote-splitting in the West, inserting himself into the campaign. Saskatchewan Social Credit secured 15.9 percent of the vote that caused the Tory party to be shut out on election night. "No one really understood Social Credit's monetary theories," Diefenbaker lamented. "Perhaps that was the reason for its popularity."[8] Diefenbaker ran on a system of health insurance and hospitalization coverage.[9] At the end of the campaign, Diefenbaker was a strong leader of a weak party. His offer to resign was refused. Reflecting on the campaign and his defeat, Diefenbaker told the press that he remained a chronic optimist. "We are not fair-weather Conservatives. We know the meaning of defeat, but we do not know the meaning of retreat."[10]

Diefenbaker was at a crossroads. "It was more in sorrow than anger that I now concluded my political ambitions would never be realized... five successive defeats. My wife was not well. My law practice was suffering. I was the leader of a party with no representation in the Legislative Assembly. What I wanted to do was gradually and responsibly relinquish my political obligations and devote the rest of my life to the practice of law."[11]

TAKING ON THE ELITES

- 4 -

OTTAWA-BOUND: DIEF THE CHIEF

We will be the next government.
We have an appointment with destiny.

Without a path to politics and a grudging acceptance that his dream of becoming prime minister would not be met, John Diefenbaker refocused on his passion for the law. However, to Conservatives in Saskatchewan, he remained a person of interest. The nominating meeting to select the federal Conservative candidate in the Saskatchewan riding of Lake Centre was scheduled for June 1939. It was the same riding where Diefenbaker had once run provincially and was a three-hour drive south of Prince Albert, where Diefenbaker then lived, so not his home constituency. Diefenbaker was unable to accept an invitation by the riding president to be the guest speaker as he was in the middle of a high-profile fraud and arson case. Unexpectedly, that case was resolved. That freed Diefenbaker to speak at the last minute to his past volunteers and supporters and to thank them both.

When nominations were called from the floor for who would be the Conservative candidate in the next election, a local Tory put forward Diefenbaker's name. Five other men were nominated. Diefenbaker was the first to speak and told the crowded room that they should select one of the highly qualified people who lived in the riding. The proceedings were delayed because of a small fire, and Diefenbaker left the building before the first ballot was counted. W.B. Kelly won the vote, but he unexpectedly rose to his feet to move his withdrawal and have Diefenbaker chosen by unanimous consent. It was a remarkable turnaround for Diefenbaker, who thought his political days were over. He attended a political meeting as a bystander and became a candidate for federal Parliament. It was accidental, if not a matter of fate.

When the writ was dropped for the 1940 federal election, Diefenbaker was in the middle of a murder trial. The accused was the Irish-born wife of a man who was an avowed Nazi and a leader in the German Bund, Henry Emele. It was a marriage arranged through correspondence that had produced several children. After being abused and beaten, Isobel Emele fled. Diefenbaker took on the case *pro bono*. She had confessed to the murder, which Diefenbaker argued was obtained under duress. He secured an acquittal, which held up under appeal. Taking the case was not a distraction from the campaign. That the murdered husband was a Nazi from Germany when Canada was at war with Hitler's regime was to Diefenbaker's political advantage.

The 1940 wartime campaign was brutal for the Tories. They were disorganized, underfunded, unprepared, and unwilling to deal harshly with Mackenzie King's Liberal government. Diefenbaker fought his campaign in Lake Centre based on his attributes and beliefs and not as his party's standard bearer. This included his view that a national unity government should be formed, similar to that which Sir Robert Borden assembled in 1917. As to issues of local concern, he advocated for higher prices for wheat crops.

Given the Conservatives' historically weak showing in Saskatchewan, Diefenbaker's decision to campaign with an independent voice was more strategic than an act of disloyalty. He carried the campaign on his back, attending multiple political meetings and rallies per day in the rural riding during the five-week writ period. He was attacked in the campaign as a lawyer who charged high fees and did not live a farming life. Diefenbaker turned that around by saying he was worth high fees, but as their MP, his highly valued work would not cost his constituents a penny. The more devastating charge was the accusation in the campaign's final week by the Liberal candidate that Diefenbaker had been a conscript in the First World War and not a volunteer. To this charge, Diefenbaker replied:

> I have been in many elections, but this is the first time a deliberate lie has been told by anyone against me. I joined up in 1916 and took my commission. I was invalidated [sent home due to injuries] in February 1917. Conscription didn't come in until after the election of December 1917.

Diefenbaker thought the shoddy Liberal tactics and overreach cost them votes. In a riding that the Liberals expected to hold, they lost by 280 votes in a tight three-way race in which Diefenbaker won 36.3 percent of the votes cast. Diefenbaker held one of the only 39 seats won by the Tories under leader Robert Manion against 179 for the Liberals under MacKenzie King. In a letter of congratulations, Diefenbaker's mother reminded him of his childhood ambition: "I can see by your letter that the aim of your ambition is to fill King's chair... well, I think you will get there someday if you work hard enough."

Once in Ottawa, Diefenbaker camped out at the Château Laurier. His wife Edna, a schoolteacher who he married on June 29, 1929, after a two-year courtship, became his parliamentary assistant, press secretary, and head cheerleader. She was known to brag openly about her husband's skills and predicted his inevitable rise to leadership. Fellow MP and friend Paul Martin Sr. remarked: "I have my ambitions too, but I have my wife better trained."[1]

Obsessed with politics, short-tempered, and moody, Diefenbaker was not the ideal husband. Naturally flirtatious, Edna was rumoured to be in the company of other men. Liberal prime minister and lifelong bachelor Mackenzie King was an admirer who said, "If I had found Edna first, John would never have got her from me."[2]

Edna became depressed, suffered from insomnia, and put herself in the care of a Toronto psychiatrist who encouraged her husband to be more attentive. She was admitted to Homewood Sanitorium in Guelph, Ontario and was given electric shock therapy. Edna pleaded with her husband to help take her away from her nightmare. Diefenbaker, dedicated to his ambition, was present but less sympathetic than what his wife required. He did not speak of her illness, likely out of embarrassment, which was not an uncommon response in that era. Not long after the 1949 election, Edna was diagnosed with leukemia. Paul Martin, then minister of health, arranged for experimental drugs from the United States. Edna died with Diefenbaker by her side on February 7, 1951. Family friend Dick Spencer wrote, "(Theirs) was an exciting and uncommon political partnership. There was love and happiness. Near the close, there was deep personal anguish."[3]

Given the length of their marriage (22 years in total) and her outspoken championing of her husband, Edna received surprisingly few mentions in Diefenbaker's memoirs. He described her in one paragraph as a most attractive and vivacious person and a faithful political helper. The only mention of her illness was as follows: "It was our tragedy that through the last nine years of our married life, she was seriously ill. She passed away in February 1951 (at the age of 49), widely mourned in Saskatchewan and in Ottawa."[4] The *Ottawa Citizen's* account of her life was filled with praise, noting that no spouse was more often present in the House of Commons, "a bright and vital component, a breath of plain prairie warmth and friendliness."[5] Her coffin was placed four feet deeper than usual to allow for her husband to rest above her when his time came.

A likely explanation for Diefenbaker's failure to give prominence to Edna in his memoirs was to avoid taking away biographical, historical and emotional attention from his beloved second wife, Olive, daughter of a Methodist minister, whom he married on December 8, 1953. Olive, who had a daughter, Carolyn, from her first marriage, was widowed three years after her marriage in 1933. She graduated from McMaster University and the Ontario College of Education, taught high school French, and served as director of child guidance for the Ontario Department of Education. Olive met her second husband and future prime minister at a Saskatoon church soon after the First World War had ended. That connection was notable enough that when both were widowed, they remembered the encounter. Olive is buried with her husband on a grassy knoll on the grounds of the University of Saskatchewan overlooking the South Saskatchewan River. Edna's remains, initially intended to be partnered with Diefenbaker's as per her 1951 burial plan, rest three kilometres away in the original Diefenbaker family plot.

***

The day Diefenbaker arrived on Parliament Hill to be sworn in as an MP, there was an ominous sign: the clock on the Peace Tower had stopped. Despite dreaming of the opportunity to engage in debate on the floor of the House of Commons, Diefenbaker was cautious and waited for a few months, easing himself into his new surroundings, before speaking. Better, he was told by the former Conservative prime minister R.B. Bennett to be asked why you do not speak rather than why you do. He was the last of the new Conservative MPs to address the House of Commons when he rose for a 30-minute speech on June 13, 1940, when the war was going horribly for the Allies. France had fallen, and the British Expeditionary Force had just been evacuated from the beaches of Dunkirk. Winston Churchill had been prime minister for one month and had resisted all calls to seek terms with Hitler. Canada was well into the fight while the Americans were on the sidelines. The matter before the Canadian House of Commons was the Defence of Canada Regulations.

The Defence of Canada Regulations were a set of emergency measures implemented under the War Measures Act on September 3, 1939, which was invoked a week before Canada entered the Second World War. The Act and its regulations enabled the suspension of *habeas corpus* and the legal rights of citizens to due process, the internment of certain citizens, bans on specified political and cultural activity, censorship of certain speech and publications, and confiscation of property. The minister of justice was given wide latitude to apply and enforce the regulations. Canadians of German descent were required to register, and some were detained. While Diefenbaker's speech occurred before the attack on Pearl Harbor, the regulations were ultimately used to intern many Japanese Canadians and confiscate their property.

As a man who had long stood for the rights and freedoms of the individual and against the power of the state being imposed on its citizens, it was expected that Diefenbaker would be wary of unchecked government overreach, the repression of free speech, and the incarceration of the innocent. That was not his response to the moment in the House of Commons on June 13, 1940.

> I ask the government to recognize the fact that we, too, are trying to do what we can to further and not, as was suggested this afternoon, to sabotage the war effort. In the beginning, there were some, and there are some today, who challenge these regulations on the grounds that they abrogate the rights of free men. In particular there is the criticism that they take away the almost inalienable rights of British subjects, the rights of *habeas corpus* and *certiorari*, and are thus the negation of democracy. My answer to that is that national safety is of paramount importance over private rights.

Having made his priority clear, Diefenbaker asked for the indulgence of time, invoking the name of the German dictator as justification:

> These rights have not been lost; they are held in abeyance until victory is attained. Their abrogation is required in the interest of the safety of the state. These rights will return to the people of this Dominion

> when victory is won. To those who criticize the Defence of Canada Regulations as taking away the liberty of the subject, I say better have the rights remain in abeyance than lose them altogether if Hitler should win.

Being of Germanic ancestry, Diefenbaker was concerned about how the government would treat Canadians of German descent. His worry was targeting Canadians based on ethnicity rather than individual risk assessments. That helps explain why Diefenbaker later opposed the policy of the Canadian government to insert a hyphen in the official census to describe the origin of anyone who was a citizen:

> How the census in Canada is taken prevents the creation of an unhyphenated Canadian nation. There is no question of the loyalty of those of German stock who were United Empire Loyalists, of those who came over in the forties, fifties, sixties. There is no question as to the loyalty of others, except the few who are today disturbing our unity and whose activities must be curbed. Other than those, the people recorded in the census as German are loyal to this country and intend to contribute to it to their best. My criticism of the census is that, regardless of the number of generations that have elapsed or the admixtures of nationality that have taken place during forty, fifty, seventy-five or one hundred and twenty-five years, so long as persons must register under the nationality of their paternal ancestor, there will never be that Canadianism which we wish to establish.

To further his point, Diefenbaker invoked the name of one of the greatest military leaders of the Allied cause in the First World War, and the former commander of the United States troops, General John J. Pershing, who was of German origin. He was, Diefenbaker pointed out, not a German-American, but simply an American:

> Let us build up in this country an unhyphenated Canadianism that is dominant, proud and strong. A naturalization certificate is an admission that the state recognizes that the person who has been accepted for

> membership in that proud heritage of British citizenship is a citizen whose loyalty is unquestionable.

To those who pressed further, he would say, "Suppose I was German; does it make for a united Canada to knock settlers?"

Going deeper into the issue of limiting rights and exposing subversives in his speeches, Diefenbaker proposed a mandatory national registration of those with the potential to serve the nation during war. More than just a precursor to a draft, Diefenbaker suggested the list would bring to light "the names of many who are today in Canada without having complied with the immigration regulations and who are in a position to carry on subversive activities." Going down a more conspiratorial hole, Diefenbaker argued that publications with an anti-British feeling should be banned from importation, citing the *Saturday Evening Post* and the *Chicago Tribune* as examples that had produced "malicious articles." He concluded as he started: one goal should be pursued without distraction or annoyance in a time of war.

> Parliament today realizes, as never before, that we have but one duty—to provide the maximum war effort to win this war. This war is being waged on two fronts—the battlefront and the home front. The Defence of Canada regulations were designed to ensure the solidarity of the Canadian people and to prevent malicious disaffection from destroying the continuity of our war effort or interfering with the production and transportation of munitions, materials, and food for our armies here and overseas. The safeguarding of our interests overseas as a nation, of our homes, of our right to live, is in the hands of our gallant boys. They will not fail us.

As a parliamentarian, Diefenbaker saw it as his duty to ensure that the minister of justice did not exceed his authority or be unnecessarily punitive or arbitrary in exercising his powers under the regulations. "Our task," he wrote in volume one of his memoirs published in 1975, "was to make certain that those interned were detained because there was evidence to suggest that they were, in fact, a threat to the security of the state, and not because the regulations had been rigidly or improperly applied." When a contractor of Italian origins was slandered by his competitors and held by the authorities, Diefenbaker assessed the evidence, which was nothing more than hearsay and secured the contractor's release. When Quebec police engaged in minority repression, the defence lawyer and civil rights advocate in him saw it as indefensible that Jehovah's Witnesses were summarily detained. However, he thought the contention that every member of the faith had the status of a church minister and was, therefore, exempt from service was preposterous.

His next most memorable moment after his inaugural remarks in Parliament was meeting Sir Winston Churchill on December 30, 1941. In conversation, he awkwardly noted to the British Prime Minister that he, Churchill, was in disgrace the last time he saw him. An astonished Churchill asked Diefenbaker, "What time was that?" Diefenbaker recalled that during the First World War, he attended British Parliamentary debates when Churchill explained his decisions in the disastrous Dardanelles campaign. But Diefenbaker admired the man and saw himself as a kindred spirit. Diefenbaker had attended the 1936 Olympic Games in Berlin and sat not far from Hitler, Goering and Goebbels. He witnessed the militarism and, on returning to Canada, made speeches about the inevitable coming war, as Churchill had been doing to far greater effect in Great Britain.

During the war, Diefenbaker believed the opposition party was responsible for being patriotic and non-partisan. The House of Commons, he said, should not be "a cockpit of contending factions, each desirous of preparing for the hustings.... (Parliament should) strengthen the resolution of the people to carry on to the end." His partisanship was for Canada.

If excusing government clampdowns on war dissenters such as Jehovah's Witnesses or overreach on other freedoms were part of Diefenbaker's public position early in the war, and well after Diefenbaker's maiden 1940 speech, the King government went too far for Diefenbaker on February 26, 1942, when it decreed that all Canadian citizens of Japanese origin would be interned, and their property confiscated. Diefenbaker later wrote that the English language does not have the words that sufficiently condemn such an atrocity. From the first volume of his memoirs:

> I did not question the proposition that, in war, security and survival are paramount. But to take a whole people and condemn them as wrongdoers because of race was something I could not accept. The Conservative Party took its stand, not officially but in fact, in favour of the government's plan for immediate forced displacement and the

> eventual deportation of the Japanese, regardless of place of birth or loyalty.... The course that was taken against Japanese Canadians was wrong. I said it over and over again; It was considered unbelievable that I would take this stand.[6]

If he did say it repeatedly, as claimed decades later, there is no published record of his protestations in Hansard or media reports of his opposition. Diefenbaker offered no reference to a conversation or proof that he spoke out against a policy he so vehemently criticized in his memoirs. Perhaps he made his views known within the confines and confidence of the Conservative caucus—or not at all. In the second volume of his memoirs, Diefenbaker addressed the criticism of his readers that his boasts of opposing Japanese internment were exaggerated or erroneous. The only reference that Diefenbaker could come up with was a statement he made in the House of Commons on April 23, 1947, well after the end of the war. That statement came in response to a question of privilege about aspersions made by another MP of his alleged support of the order-in-council ordering the forced removal of Japanese Canadians from the Pacific coast: "I want to say that my attitude has never changed, and do not detract from the fact. I am opposed to any discrimination against Canadians, regardless of their race or creed."[7] This was a meek and unconvincing defence, at best.

A somewhat stronger defence was his opposition in 1945 to the government's likely popular proposal to deport Canadian citizens of Japanese origin: "To deport Canadian citizens was the very antithesis of the principles of democracy," Diefenbaker bellowed in the House of Commons, "one of the first of which is that minorities are entitled to protection."

Diefenbaker's proof of defending minorities who originated from hostile nations was never convincingly produced. He was not alone in lacking the courage to condemn unwarranted and arbitrary oppression during the war. For example, Earl Warren, as Attorney General of California (and later Chief Justice of the Supreme Court), was, during the Second World War, in favour of the internment of Japanese Americans, citizens or more recent immigrants. But Warren would admit he was wrong. As with many during the war, Diefenbaker may have been selective with his outrage given the prejudice of his era. While Diefenbaker may have been less vocal than he claimed about those of Japanese origin who took up Canadian citizenship, at the height of the war, he did chastise the government on the record for restricting the free speech of communists and

Jehovah's Witnesses. "I don't believe in communism," he said before the press in 1943, but the curtailment of free speech "is being used to curtail the tongues of political opponents."[8]

There is no question that Diefenbaker pressed the government in the House of Commons for its excessive use of orders-in-council, or executive proclamations, to manage the conduct of the war rather than to exercise its authority more transparently through debate, resolution, and legislation in Parliament. Through persistent questioning during the conduct of the war, he ascertained that about 90,000 orders-in-council had been issued, a level suggesting to him that Parliament was "nothing more than a decorous necessity."

***

In the June 11, 1945 election, Diefenbaker set a course distinct from his leader, John Bracken, and his party. He supported the South Saskatchewan River Dam and opposed sending Canadian troops to Japan. This was likely a wise move on his part because Diefenbaker was the only Conservative to win in Saskatchewan. He was dismayed that out of the 66-member Tory caucus elected in 1945, 48 came from Ontario and only ten from Canada's four western provinces. The heavy influence of central Canada in the caucus frustrated Diefenbaker.

After the war, there was renewed interest in building up the United Nations as an organization that would promote dialogue and sustain peace among countries around the globe. This was a priority of a Diefenbaker hero, Winston Churchill, who saw some form of international cooperation necessary for a stable postwar world. Likewise, despite being a Canadian nationalist, Diefenbaker favoured giving up some Canadian sovereignty to the proposed United Nations "in the cause of stemming the sources of war."

He was an observer and advisor to the Conservative member of Canada's delegation, Gordon Graydon, to the founding San Francisco Conference held April-June 1945, and later wrote, "For the first time in all history, the various nations would provide forces to a strong international army that would serve under the aegis of the international organization to ensure that whenever and whatever aggression took place, it would be met and defeated."[9] But he understood the inherent weakness of the United Nations. As he said in the House of Commons, "The U.N. Charter provides the basis to end war, but it does not terminate the prerogative of any of the great powers to wage war. It prevents aggression among the small nations." He urged that the U.N. charter be amended such that it holds the "power to control the atomic bomb."[10] It was a naïve proposition that would have been a non-starter with the United States but was an early indication that he viewed Canada's closest ally with some suspicion.

Diefenbaker had great hopes that the United Nations would settle the question of establishing the state of Israel. He paid tribute to the "magnificent record" of Jewish soldiers serving in the Canadian military in the Second World War and how 480,000 Jews had settled in Palestine, and who had raised the cultural and living standards of that country.[11] This contrasted with the position of the Liberal government during the Second World War when Jewish refugees were denied entry into Canada, after the official in charge, Frederick Blair, infamously responded, "None is too many" when asked how many Jews should Canada admit.

***

During and immediately after the end of the war it was not politics as usual on the Canadian scene. Unlike during the First World War, when the Conservatives established the Unionist Party to bring in Liberals who favoured conscription, the Tories remained within their ranks, but were largely aligned with the Liberal government's conduct of the war. The leadership and vision of the Conservative party were either absent or invisible to Canadians. It was an undefined entity. They had lost three consecutive elections with no prospect of winning government anytime soon.

Diefenbaker was not alone in thinking that the Conservative party had something of a death wish after enjoying a glorious beginning under Sir John A. Macdonald. "My first insight into what now seems a predisposition on the part of the Canadian Conservatives to self-assassination," noted Diefenbaker, "came with the political destruction of Dr. Robert Manion." Manion had become the leader in 1938 and was in the chair when Diefenbaker was elected in 1940. Diefenbaker detected a sentiment in the Conservative caucus that Manion was a loser because he was a Roman Catholic and had a French-Canadian wife. Diefenbaker thought that prejudice of any form was abhorrent and that Manion deserved better.

Manion honourably offered his resignation to the caucus after losing the 1940 election, which was a formality in such circumstances. To his astonishment, and Diefenbaker's, the offer was accepted. The party thought Arthur Meighen, the leader who lost the 1920 and 1926 elections for Conservatives and was sitting in caucus as a Senator, should be given yet another shot at Mackenzie King.

Diefenbaker admired Meighen and did not get in his way, but he cautioned that it would be unwise for him to lead from the Senate, believing that to be the legitimate leader, he needed a seat in the House of Commons. Mackenzie King hated Meighen and did all he could to facilitate his demise. Indeed, King refused to run a Liberal in the by-election that Meighen pursued, a wise strategic move as Liberals and CCF voters got behind the CCF candidate, J.S. Noseworthy. Meighen lost the byelection and was finished for good.

After Meighen stepped down in 1942, Diefenbaker assessed his leadership prospects. A Toronto friend advised against it. After canvassing establishment figures in the party, lawyer David Walker gave Diefenbaker his grim assessment in writing:

> Most people that knew you conceded that you were one of the most brilliant debaters in the House of Commons with one of the keenest minds and a tremendous fighter. Admitting all your qualities, the people I talked with, for one reason or another, including such silly reasons as your name and physique, refuse to consider you seriously as their choice as leader of the party. Every one of them conceded that you would be and should be a member of the cabinet. Since our friendship would not be worthwhile unless we were frank with one another, I know that you will accept this letter in the spirit in which it is written.[12]

Diefenbaker was not dissuaded and decided to run anyway, but made few preparations before the convention, which meant no campaign team or written material supported his candidacy. However, he was encouraged by the party's openness to a leader from the West. The front-runner was Manitoba premier John Bracken, the choice of retiring leader Arthur Meighen. Bracken was an enigma to Diefenbaker: "Mr. Bracken had never evinced even the slightest interest in being a Conservative. He had been a Progressive, a Liberal Progressive, and, finally, a Liberal."[13] Holding the convention in Winnipeg gave Bracken a home-field advantage.

Diefenbaker's strengths—his theatrical manner and oratorical gifts—were not in evidence when he delivered his convention speech. Atypically, reading from a text, he stiffly reiterated the themes that had characterized his political life:

the security of the common man, a fight for democratic institutions, a fair deal under a system of private initiative, and national unity based on a Canadianism with no racial basis. His closing pitch was, "I believe that Canadian unity must be assured; that it must be built on the basis of a Canadianism that knows no racial origin; that of the various races and creeds of this Dominion must evolve a united Canada."

Bracken intended to move the party to more socially progressive views, as was articulated at a party conference in Port Hope, Ontario in September 1942. Bracken stipulated the change in party name to Progressive Conservative, a change that Diefenbaker thought unnecessary and unwise. However, Diefenbaker was more progressive than most of his caucus colleagues. Still, he said, "It is only the Conservative party that had the courage to stand up to the bureaucracy... and the Canadian Broadcasting Corporation."[14] He knew from the outset he had no chance of winning but wanted his vision and persona to gain profile before convention delegates. "I wanted to plant at least the seed of my idea: This is one nation, one Canada."[15] The only other contender, Howard Green, fainted on the platform and had to be carried away on a stretcher.

Finishing third in a field of five gave Diefenbaker a respectable position on the first ballot, which was enough to assure him prominence on the front benches of the party under Bracken's leadership. When Bracken declined to enter the House of Commons through a by-election, the position of House leader was up for grabs. Bracken decreed a vote of caucus members would select the leader. Diefenbaker put himself up for the position, but honourably voted for his opponent and lost by one vote.

The 1945 election, held on June 11, after the war in Europe had ended but two months before the surrender of Japan in Asia, produced a minority Liberal government. The Grits lost 61 seats, with the Tories picking up 28 and the CCF 20. There were also eight "independent" Liberal MPs who ran in opposition to Mackenzie King's meandering position on conscription.[a] However, they were MPs that Mackenzie King could rely upon, sufficient to give him a working majority. In that election, Diefenbaker defied his party by opposing the continuation of

---

a King had opposed conscription at the outset of the Second World War, but held a referendum on April 27, 1942 to relieve the government from its earlier promise. King described his position as, "not necessarily conscription, but conscription if necessary."

conscription while war was ongoing with Japan. He said farmers needed young hands to return to the fields after Europe had been secured.

Progressive Conservatives had made gains, but there was no patience for a leader who did not meet expectations. Bracken held on until 1948 but was ultimately hounded from his position by MPs and party officials who believed he had no prospect of improving on his result in 1945. The eastern bosses looked to Ontario, where George Drew, the provincial premier, had the feel of a winner. To those in the East, Diefenbaker was dismissed as a "Western populist." However, it was not just westerners that George Drew struggled with. Drew opposed family allowance benefits as a scheme to "breed slackers" in Quebec. He said he would not support legislation that brought about any more of those "French Canadian bastards." It was an offensive, unbecoming, and counterproductive comment for anyone aspiring for national office. By contrast, Diefenbaker broke with his party in 1944 to support the passage of the Family Allowances Act.[16]

Diefenbaker was the first to enter the 1948 leadership contest. On September 17, he reiterated the themes that he carried with him throughout his political life: a love for Canada and the protection of civil rights:

> I have something to contribute to Canada in the crusade to mobilize Canadians everywhere for Canada.... To restore parliamentary authority, the protection of provincial legislative powers, the promotion of free enterprise, the preservation of liberty under a national bill of rights, and generally fair and just treatment for all Canadians.[17]

Diefenbaker was a longshot to the press but demonstrated his capacity for political spin. "Of course, I will win. I mean that seriously." With a nod to the importance of momentum, he added, "although I would not have said it two weeks ago."[18]

Diefenbaker was indeed an underdog to win the leadership. But he had new supporters, including feminist Nellie McClung, who wrote to Diefenbaker, "I have admired your courage and clear thinking for a long time and hope you will be the new leader. You are young, modest, straightforward, and have an open mind."[19] It isn't easy to imagine anyone, at any time, suggesting that Diefenbaker was modest.

Contra McClung, fellow Tory Donald Fleming, who entered the House of Commons in 1940, had reservations about Diefenbaker's leadership qualities.

He thought Diefenbaker was a "loner" and a "*prima donna.*"[20] He worried about Diefenbaker's instincts and believed his colleague's only path to power would be from the party's grassroots, not the power brokers who were then at the centre of decision-making.

The Diefenbaker team was better organized for this contest than the 1942 version. Buttons, pamphlets, posters, and ribbons filled the boisterous Ottawa Coliseum. There was glitz but no alcohol to ply delegates, cash or otherwise.[21] Diefenbaker's campaign speech was a continuation of his views that were becoming well-known within his party.

> Canadians are asking for a party that will honestly try to end class warfare and hatred: that will regulate injustice and exploitation in enterprise while retaining an expanding free initiative, accept social security as a means, not an end... while continuing to provide adequately for the aged and afflicted... that only under responsible free initiative is there opportunity to rise to the top however humble one's origins; that will protect our people against unfairness.[22]

With a predisposition to believe people in authority stood in his way, Diefenbaker alleged foul play and suspected that many of his supporters were targeted for removal from the list of delegates-at-large. Nonetheless, Diefenbaker improved his standing from the last leadership convention by one spot, finishing second to George Drew, who won easily on the first ballot with the support of two-thirds of the delegates. It was not a surprise to Diefenbaker—who came in second with 25 percent support of the votes—having written to his mother, "I cannot hope to win, but it's a good fight."

However, it would turn out to be a prickly relationship between the winner and the runner-up, starting with the first night. Diefenbaker may have then, or later in his re-telling, concocted much of the animosity to maintain a distance from Drew, but Diefenbaker pointed to an incident where he felt shabbily treated. "On the night after his victory, I was an intruder. I went to congratulate him. I walked into that gathering, and it was as if an animal not customarily admitted to homes had suddenly come into the place." It was not the first time the Prairie populist would feel out of place among those who today might be called "Laurentian elites." It would not be the last, either. But Diefenbaker was not necessarily in error about Drew's aloofness, which would soon become evident during and after the election with Drew at the helm.

In the 1949 election, Diefenbaker once again pursued a path independent of his party. When campaign material arrived from national headquarters, he loaded it into a boat and defiantly threw it overboard. A poster of Drew never appeared in a Diefenbaker campaign office.[23] His primary challenger came from the Cooperative Commonwealth Federation, or "CCF" (the precursor to the New Democratic Party), the party Diefenbaker said would be the choice of most communist sympathizers. When challenged by the CCF premier of Saskatchewan, Tommy Douglas, to name them, Diefenbaker replied that it would cost too much money to read them out on the radio, but if he wanted him to read the list of the communists who were not going to vote CCF, he would read that.[24]

The Liberals had tired of being tormented by Diefenbaker in the House of Commons from the time he had entered the chamber in 1940 and wanted to take him out by any means necessary. This included the federal government renting an empty home next to Diefenbaker's residence in Prince Albert to have it converted into a foster residence for "unwed Indian mothers" during the campaign. As it happened, Diefenbaker retained his seat with a healthy margin, but it was one of only seven for the Progressive Conservatives in western Canada.

Drew could not win Ontario, let alone the nation. The Liberals under Louis St. Laurent picked up 73 seats and earned a comfortable majority government. The Tories were reduced to a rump of 41 seats. Given his earlier comments about the French, it was not surprising that Drew won only two seats in Quebec. One writer remarked that Drew was a "big, handsome aristocrat, the least common man [I had ever] come across." During the election campaign, the press nicknamed him "Gorgeous George." It was another way of saying he could not relate to voters.

Despite that loss, Drew remained the leader, only to flounder yet again in the 1953 election, earning just 51 seats compared with 171 for the St. Laurent Liberals, and this was when total parliamentary representation was just 265 seats. It was the fifth consecutive election loss for the Progressive Conservatives, and the prospects ahead remained bleak. Drew may have been ready to continue, but his party was broke, morale was low, and his political capital was spent. He had thrown every accusation he could at the Liberals in the election without any results to show for it. The only good news for the Tories was that with a succession of Liberal majority governments, the Grits had a sense of invincibility, and their arrogance reached new heights.

***

The Tories had no grand plan for the parliamentary session that began in January 1956. It was their good fortune that it included a debate that resulted in the most serious parliamentary upheaval since the conscription crisis in 1944. The Liberal government sought rapid construction of a natural gas pipeline from Alberta to Eastern Canada, and C.D. Howe, known colloquially as the "minister of everything," led the government charge. American-owned TransCanada Pipelines would construct and own the pipeline, but a government loan of $80 million was required to get started. The bill was delayed in cabinet, and Howe gave parliamentarians little time to debate. So tight was the deadline that the bill to finance the pipeline was introduced on May 8, 1956, with construction to begin in July. Before the bill was introduced, the government announced it would use closure to limit debate, which it did on four occasions. This was contempt for Parliament beyond anything the Liberals had attempted in the past. Closure is sometimes used after extensive and protracted debate along with political brinksmanship. Invoking closure on the day a bill is introduced was not a tactic used even during times of war.

Tories were outraged less by the content of the bill—although they were uncomfortable with the extent of American influence—than by how their duties as parliamentarians were nullified. In opposition, the Conservatives used every delaying mechanism and obstructive tactic left to them to prevent the legislation from passing through the various stages of debate.

When Howe was questioned in the House of Commons about the TransCanada Pipeline as "socialism personified," the minister replied, "That's not public enterprise; that's *my* enterprise." When questioned about reneging on government commitments, the same minister replied, "Who would stop us? If we wanted to get away with it—who would stop us?" Never repentant, Howe said, "If we have overstepped our powers, I make no apology for having done so." The Liberals got their pipeline, but the Tories won the debate in the public square. Rising Tory fortunes resulted from Liberal arrogance rather than Drew's cunning political wizardry.

For his part, Diefenbaker had been earning comfortable margins over four elections, and his status among party faithful was on the rise. He had considered retiring from politics in 1952 when it appeared that Drew was not going anywhere. However, the government redrew the electoral map in a manner that Diefenbaker believed was aimed at his defeat. In 1953, He ran not in Lake Centre but the new riding of Prince Albert to make the point that he could not be pushed around. He was not confident of victory but nonetheless had determined to go to London for the Coronation of Queen Elizabeth rather than campaign in Prince Albert. His wife, Olive, persuaded him to forgo the trip. It may not have been necessary, and the proud monarchist might have been fine in London for a spell as Diefenbaker won Prince Albert by a significant margin.

Just as Liberal arrogance peaked and Drew's political prospects shone brighter, the fatigue of nearly 20 years in politics had taken its toll. Drew was sidelined with a viral infection not long after the pipeline debate. His doctors told him he would not recover unless he relinquished the leadership. This was Diefenbaker's opportunity. Local Conservative constituency associations across the country saw Diefenbaker as the party's star attraction for fundraisers. His skill was cutting through Liberal hypocrisy with lines delivered like lightning bolts.

He made no friends on Bay Street, including when he told a Toronto audience that business executives convicted of anticompetitive conduct should be "thrown in the slammer" rather than slapped on the wrist with a fine. Some members of the parliamentary caucus resented Diefenbaker's lack of team play. His colleague who had his doubts previously had them again: Donald Fleming observed a fault in Diefenbaker: "To deserve loyalty on the part of others, a leader must have proven themselves loyal as a follower."[25]

Fleming was not wrong. Increasingly, Diefenbaker drew the limelight to himself more so than his party. It helped his cause that the press could always count on Diefenbaker for a pithy quote. This, combined with a short temper and unwillingness to do committee work, left him isolated from his fellow caucus members. He was beginning to exhibit the traits that would have him labelled a renegade much later in his career. According to party backroom organizer Dalton Camp:

> John Diefenbaker was an enigma. Popular with the press, presumably admired by Liberals, greatly in demand as a platform orator, Diefenbaker maintained a distance from his parliamentary colleagues. He rarely

> attended caucus, was not usually available to the Whip's office when it was attempting to organize the schedule of opposition speakers, and beyond the call of the duty roster for attendance in the house.[26]

Surprisingly, a man with leadership ambitions had little interest in connecting with parliamentary colleagues. His constituency was the common man, the disadvantaged, the dispossessed, and the persecuted. In short, the people, not the elites or even his fellow caucus members.

Diefenbaker had the first of many confrontations with Camp after a formal dinner in Winnipeg in 1955 to honour Sir John A. Macdonald. George Drew was the keynote speaker, and Diefenbaker and his wife were guests. Diefenbaker was displeased over the treatment given to his wife, Olive, whom he had married in 1953. He raised an issue from that evening a year or so later with Camp, as was described in Camp's autobiography:

> Diefenbaker: Sit down. I want to tell you something. I don't want my wife to be insulted again, you understand?
>
> Camp: I don't understand.
>
> Diefenbaker: I don't blame you. I know how they do these things, but I want you to know. I want to know that wherever I go, my wife goes. If I'm asked to sit at the head table, my wife sits with me. You see, that's the way it is with me. My wife does not sit below the salt.
>
> Camp: There were too many people for the head table. We had to ask all the wives to sit together at another table.
>
> Diefenbaker: I believe Mrs. Drew was at the head table.
>
> Camp: She was the only exception, except the mayor's wife.
>
> Olive Diefenbaker: Camp explained it couldn't be helped. Let's not talk about it.

Diefenbaker: Just a minute. I know how these things happen. But I want you to know, you see, there will never be a next time. That's all. If my wife can't be there, then I won't be there. Is that clear?[27]

Camp concluded Diefenbaker was paranoid and a troublemaker. He certainly did not see him as a future leader of the party. Neither did the Conservative establishment, none of whom Diefenbaker sought to court.

Over a year later, as if somewhat aware of his deficiencies and trigger-happy reflex when it came to perceived slights, Diefenbaker attempted to portray uncharacteristic humility as he announced his candidacy for the leadership with a vote scheduled for December 14, 1956. "[I]f Canadians generally believe that I have a contribution to make, if it is their wish that I let my name stand at the leadership convention, I am willing." Willing indeed—for the third time.

Just as the Conservative leadership race took shape, an international crisis over the Suez Canal erupted. Liberal Minister of External Affairs Lester B. Pearson was involved in settling the dispute for which he was awarded the Nobel Peace Prize. Diefenbaker was his party's critic for foreign affairs and labelled Pearson an "errand boy" for the Americans. The Nobel was an award Diefenbaker thought was wrongly given, a point he reiterated at Pearson's passing in 1972.[28]

A feeling of inevitability surrounded Diefenbaker's rise to the leadership. "Stop Diefenbaker" campaigns were launched but faded quickly. Word around the circles close to George Drew was, "If Diefenbaker wants it, let the crazy son of a bitch have it. People want John Diefenbaker, and there is no use kicking against the pricks." Donald Fleming cautioned that "even those who were not ready to support Diefenbaker were reluctant to show their true colours against him. This was based in some cases on the belief that he was bound to win, in others on fear of his reputed vindictiveness." Given how Diefenbaker had bucked the party in past elections, the question was asked whether he was really a conservative. After losing five consecutive elections, the party was ready to take the risk.

Diefenbaker was 61 when the convention gavel was struck at the Ottawa Coliseum in December 1956. "I have one love... Canada; one purpose... Canada's greatness; one aim... Canadian unity from the Atlantic to the Pacific." He declared he would lead a people's party that would help those most in need.[29] Sounding like a winner, Diefenbaker boasted there was no need for patience or a long period before Progressive Conservatives would hold power: he claimed he would win the next election.

Victory in the leadership came on the first ballot, although not without controversy. Diefenbaker chose a proposer from the Atlantic and a seconder from the Pacific, foregoing the tradition of an English and French introduction. The original plan was for Pierre Sévigny from Quebec to second the nomination, but Diefenbaker decided he wanted to do things differently. It was a mistake for which he was rebuked. Léon Balcer, a Quebec MP and co-chair of the convention put it bluntly: "This break with tradition is interpreted by Quebec delegates as an indication that Mr. Diefenbaker thinks he doesn't need Quebec support and doesn't care for it."[30] Many Quebec delegates walked out of the convention when the Diefenbaker's seconder was announced. In his acceptance speech, Diefenbaker pleaded for unity:

> I know some of you have a defeatist attitude. I leave you with a message that raised the spirits of Canadians in the First Great War. The officers were asked to do a formidable task and each one in turn was fearful of the result and said it could not be done. Finally, the officer commanding said: 'Now, gentlemen, you have given me every reason why it cannot be done. Now go and do it.' My friends let us unite and go and do it.[31]

When accepting the burden of leadership, he signalled that those entrusted with such positions had to know when to leave: "I say to you in all humility that the great trust that you have given me, the trust of the party of [John A.] Macdonald and of [George-Étienne] Cartier and their successors, will be handed on by me to whomever my successor may be, unimpaired and enhanced to the limits of my capacity and ability."[32]

Sympathetic to his fellow Quebec delegates who felt slighted, a young delegate from the province, 17-year-old Brian Mulroney, wrote in his memoirs of the difficulties Conservatives had faced in *la belle* province since the days of Macdonald. "It was my first experience with the self-destructive instinct of the PC Party, and I remember it troubled and embarrassed me greatly."

A prominent journalist, Bruce Hutchison, who was linked to the Liberal establishment, predicted that under Diefenbaker, the Tories would be reduced to sixteen seats. A journalist for the *Chicago Tribune* reported that a U.S. Embassy official confided, "It was like a bunch of guys from Mars had taken over."[33]

After the convention, Diefenbaker gave Dalton Camp a mission at party headquarters. "I just want to know what's going on down there, you see. Will you do that?" Perhaps it was a half-hearted effort to bring Camp into his fold. Camp, who earlier predicted the demise of Diefenbaker, remained skeptical and decidedly hostile towards his future leader, writing:

> Even though [his win was] certain, the achievement will not be graceful or painless.... (Diefenbaker) will be constantly reminded of the perils outside his door, where wicked forces combine to thwart his victory, even though the Conservative party has no other choice or purpose than to elect him and is, in fact, eager and anxious to do so.

Today's media, at least of the traditional variety, is often accused by conservatives (small or large 'c') of being left-wing or sympathetic to liberal causes and parties. While there is some accuracy in that complaint, in the 1950s, the press loved Diefenbaker for his crisp and colourful quotations.

Thinking he was something of a buffoon, the establishment Tories from Toronto underestimated the Prairie scrapper and waited for Diefenbaker to fall flat on his face. But the firebrand politician was what Canadians wanted after successive plodding, uninspired, and arrogant Liberal administrations. John Diefenbaker now had to fulfill his commitment to party members telling the faithful "We have an appointment with destiny."[34]

- 5 -

1957: FROM OPPOSITION TO MINORITY

I caught the big one yesterday.

After winning the leadership of the Progressive Conservative Party of Canada, Diefenbaker's priority was unity. He knew he was not the first choice of eastern-establishment Tories, who did not hide their displeasure before the CBC cameras when the first and only leadership ballot was tallied. "There was no doubt," wrote Diefenbaker in his memoirs, "that they regarded me being chosen leader an unmitigated disaster, a catastrophe, a judgment that they now considered beyond doubt."[1]

Diefenbaker proffered up an olive branch to the man whose 1949 campaign literature he discarded and whose wife Diefenbaker thought should not have had a seat at a Winnipeg dinner. Diefenbaker invited George Drew to be his seatmate in the House of Commons, but Drew declined the offer owing to ill health. But it was more than illness. Drew told his friends, "The party is finished. It won't be three months before Diefenbaker has lost control. He gets his eye on one thing, and he concentrates on it, and he gets up and makes a speech on it. Then he goes away for two weeks to recover."[2] At least that was Drew's assessment of Diefenbaker when roles were reversed, and Drew served under him in caucus.

Diefenbaker then asked his leadership opponents, Davie Fulton and Donald Fleming, to take senior positions on the front benches, which they readily accepted. But, as Drew predicted, cracks quickly appeared. After being reassured by the party's national director that he was committed to Diefenbaker's success in the next election, his resignation letter appeared in the *Ottawa Journal* a few weeks later. Diefenbaker sensed danger. "What I did not need was a national headquarters full of people whose chief desire was to torpedo me so as to bring about a new leadership convention as quickly as possible."[3] This led to hiring Allister Grosart, an advertising agency executive, as the party's new national director. He was loyal to Diefenbaker in even the most trying of circumstances.

When Parliament resumed sitting on January 8, 1957, Diefenbaker sensed jubilation on the Liberal front benches. He was happy to be underestimated, as he had been over most of his political career. When the Liberal budget augmented the Old Age Pension by six dollars per month—not necessarily an insubstantial lift when OAS started in 1952 at 40 dollars a month but where it still stood five years later—Diefenbaker labelled the Liberal cabinet the "six-buck boys." He contrasted this parsimony with tax breaks for large businesses the St. Laurent government offered up.

When the *Royal Commission on Canada's Economic Prospects'* first report was tabled in the House of Commons in 1956, Diefenbaker pounced on its conclusion that Canada's economic independence was vulnerable to American control of our strategic national assets. This included our natural resources and many large businesses. It was then that Diefenbaker conceived of a vision for developing a made-in-Canada program to develop our natural resources in the North and Far North. It was a 20th century version of Macdonald's national policy that had defined his career. It became known as the New Frontier Policy, a name that Diefenbaker claims was later "borrowed without attribution" by John F. Kennedy in the 1960 American election. Diefenbaker's vision also included major infrastructure projects such as a national electricity grid, hydropower from the Fraser, Hamilton and Columbia Rivers as well as the Bay of Fundy and the South Saskatchewan Dam.

The Liberals chose June 10, 1957, as Election Day. The campaign began with Louis St. Laurent polling at a comfortable 48 percent. Believing defeat was impossible, he left 16 coveted Senate seats vacant. The Liberals ran on a long record in governing Canada during unprecedented growth. They offered little new policy to confront the challenges facing the agricultural sector or a deepening trade imbalance. Diefenbaker was intent on capturing the imagination of Canadian voters, believing that government "was as much a matter of inspiration as it was administration."[4]

Diefenbaker was more confident about victory than those on his campaign team. When they cautioned against booking Toronto's Massey Hall for a campaign event, fearing a sparse crowd would reflect poorly in the press, Diefenbaker told them, "If we can't fill it, we might as well forget the whole campaign."

Diefenbaker's confidence and challenge were met as the hall was packed with supporters on the evening of April 25. In a speech he would echo for the remainder of his time as leader, Diefenbaker said his abiding faith lay in the freedom of the Canadian people and the sovereign independence of Canada where "the state shall be the servant and not the master of the people."

On the stump, Diefenbaker's team remarked that he had three speeches in mind when he went to the podium. First, the one he intended to give. Second, the prepared remarks that were given to the press. Third, the speech he finally delivered to the audience. Diefenbaker believed he was at his best when he got a sense of the crowd and a feeling for what moved them. Teleprompters were in use in the 1950s, but not by Diefenbaker, who observed the device turned speakers into amateur announcers. He preferred that desks be removed from the House of Commons so members would have to stand without notes nearby. "There is no nervousness in reading a script," Diefenbaker noted, "nor is there any debate." He was an early advocate of television cameras in Parliament to encourage attendance and more lively debate. In short, he was a performer who rose to whatever challenge was in front of him.

Dalton Camp conceded that when on the stump, absent artificial stagecraft, Diefenbaker elevated written speeches:

> He seemed to know where the knife met the bone, and he knew how to get it out and put it over to the audience, and he had a way then, in that particular year, of touching people or reaching people. He made Conservatives feel and made people hopeful... He had time for everybody. He had time for waitresses and time for taxi drivers.... It was as though the whole country was Prince Albert.[5]

Historian and author Conrad Black observed that Diefenbaker had a jerky delivery style in his speeches but had "perfect timing, great wit, a fine ear for the absurd and the incongruous, and a possessed quality, earnest and even fanatical that commanded attention and, among an irreducible group of followers, adherence."[6]

He sparred with hecklers but almost always with humour. To one detractor who refused to shake his hand, "Not now or ever?" Diefenbaker asked. "Well. I admire you for your clarity of expression and your loyalty to your party."[7] After gaining the backing of a woman voter, Diefenbaker asked if he would also get her husband's support. "My husband? He hasn't supported me for the last seven years," which reflected how Canadians would share their stories with him.

The campaign revolved not around the party but on its leader. "It's Time for a Diefenbaker Government" was the slogan on Tory banners at rallies and in campaign material. There was little attachment or support for the Conservative brand in the country, but sentiment for a change in government was building. Diefenbaker represented not only change for the country but change for his party. In one respect, Diefenbaker wanted to modernize the party by returning it to its roots. Campaign posters featured pictures of the two Johns—Diefenbaker and Canada's first prime minister, Sir John A. Macdonald—both ardent nationalists inherently wary of American influence.

In speeches, Diefenbaker lamented that 65 percent of our national income was foreign-controlled: "How long Canada can continue as a separate existence is the problem before Canada today." Through his northern vision, he promised Canadian ownership and control over a development that would create hundreds of thousands of jobs. It was not a partisan statement, as all parties advocated for greater Canadian control of our economy. But Diefenbaker was a more convincing crusader.

According to Diefenbaker, the turning point in the campaign was a meeting in Vancouver on May 23. The auditorium was filled with 10,000 people. The momentum became evident to those who thought Liberals could not lose.

However, Quebec remained a question mark for Diefenbaker, as it had been for Conservatives since the days of Macdonald. The hanging of Louis Riel in 1885 when Macdonald was in power, the support for conscription in two world wars, and the failure of the Tory party ever to nominate a leader from Quebec (unlike the Liberals that alternated French and English leaders) left the Conservatives on the sidelines in Quebec for much of the 20th century. In his speech in Montreal on March 12, Diefenbaker outlined an eight-point plan on what a Conservative government would do for Quebecers. The plan included respecting provincial rights, halting the centralization of power in Ottawa, respecting parliamentary democracy, reversing the trend to socialism, supporting the agricultural sector, respecting labour rights, and maintaining social security measures. The speech and its content were politely received. Quebecers remained uneasy about what he meant by "One Canada—One Nation" when they mostly viewed the country as a partnership of two founding languages and peoples.

The Chief brought the evangelical zeal of a preacher to campaign events, mesmerizing and energizing party supporters. Diefenbaker spoke in grand terms, much the way he had to his mother when he was a boy. "I'm one of those who believe that this party has a sacred trust, trust in accordance with the traditions of Macdonald. It has an appointment with destiny.... one Canada, with equality of opportunity for every citizen."

Diefenbaker knew that to win, he needed more than the traditional Tory supporters in the countryside. In the previous five federal elections, the best the party had mustered in the popular vote was 30.3 percent. The Tories needed to attract and motivate the undecided, the apathetic, and the disenchanted to their side. The key was not party ideology but the populist Diefenbaker. He appealed to the average Canadian: "My abiding interest is your interest; my guiding principle is the welfare of the average Canadian." This was not micro-targeting of different blocks of voters in different regions but a plea to gain a wide swath of support nationwide. Whenever local Tory organizers tried to impress their leader by arranging transportation in a shiny new Cadillac or limousine, he declined, preferring to ride with campaign workers in a nondescript Chevrolet.

Canadian ownership of industry was an objective as well as increased immigration and reduced taxes. Another key platform plank was support for farmers. Diefenbaker favoured price supports, producer marketing boards, government lending programs, favourable freight rates, and crop insurance for farmers. For seniors, he ridiculed the six dollars per month increase in Old Age Security as a mere 20 cents per day, leaving them with less purchasing power than they had six years before. Rather than periodic and discretionary increases, Diefenbaker proposed pension increases that kept pace with the cost of living. He also promised to extend national health insurance to cover tubercular and mental health patients.

Conservatives had lost long enough and so were willing to allow Diefenbaker to remake their party in his image. Party president George Hees remarked to his fellow candidates across the land, "I don't care if they like acrobats or cream cheese. If they like it, give it to them. It's about time we realized that people would rather be entertained than educated." Hees told his party's candidates, "Whenever I see a hand sticking out of a sleeve, I shake it." Hees was not taken seriously by Liberal C.D. Howe, who described Hees as a man with "the build of Adonis and the brains of a gnat."

***

As leader, Diefenbaker used the 1957 election to advance the cause central to his involvement in public life: a Bill of Rights. To most Canadians living paycheque to paycheque, it was not an issue that captured many imaginations. But it did place Diefenbaker on a different level as a politician, and it was something they had not come to expect from a Conservative leader. The typical Tory was more in tune with business and economic interests, more at home in a chamber of commerce or Rotary Club meeting than being preoccupied with what seemed like philosophical positions. As he had proposed in private members bills, a Bill of Rights would make Parliament more conscious of freedom. "It would act as a landmark by means of which Canadians, through Parliament, would have redeclared those things which have made Canada great.... Canada that stood for prejudice towards none and freedom for all. There were to be no second-class citizens, no discrimination based on race, creed, sex, or economic station in the Canada of my dreams."[8]

Audiences across the country responded enthusiastically to Diefenbaker's optimism and hope. The Liberals, encouraged by favourable polls, dismissed evidence of Diefenbaker's rising popularity. When Diefenbaker openly predicted his party would win 97 seats, a press gallery member declared it wishful thinking. So did his campaign team, who were hoping for 80 seats. A poll taken June 8, two days before Election Day, had the Liberals ahead by five percentage points. St. Laurent said he had no doubt about the outcome and planned to attend the Prime Ministers' Conference in London on June 26.[9] *Maclean's* went to press before the votes were counted and presuming a Liberal victory declared, "For better or for worse, we Canadians have once again elected one of the most powerful governments ever created by the free will of a free electorate. We have given that government an almost unprecedented vote of confidence, considering the length of its term in office." At the CBC, reporter Charles Lynch was chastised by management for stating Diefenbaker might win the election. The broadcaster wanted him, "to stick to the straight and narrow, which meant the assumption of yet another Liberal victory."[10] Meanwhile, the *Globe and Mail* editorialists in Toronto meekly endorsed Saskatchewan's Diefenbaker as "fully competent to become Prime Minister."

When the results were tallied up on June 10, 1957, Louis St. Laurent's Liberals won the popular vote count, besting the Tories by almost two percentage points.

However, because of the huge Liberal pluralities in Quebec, the larger popular vote did not translate into a greater number of seats. Nearly half of St. Laurent's cabinet went down to defeat.

The final seat count was 111 seats for the Conservatives, 104 for the Liberals, 25 for CCF, and 19 for Social Credit. The increase from four to a modest eight seats in Quebec for the PCs made the Tory entry into government more likely than a Liberal return with the help of the CCF. Voter turnout was 74.1 percent, a significant increase from 67.5 percent in the previous election, another indication that Diefenbaker had inspired the nation and that the country wanted a change in government.

The contest was close enough that Prime Minister St. Laurent did not concede until after the military vote was counted. When the final vote did not change the tally, Liberal ministers urged their leader to form a government and face Parliament. Liberals had played this card once before, in 1925, when they were 15 seats short of the Tories but clung to power briefly with the help of the 22 Progressive MPs. St. Laurent wisely rejected the advice because of his lower seat total and the lack of Liberal seats outside Quebec. Liberals had won 82 percent of the seats in Quebec but only 22 percent in the rest of Canada. It's not that everyone on the Liberal front bench was enamoured with St. Laurent. During the pipeline debate C.D. Howe was rumoured to have said St. Laurent, who was 75, would carry the Liberal banner in the 1957 election "even if we have to run him stuffed."[11]

On election night, Diefenbaker, 61, visited his mother in a hospital in Saskatoon. "You've been given the opportunity to do something for your country. Do not forget the poor and afflicted. Do the best you can as long as you can," she told him.[12] In an address before the national media in Regina, Diefenbaker said that when he accepted his party's leadership, he indicated this scripture would guide him: "He who would be chiefist among you shall be the servant of all."[13] Then, "Dief the Chief" became widely used as the moniker for Canada's 13th prime minister.

One day after the election, Diefenbaker went fishing with a few friends and some reporters at Saskatchewan's Lac La Ronge. After observing a small catch by the Chief, a friend said, "Not much of a fish you got there, eh?" Diefenbaker, who enjoyed having his picture taken while fishing to portray his rural roots and connection to ordinary Canadians, replied, "I caught the big one yesterday." Four days after the election, Diefenbaker and his wife took a regular overnight commercial flight to Ottawa, which he paid for out of his pocket. Three days later, St. Laurent announced his decision to resign. When Diefenbaker was summoned to Rideau Hall to meet with the Governor General, he travelled by taxi.

***

Diefenbaker's cabinet differed little in structure from its predecessor except that with 23 ministers, he had one less than the previous administration. His general view was that a cabinet beyond that number would be dysfunctional and a glorified extension of the House of Commons. Further, a large cabinet, he thought, inevitably resulted in a large bureaucracy with added cost and reduced political influence. He restricted his cabinet to previously elected MPs, which left him with few options from Quebec. Because the Liberals had held power for the past 22 years, every minister, including the prime minister, had virtually no experience at the cabinet table.

Diefenbaker drew inspiration from past world leaders who filled critical posts in their administrations with political rivals. As Diefenbaker remarked to Ellen Fairclough, a chartered accountant by training and whom he appointed as Canada's first female minister, "Looks to me as if I have to compose a cabinet of my enemies." She had not supported Diefenbaker in the leadership contest. Diefenbaker endeavoured to appoint Ottawa Mayor Charlotte Whitton an Ambassador to Eire (Ireland). But just before assuming the post, she had a physical altercation with a city board of control member, and the appointment was terminated.[14] Diefenbaker would later appoint Canada's first female ambassador when Margaret Meagher became our head of mission in Israel.

Fairclough's cabinet appointment set a precedent that others would follow. Lester B. Person appointed Judy LaMarsh to the cabinet in 1963. However, when Pierre Trudeau became prime minister in 1968, his first cabinet comprised only men. While common sentiment then was that "conservatives" were slow to embrace change while Liberals were naturally progressive, the record is that over Trudeau's 15 and-a-half years in office, only three women made it to his cabinet table, making Diefenbaker's ground-breaking appointment all the more exceptional.

Diefenbaker set other precedents: Michael Starr, of Ukrainian descent, was the first MP of neither British nor French origin to enter the cabinet. It was, at the time, a breakthrough appointment. As Starr put it, when he spoke Ukrainian to some of his constituents, they would cry out of disbelief, with one saying, "Now I can die. I have met a minister of Ukrainian extraction." The voters gave Diefenbaker another first: Douglas Jung became the first MP of Chinese descent and from a visible minority. He was also a lawyer and a war hero.

Some ministers filled multiple roles. In addition to being the first minister, Diefenbaker was president of the Privy Council and secretary of state for External Affairs, albeit briefly. A few months after the election, Diefenbaker recruited University of Toronto president Sidney Smith to the position.

There was criticism that his cabinet included only three ministers from Quebec, and only one, Léon Balcer, was a francophone. Ontario had five ministers. Diefenbaker responded that there had been four ministers from Quebec in 1940. For a time in 1942, due to various resignations, the only francophone in the Liberal cabinet was the prime minister. This was cold comfort to Quebecers who felt they deserved better from Diefenbaker.

Despite winning the first Tory government in 22 years, members of Diefenbaker's cabinet remained skeptical that he could lead the country. Governing was an enormous challenge for Diefenbaker, whose experience running an organization was limited to a small Saskatchewan law office and a national political party for a brief period.[a] He wisely retained and relied on the clerk of the Privy Council, Robert Bryce, for sound advice. For a man known to be vindictive, he made surprisingly few changes in the public service and even retained some ministerial assistants who were Liberal partisans.

Diefenbaker listened to his cabinet but always sought consensus or unanimity that aligned with his position. As prime minister, he averaged 140 cabinet meetings annually, almost double that of the previous Liberal administration.[15] But there were limits to what cabinet ministers could do. "If there are any statesmen here," he told his ministers, "they'd better resign. I want politicians."

He established strict rules for ministers and enacted a code of conduct to limit or eliminate conflicts of interest. Cabinet deliberations were secret, with communications strictly controlled by the prime minister. Ministers were threatened with termination should they break these rules. Diefenbaker regarded each of his ministers as equals at the cabinet table, with all enjoying the right to

---

a Stephen Harper was similarly inexperienced, having run only a small advocacy group, the National Citizens Coalition. Harper lasted in power for nine years compared with Diefenbaker's six.

place an item on the agenda for consideration. He left it to himself to determine the matters to be discussed.

External Affairs and the roster of ambassadors that filled Canadian embassies abroad worried the prime minister.

> The department had built up an inbred elite of personalities, which had been allowed to establish its own rules, a kingdom within a kingdom where diplomatic initiatives and negotiations were too often governed by democratically irresponsible perceptions of Canada's needs. I wanted to change this. I thought that something midway between the Canadian practice and that followed by the United States, where almost every head of post was a political appointee, would serve Canada well.[16]

He also believed that Canadian ambassadors or high commissioners should have a direct line to the prime minister on essential matters. He appointed his predecessor, George Drew, as high commissioner to Great Britain over the objections of the senior ranks at External Affairs.

Diefenbaker worried that those at the deputy minister rank had "absorbed the political faith" of the previous Liberal government. While judging each deputy on their merits, he directed ministers not to allow themselves to be led around by their deputies or cowered by their deputies' superior command of relevant data.[17]

While holding a slim minority government, Diefenbaker acted as if he had a majority, ready and willing to go to the people at any moment should his government be defeated. He wanted another election partly because his economic briefings indicated a recession was imminent. His government's response was to add stimulus to the economy as he did not want to follow the early years of R.B. Bennett, who had the misfortune of governing during the Great Depression. Better, thought Diefenbaker, to convert his minority to a majority before the economy tanked.

It was Diefenbaker's good timing that the former Liberal government had invited Queen Elizabeth to open the postelection session of Parliament for October 14. Breaking with protocol, Diefenbaker agreed to allow CBC cameras to broadcast the Throne Speech, where he would be seated next to Her Majesty. On the side of bad timing, it was the day the Nobel Prize committee announced its award for peace was going to Lester Pearson

In the throne speech, the Diefenbaker government was generous with the public purse and committed to enhancing old age security while providing additional support for farmers. It also pledged to eliminate discrimination against married women in unemployment insurance by extending their unemployment benefits from sixteen to twenty-four weeks, another indication that Diefenbaker cared about the average Canadian and was pro-women before feminism became associated with more liberal politicians later in the 1960s and the 1970s. The Tory party, which had a generation of leadership that had condemned socialism and government largesse, was now helping people who were down and out with taxpayer funds. To Diefenbaker, it was not social welfare but social justice.

Diefenbaker brought about a fundamental change that led to the implementation of a universal national health-care system that the Liberal government of Louis St. Laurent had resisted. The premier of Saskatchewan, Tommy Douglas, had sought to establish a single-payer hospital plan under a 50-50 cost-shared arrangement with the federal government. The St. Laurent government agreed to such a plan in 1955 under the Hospital Insurance and Diagnostic Services Act based on uniform terms and conditions, provided that a majority of provinces comprising a majority of the population had qualifying hospital insurance programs. University of Toronto professor Gregory P. Marchildon wrote that Douglas was "infuriated by the double majority rule and perceived it as a political ploy by Prime Minister St. Laurent to delay, perhaps indefinitely, the implementation of national hospital coverage."[18] Diefenbaker believed in medicare and had the double-majority clause removed from the legislation. On July 1, 1958, Saskatchewan began receiving 50 percent funding for its universal hospital coverage. Soon, Alberta, British Columbia, and Manitoba altered their programs to become eligible for federal funding. By 1961, every province became part of the system, providing all Canadians with universal access to hospital care. This placed a significant demand on federal finances. From $27 million in 1958, the federal contribution rose to $150 million in 1959, $170 million in 1960, and $260 million in 1961.[19]

***

Diefenbaker's proposals, which included reductions in corporate tax rates for small businesses and support for major infrastructure projects, constituted significant financial investments in Canada's future. He was determined to see the construction of the South Saskatchewan Dam, and he "would not allow a national need to be frustrated by cost-benefit bureaucratic studies."[20] This meant he would go over the heads of the bureaucrats who had known nothing but Liberals for the previous 22 years. And he was in a hurry to get things done. The South Saskatchewan Dam was started in 1959 and was operational in 1967. It created *Lake Diefenbaker* by diverting a significant flow of the South Saskatchewan River into the Qu'Appelle River. The dam was named after a former Liberal premier of Saskatchewan, James G. Gardiner.

If Diefenbaker had any doubts that he had reached the pinnacle of political success, reality sank in when he met Winston Churchill and the Queen a few months after being sworn in at his first Commonwealth meeting. Lady Churchill told Olive that when the election result was announced, her husband was so excited he danced. Diefenbaker often recounted his conversation with Churchill when asked to join the recently retired British PM for a drink.

Churchill: Are you a prohibitionist or a teetotaler?

Diefenbaker: A teetotaler.

Churchill: Good. In that case, you only hurt yourself.[21]

Olive added that her husband was not an absolutist about alcohol and would very occasionally have a glass of sherry.

Diefenbaker's wariness of American dominance appeared early on when he pressed for increased trade with Britain to diminish Canada's economic reliance on the United States. A goal of diverting 15 percent of imports from the United States to the United Kingdom was established, an arbitrary target that Diefenbaker described as "reasonable, equitable and obtainable." He went further, suggesting that a free trade agreement with Britain be explored. However, his proposals lacked any form of realism, insight, or meaningful analysis. Discriminating against the Americans in trade would place Canada against the General Agreement on Tariffs and Trade (GATT), not to mention the plain economic common sense of fully exploiting trade opportunities with a next-door neighbour.

Diefenbaker's trade and commerce minister, George Hees, was less concerned with whom Canada traded so long as it traded. His tie clip was decorated with the letters Y.C.D.B.S.O.Y.A. In meetings, he would fiddle with the clip until, invariably, someone would ask what the letters stood for. "What's it mean, you ask? Well, you can't do business sitting on your ass."

When the prime minister travelled to the United States in September 1957 to meet President Dwight Eisenhower, he remarked that issues and problems were best solved in an atmosphere of unity and friendship. Diefenbaker wanted Canada to be less of an exporter of raw materials and more of an exporter of finished goods. He also wanted greater Canadian ownership and control of industries. However, it was national defence that dominated Canadian-American relations during Diefenbaker's term as prime minister.

***

Diefenbaker wanted to convert his parliamentary minority into a majority as soon as possible, but that would take a political opening he could not conjure up on his own. Diefenbaker's energy remained high, and he continued campaigning as if an election was imminent. He positioned his government in the political center to broaden the Tory appeal before the next election.

Nation-building projects commenced in all regions, which included electric power development in the Atlantic provinces, a Winter Works Program, the construction of six ships, and work on the Mackenzie Highway. As to how these investments impacted the federal debt load, Diefenbaker told the House of Commons on January 21, 1958, "We are not going to put a balanced budget above our firm determination to provide, through the agency of public works, jobs for unemployed Canadians."[22]

Diefenbaker enjoyed being prime minister and was not overwhelmed by the trappings of power. He typically woke up at 5:30 a.m. after three to four hours of sleep and began his day with a grapefruit and coffee.[23] He would dictate letters for an hour before heading out for a morning walk of about two kilometres with no security detail, although he changed his route each day as a precaution. His workday was about 14 hours, which included lunch at his desk. He rarely visited the posh and storied Rideau Club, an institution that over its history discriminated against women and minorities and was the only prime minister who never sought a membership. In his memoirs, Diefenbaker explained his rationale: "We ended discrimination and I have refused over the years to join any club that discriminates on the basis of colour or religion."[24] He naturally resisted elite cultural institutions and kept formal dinners to a minimum. His focus was on maintaining his connection to ordinary Canadians.

- 6 -

1958: MINORITY TO MAJORITY

This is a victory not for any one person or party but rather a victory for the kind of Canadianism in which we all believe.

In January 1958, the Liberal Party chose Lester B. "Mike" Pearson over Paul Martin Sr. as leader. Diefenbaker watched the convention on television and confidently remarked, "I saw one of the banners that the Young Liberals carried which was entitled, 'Diefenbaker—'raw deal.'" He loved the attention, remarking, "Advertising, wherever it comes from, is always acceptable so long as one doesn't have to pay for it."

With the polls heavily in the Tories' favour and the Opposition in disarray, talk of an election buzzed around Parliament Hill. When the former diplomat and Nobel Prize winner took his seat in the House of Commons on January 20, 1958, as leader of Her Majesty's Loyal Opposition, he immediately went on the offensive and challenged the Diefenbaker government to resign. But Pearson was not throwing down the election gauntlet and putting the seats of his Liberal caucus members on the line. He wanted a one-way ticket directly to the prime minister's chair in a minority parliament. "I would be prepared, if called upon, to form... a government to tackle immediately the formidable problem of ending the Tory pause and getting this country back on the Liberal highway of progress from which we have been temporarily diverted."

Temporarily, indeed. It had barely been seven months since the 1957 election. His motion read in part, "in view of the desirability, at this time, of having a government pledged to implement Liberal policies, His Excellency's advisors should... submit their resignations forthwith."[1]

The attitude on the Liberal benches was that they were the natural party of government, and it was plain wrong to have a Tory sit in the prime minister's chair. St. Laurent had admitted that Canadians had "got tired of having us around," but the question remained: How long should they be kept in opposition? Party stalwart Jack Pickersgill said, "We are the party of government; the Conservatives are like the mumps; you get them once in your life."[2]

Diefenbaker sensed a golden opportunity to belittle his unworthy opponent and keep the Liberals on the opposition side of the House for an extended period. "This is it," Diefenbaker said to his seatmate in the House of Commons, Howard Green. In an unscripted address that lasted two hours, Diefenbaker portrayed the new Liberal leader, not inaccurately, as arrogant, which weakened Pearson in the public imagination:

> On Thursday, there was shrieking defiance; on Monday, there was shrinking indecision... The only reason this motion is worded as it is, is that my honourable friends opposite quake when they think of what will happen if an election comes.... It is the resignation from responsibility of a great party.

Diefenbaker later told his associates he had "operated on Pearson without an anesthetic."[3] He added, "Pearson must have had help drafting that motion. Could one person, without assistance, have produced anything so stupid?"[4]

Lester Pearson could not counter the takedown. As he wrote in his memoirs, "Diefenbaker tore me to shreds." His seatmate, Paul Martin Sr., said Diefenbaker had delivered "one of the greatest devastating speeches (in Canadian history)." CCF MP Colin Cameron agreed and said in the House of Commons, "I wonder if the Prime Minister really believes in the humane slaughtering of animals."[5] CBC's Charles Lynch noted the same in his coverage, pointing out that Diefenbaker, "smote Pearson, hip and thigh." But CBC management reprimanded Lynch for "editorializing." Lynch claimed truth as his defence.[6]

Worse for Pearson, Diefenbaker could use Pearson's motion to turn over the government to the Liberals as justification for the election he desperately wanted and an opportunity to win a majority government that he coveted. There was another reason why Diefenbaker wanted to go to the polls. Government revenues were falling because of a weakening economy, and some economists predicted a recession. Diefenbaker wanted to act fast so he could blame the economic downturn on the Liberals for failing to disclose or respond to a pending crisis. Diefenbaker laid his hands on a report prepared by the former associate deputy minister of trade and commerce, Mitchell Sharp, that contained damaging evidence held by the previous Liberal government that they kept from the public. Diefenbaker made his case in the House of Commons:

> I intend to establish as clearly as the printed word will make possible that my honourable friend concealed from the Canadian people the facts. You [Mr. Pearson] secured the advice of the economists in your own departments and were advised as to what the situation was in March 1957.... They had a warning... did they tell us that?.... Why did they not act when the House was sitting in January, February, March and April?.... You [Pearson] concealed the facts; that is what you did.

Diefenbaker went to Quebec City on February 1 to meet Governor General Vincent Massey and claimed obstruction in Parliament. The reality was that the Liberal party was weak, and Diefenbaker was exploiting Pearson's rookie error. Parliament was dissolved, and an election was scheduled for March 31, 1958, just nine months and three weeks since the last campaign. It was not much longer a term than when Joe Clark held a Tory government in 1979–80 but with an entirely different outcome.

In the 1958 campaign, Diefenbaker's "northern vision" took shape. He promised "Roads to Resources" and respect for northern native communities. With this call and ambition, voters could hear the echo of Sir John A. Macdonald's national vision for Canada, a sentiment Diefenbaker bolstered:

> This is the vision: One Canada. One Canada, where Canadians will have preserved to them the control of their own economic and political destiny. Sir John A. Macdonald saw Canada from east to west: I see a new Canada—Canada of the North.... this is the vision.

Pearson could not grasp the appeal of Diefenbaker's approach and criticized the merits of "building roads from igloo to igloo." In response, Diefenbaker brought his vision to life: "I think of a vast program on Frobisher Bay on Baffin Island in the Canadian Arctic. We intend to start a vast roads program for the Yukon and Northwest Territories, which will open up exploration of vast new oil and mineral areas—thirty million acres."

Diefenbaker saw himself as a man of the people who campaigned under the slogan "Follow John." He pursued Napoleon's maxim: a leader peddles hope. "Instead of [the] helplessness and fear the Liberals generate," said Diefenbaker, "we have given faith; instead of desperation, we offer inspiration." As the northern vision took hold, Diefenbaker added other elements: "We'll build a nation of fifty million people within the lifetime of many of you here. I'm asking you to catch the vision of the greatness and the potential of this nation."

He gave life and credibility to the slogan offered by the late 19th-century/early 20th-century Liberal leader Sir Wilfrid Laurier, "The twentieth century belongs to Canada." With Diefenbaker at the helm, Canadians thought that it might. With Diefenbaker, Canada also had a leader who stood up to the conservative establishment. The Tory party had redefined itself in one quick and easy step: the stiff-shirted Bay Street banker was out; Canada's new folk hero was in. In Quebec, Tory minister Pierre Sévigny experienced first-hand the evangelical zeal of his leader: "I saw people kneel and kiss his coat. Not one, but many people were in tears. People were delirious."[7]

After Diefenbaker cemented a political relationship with Maurice Duplessis of the Union Nationale government in Quebec, the cradle and nexus of traditional Liberal support, Pearson was dead in the water. It was Duplessis's opportunity to return the favour the Liberals had done him when they intervened in the Quebec provincial election in 1939. Duplessis had resisted previous involvement in federal politics so long as St. Laurent, a Quebecer, was leading the Liberal party. With the unilingual Pearson at the helm, Duplessis saw an opening to bring the Liberals down and have a federal prime minister who would owe him some favours. Duplessis biographer Conrad Black was told the story of Yvon Tassé, a school architect, who was awakened by the Quebec premier one evening and told to get dressed and get into the premier's car waiting at his front door to accept a draft as the Tory candidate. Tassé said he didn't want the nomination. Duplessis told him to do as asked if he wanted to keep designing schools in Quebec.[8]

Duplessis personally selected the Progressive Conservative candidates in his home province and ensured that $15,000 was made available in each of 50 winnable constituencies. His Union Nationale political machine was activated, and voters in these ridings were canvassed by Duplessis loyalists at least twice during the 1958 campaign. Despite the momentum, there was evident tension between Diefenbaker and party organizer Dalton Camp. "Your stuff is not as good now as it was last time," Diefenbaker told Camp. For his part, Camp thought Diefenbaker was more demanding and imperial now that he was campaigning as the prime minister. When Camp suggested to Diefenbaker that Tory candidates should not disparage the awarding of the Nobel Peace Prize to Lester Pearson, he was not aware they were following Diefenbaker's instructions.[9]

Pearson was a weak opponent, at one point criticizing Diefenbaker for putting the country through a winter election before being reminded that his intervention in the House of Commons precipitated the contest. He told his colleagues he hoped Liberals would win 100 seats.

On election night, Quebecers jumped on the Tory bandwagon in full force, giving Diefenbaker a majority of the popular vote nationwide and 50 of Quebec's 75 seats. Tory candidates swept Prince Edward Island, Nova Scotia, Manitoba, and Alberta. The CCF was reduced to eight seats, and the once mighty Liberal party became a rump of 48 members, its lowest number since Confederation. The Tories took their Social Credit first cousins down from 19 seats to zero. By taking 53 percent of the popular vote, compared to 33 percent for the Liberals, the Conservative caucus swelled to 208 members. With 78.5 percent of total seats, no Canadian government of any stripe has ever held such command of the House of Commons before or since. Pearson's wife described the fate that had fallen upon her partner well: "You have lost everything, Mike. You've even won your seat."[10]

Sir John A. Macdonald once said, "Given a government with a big surplus, a big majority and a weak opposition, you could debauch a committee of archangels." Now, with an overwhelming and unprecedented majority, the Chief was burdened by high expectations and a caucus too large to be manageable, especially in Quebec. Politically, he had only one way to go: down.

Diefenbaker claimed his government was truly national, representing all people and races. "This is a victory.... not for any one person or party, but rather a victory for the kind of Canadianism in which we all believe." This may have been what Diefenbaker believed, but it's more likely that Canadians responded to an enigmatic leader's charisma, conviction, and charm with a fortuitous boost from a Quebec premier.

Richard Nixon, then vice president of the United States, wrote to Diefenbaker to congratulate him on his overwhelming victory, "History will record that you are one of the truly great political campaigners of our time. The fact that within the space of just a few months you were able to do what you did against what appeared to be impossible odds is an achievement which has seldom been equaled in history."

Despite the trappings of office and the strict protocol attached to being prime minister, Diefenbaker did not lose touch with ordinary Canadians and never forgot his Prairie populist roots. "One thing which must be guarded against is complacency and its twin, arrogance, which are often the aftermath of great political victory.... I intend to maintain as close a relationship with the people as possible and ask various outstanding Canadians to give me the benefit of their views from time to time." He is the last prime minister who would see citizens in his office without an appointment. Students touring the Parliament buildings could stop by Diefenbaker's office. He liked to quote Abraham Lincoln, saying, "God must have liked the common people. He made so many of them."[11] Diefenbaker said, "I like people. Their problems are your problems. Their heartbreaks are your heartbreaks.... I did not set out to be just to the powerful. They can look after themselves."

Another American president Diefenbaker admired was Harry Truman, who had similar populist and down-to-earth instincts and preferences. As Truman put it, "My own sympathy has always been with the little fellow. The man without advantages.... Whether discrimination is based on race, creed, or color, or land of origin, it is utterly contrary to American ideals of democracy." As to vision, Truman said, "Make no little plans. Make the biggest one you can think of and spend the rest of your life carrying it out." That vision and purpose for Diefenbaker was to stick up for ordinary citizens and ensure equality for all Canadians.

It wasn't easy, however, for the mostly unilingual Diefenbaker to connect with Quebecers. Diefenbaker didn't mind poking fun at himself on the subject. "Apparently, I just can't pronounce French well while talking. An English-speaking friend joked to me, 'I love to hear you talk French on television. When you do, every English-speaking person in the audience, who doesn't know a word of French, can understand every word you say,'" he wrote. Oddly, not much was said at the time that Olive Diefenbaker spoke French "flawlessly" and was a voracious reader of French literature.[12]

Publicly, Diefenbaker continuously aligned himself with the views of Sir John A. Macdonald, who had brilliantly assembled a coalition of voters in both English and French Canada. "I have no accord with the desire expressed in some quarters," Macdonald said in the House of Commons, "that by any mode whatever there should be an attempt made to oppress one language at the expense of the other; I believe that it would be impossible if it were tried, and it would be foolish and wicked if it were possible."[13]

It was inevitable that Diefenbaker's vision of One Canada would clash with the nationalist aspirations that would soon be expressed in Quebec's Quiet Revolution. Despite having won a majority of Quebec's seats, Diefenbaker did not have enduring political antennae on the ground in Quebec. On a more practical level, he failed to give adequate personal attention to the French-speaking MPs in his caucus, which resulted in grumbling.

With tunnel vision and the blindness resulting from natural stubbornness combined with political power, Diefenbaker believed his position within his party and as prime minister was unassailable. Thus, he revelled in the adulation he had received in the 1958 election to the point of addiction. He was not the leader of a team or a party; he led a movement transfixed on one man's personal qualities, charisma, vision and innate sense of destiny. Despite the responsibilities of office and a vast parliamentary majority, Diefenbaker continued to travel the country and make speeches as if locked in campaign mode. Being with ordinary Canadians was where he was most comfortable.

Parliament opened on May 12, 1958. The government put forward a set of policies designed to enhance the nation's social welfare, with new support for seniors, the unemployed, and farmers. Among other priorities, Diefenbaker's government would establish a regulatory agency for radio and television, respond to a declining economy, curtail inflation, and minimize a projected deficit. Proceedings of the House of Commons were to be translated. But the crowning jewel of his government's throne speech was a bill of rights.

***

In 1958, Diefenbaker went on an international tour. He enjoyed being among world leaders and showed no signs of intimidation on a grand stage. Those who travelled with Diefenbaker said he did not hesitate to take instinctive positions on issues on which his knowledge was limited. For example, he did not consult his advisors before declaring Canadian support for admitting communist China to the United Nations, a policy that annoyed the Americans. However, most of his instincts were proven correct in time.

Tellingly, and perhaps as the result of a politician heading a minor world power concerned with the more dominant nation-state next door, Diefenbaker had been an early supporter of the United Nations as an instrument to avoid war and resolve conflict—and to serve, at least in theory, as a counterweight to any American imperial ambitions post-war.

> I saw the United Nations as man's last chance. I was enthusiastic about the results. I felt that for the first time in all history the various nations would provide forces to a strong international army which would serve under the aegis of the international organization to ensure that whenever and wherever aggression took place, it would be met and defeated. This dream has not been attained and I doubt whether it will be attained in generations to come. The reason was simply that the Great Powers were entirely opposed to doing that, to which they gave their vocal support. Like most people, I suppose, I hoped against hope while aware of the weaknesses in the United Nations Charter from the very beginning. As I said in the House when we debated the U.N. Charter, the Charter provides the basis to end war, but it does not terminate the prerogative of any of the great powers to wage war. It prevents aggression among small nations. In theory, it allows powerful nations, who alone have the power and resources to make war, to go unpunished if any of them commit acts of aggression.[14]

With unparalleled numbers in the House of Commons, Diefenbaker was challenged by the issues of his time and the difficulty of implementing his vision for Canada. He was a better campaigner than a manager of issues. His primary skills were as an advocate for his clients in the courtroom, a prosecutor of his opponents in the House of Commons, and his ability to interpret the hopes of ordinary Canadians. He had his indefatigable political energy on the campaign trail, but his patience was taken to the brink when working with his cabinet and officials in his party.

Diefenbaker birthplace, Neustadt, ON.

Formal family portrait of William, Mary, John and Elmer Diefenbaker, 1902.

Diefenbaker in uniform Kitchener, Ontario.

John Diefenbaker in uniform Great War, England, 1916.

John Diefenbaker with Cousins, c. 1920s.

Diefenbaker, 1925 General Election.

Edna, John Diefenbaker with mother Mary, c .1930s.

Diefenbaker walking in downtown Vancouver c. 1940s

John, William, Edna and Mary Diefenbaker in front of William and Mary's home in Saskatoon, 1941.

Diefenbaker and George Drew, 1948.

John Diefenbaker seated with two supporters at Lake Centre Nomination Convention 1949.

Diefenbaker, 1949.

ISSUES AT HOME AND ABROAD

- 7 -

THE 1960 BILL OF RIGHTS

I am a Canadian, a free Canadian, free to speak without fear, free to worship God in my own way, free to stand for what I think right, free to oppose what I believe wrong, free to choose those who shall govern my country. This heritage of freedom I pledge to uphold for myself, and all mankind.

When Canadians think about individual rights, it is likely the Charter of Rights and Freedoms, proclaimed into law by Queen Elizabeth II on April 17, 1982, that comes to mind and not the Bill of Rights that Diefenbaker's government passed in 1960. The latter was a law on the books that was an aspirational statement of beliefs and principles to guide legislators and possibly judges that applied only to the federal domain. The former was a constitutional provision that constrained the powers of federal and provincial governments alike. Yet, it is difficult to imagine the construction of the 1982 Charter that came into being under Pierre Trudeau without the foundation of the Bill of Rights that John Diefenbaker championed his entire life.

Diefenbaker's commitment to individual liberties and freedoms was "baked" into his belief structure in his youth. As he wrote in his memoirs:

> At an early age, I developed a consciousness of injustice, which has never left me. The idea of the poor being treated differently, the working man looked down upon as a digit, filled me with revulsion. I was beginning to add to my highland inheritance an acquired distrust of powerful forces and a concern over their overwhelming impact on the helpless.[1]

He recalled making friends with three or four black boys when he was five or six whom he thought were badly treated. His father chastised him when he unknowingly used a word of profound derision in a conversation with his friends, a castigation he said he never forgot. Diefenbaker did not reveal the word in his memoirs, but the implication was clear it was the "N" word. It was the first, last, and only time he said he uttered the word.

Diefenbaker's 1960 Bill of Rights was preceded by early templates in the same vein. When he became the leader of the Saskatchewan Conservative Party in 1936, he made a bill of rights a personal political priority. He was well ahead of his time—and the rest of the country: Ontario passed the Racial Discrimination Act in 1944, and Saskatchewan passed the Acts to Protect Certain Civil Rights a few years later. Internationally, it was only in 1948 that the United Nations adopted a Universal Declaration of Human Rights that spoke to the rights and freedoms that could not be infringed on the grounds of race, colour, sex, language, religion, political beliefs, or place of birth. It also banned enslavement, torture, and arbitrary arrest and detention and enshrined the right to be presumed innocent. Not to overstate its importance, the U.N. declaration is ignored by every repressive regime that is a signatory without consequence.

The commitment of Diefenbaker and other Canadians to free speech was regularly tested. After the end of the Second World War, the public was shocked to learn of the Soviet spy network operating in Canada, which came to light following the defection of a cipher clerk operating from the Soviet embassy in Canada. The Liberal government sought to keep Igor Gouzenko's defection a secret.

Using the National Emergency Powers Act, the government, through undisclosed orders-in-council, detained fourteen Canadians suspected of being spies without due process or access to legal counsel. British and American security officials leaked the story to the press in 1946. This led the committed anti-communist Diefenbaker to attack the prime minister in the House of Commons. It was also an opportunity to use the government's infringement of personal liberties to advance his cause for legislative protections and, in so doing, give the government and those paying attention a history lesson in the centuries-long tradition of freedom:

> Mr. Speaker... I do not believe the minds of liberty-loving Canadians, however much they hate communism, have become so apathetic in six

> years of domination by a state in a period when the political doctrines of regimentation have been in effect. I believe the time has come for a declaration of liberties to be made by this Parliament. Magna Carta is part of our birthright. *Habeas Corpus*, the Bill of Rights, the Petition of Right, are all part of our tradition. I think out of the events of the last few years, a responsibility falls upon Parliament to assure that Canadians, as well as others in the empire... should have established by their legislature a Bill of Rights under which freedom of religion, of speech, of association... freedom from capricious arrest and freedom under the rule of law, should be made part and parcel of the law of the country.[2]

The Liberal minister of justice, James Lorimer Ilsley, responded that liberties resulting from principles established under the Magna Carta were "great and glorious privileges... [b]ut they are privileges which can be, and which unfortunately sometimes have to be, interfered with by the actions of Parliament."

Since there was a willingness by the public to trust the government on matters it determined impacted national security, Diefenbaker knew he had work to do to establish a counterweight to arbitrary and unchecked government decisions. He believed it required a federal statute or, if possible, a constitutional amendment to protect individual rights. This caught the attention of the editorial writers at the *Globe and Mail*, who observed, "Too few members of the House of Commons have interested themselves in the liberties of their constituents. There has been one outstanding exception among them. He is John Diefenbaker... a tenacious but a brilliant and rugged guardian of all civil liberties."[3]

In January 1947, Diefenbaker placed on the order paper a private member's resolution calling for a Bill of Rights:

> A Bill of Rights must deny the right of government to interfere with my right to speak within the law, my right to serve my Maker as my conscience demands, my right to be free from the threat of a police state... my right to live my own life... without regard to race or colour or creed... my rights to have recourse to the courts to guard me against the intrusions or the invasions of the state.[4]

In 1948, Diefenbaker highlighted to a national CBC radio audience how the government had abrogated the liberties of individual Canadians. He asserted that a Bill of Rights was the only way to curb the arbitrary power of government. In the years thereafter, while an opposition MP, Diefenbaker routinely introduced a private member's resolution before the House of Commons on a Bill of Rights. For example, on June 10, 1948, in Winnipeg, he led the charge in this manner:

> The time has come to assure that this government shall be shorn of its arrogant disregard of the rights of the people. It does not rule by Divine right as did the Stuart King... A Bill of Rights for Canada is the only way in which to stop the march on the part of the government towards arbitrary power and to curb the arrogance of men 'clad in a little brief authority.'... Some say that it is unnecessary, and our unwritten constitutional rights protect us. They have not in the past.[5]

On February 7, 1955, Diefenbaker rose in the House of Commons to connect his proposed Bill of Rights to the discrimination facing Indigenous Canadians, who had no right to vote, faced harsh limitations in gaining access to the courts, and were uniquely restricted in their freedoms because of their Indian status:

> I believe that today, our Indians should no longer be in the position of second-class citizens in the country in which they indeed were the first citizens. The rights of individuals are undermined, I submit, in the commissions that today are hearing evidence at various Indian reserves in this country; and I believe these commissions, which are causing division in the reserves to a degree that few in Parliament understand, should cease to operate. Evidence is not the requirement before those commissions. Hearsay is too often accepted. I conclude by summarizing what I have tried to place before the house. I have made certain recommendations that I believe deserve serious consideration. The resolution should be permitted to come to a vote in which members of the house, without regard to party, may freely express, by their votes, their viewpoint on this matter.

Seven decades after that speech, it is too easy to forget the context of the 1950s, which included fear of another war, this time potentially nuclear, but also the threat of worldwide communism and its repression. Both created a heightened state of anxiety and a willingness to sacrifice and suppress freedoms. Diefenbaker continued that Canada and the world were living in an age of fear and whether "freedom everywhere in the world is being weighed in the scales... cynical as to whether or not it can be preserved in the tumultuous present... in an age of the all-powerful state created as the result of war or threatened war." He worried that political expediency to maintain security would ultimately constitute a mortal threat to freedom. "I ask this question. Must free nations desert their faith in the fundamentals of freedom? Can freedom-loving nations preserve freedom and defend themselves without destroying it? Do we have to emulate the enemy? I do not think so."

Hearkening back to John Stuart Mill's arguments, Diefenbaker argued that it was through freedom that people were able to exercise their creative genius. "We have learned today, with the experience of the years of war and a cold war, that freedom has to be paid for in every generation; that it cannot be purchased at bargain counters; it cannot be purchased on credit with payment to be made in the future. It can only be purchased by action."

Before Diefenbaker, individual rights had not been a feature of any Conservative platform or a cause that any party leader espoused. It is unlikely that a bill of rights was a key factor in the outcomes of the 1957 and 1958 Conservative victories. Still, it was an element that Diefenbaker included in his election manifestos and something he raised on the campaign trail.

***

Diefenbaker viewed the Canadian Bill of Rights as his government's most important legislation. When he introduced the bill on September 5, 1958, Diefenbaker encouraged extensive discussion, review, and amendment. He knew that failing to put the Bill of Rights in a constitutional amendment limited its application. One critic called the narrow applicability of the bill a "timid and tepid affirmation of a political and social tradition." The Canadian Bar Association called it "window dressing." An unattributed quote was used to diminish the bill's importance: "It provides protection to all Canadians, just so long as they don't live in any of the provinces."

Diefenbaker underscored the declaratory and symbolic power of a Bill of Rights not just in Canada but its significance around the world. Again, the context for the era matters: Soviet communism, led by the only recently deceased Josef Stalin, had been and was brutally repressive. China had fallen to communism in the 1949 revolution led by Mao-Tse Tung. Diefenbaker thought the proposed Bill of Rights was needed not only for its own sake but as a symbol of a superior West vis-à-vis a repressive Russian regime and the possible attraction communism held for others around the world. He told international leaders of democratic nations that "the free world is not getting out its message... that time and time again he had encountered those with no appreciation of what the United States or others in (the) free world have been contributing," calling for a "declaration of freedom's creed... so that uncommitted peoples can understand the worth and superiority of freedom when compared with communism."[6]

Following the 1958 election, the Bill of Rights was reintroduced on Dominion Day, July 1, 1960, and it was passed with the unanimous support of the House of Commons and proclaimed into law the following month on August 10. Diefenbaker considered the bill an expression of Canadian values rather than a raw legal instrument. To raise its standing in the hearts and minds of Canadians, 20,000 copies of critical portions of the bill were printed on high-quality parchment and distributed to classrooms for $1.00, with the prime minister's signature prominently affixed.

One bill provision not included in the parchment version was a so-called "notwithstanding clause," which limited the bill's application in certain circumstances, such as in a period of war. A variant of this clause would become a prominent feature of Trudeau's 1982 constitutional initiative, primarily to ensure that the ultimate power rested with elected politicians rather than appointed and unaccountable judges. It was a provision that various premiers had demanded; otherwise, there would have been no Charter or patriation of our constitution. Some today might see it as limiting rights, as has happened in Quebec with restrictions on the use of the English language. Others might hew to the original purpose of the notwithstanding clause: to prevent judicial usurpation of legislatures and Parliament.

One consequential amendment to the War Measures Act was attached to Diefenbaker's Bill of Rights, which stated that anything done under the War Measures Act was to be deemed not to be an infringement, abrogation, or abridgement of any right or freedom recognized in the Canadian Bill of Rights. This was consistent with the view Diefenbaker took in the Second World War, which was that when the country was facing an existential crisis, liberties may have to be suspended so that they could be restored permanently.

The Canadian Bill of Rights preamble declared that Canada "is founded upon principles that acknowledge the supremacy of God, the dignity and worth of the human person and the position of the family in a society of free men and free institutions." It also affirmed that people and institutions remain free only when freedom is founded on respect for moral and spiritual values and the rule of law.

Diefenbaker saw the bill as an expression of Canadian values written in plain language. Years later, he reflected on the meaning of the Bill of Rights. "Those law professors and politicians who condemned it had closed their eyes to what was happening. All the laws of this Dominion were made to conform to it. It became the standard and the pattern for those Canadian provinces that wished to enact their own provincial Bill of Rights." The Bill, still in effect, recognizes the rights of individuals to life, liberty, personal security, and enjoyment of property. It does not recognize property rights since that is a matter of provincial jurisdiction. The bill protects rights to equality before the law and ensures the protection of the law. It protects the freedoms of religion, speech, the press, assembly, and association. It also guarantees legal rights such as counsel and a fair hearing. Legislators were effectively directed to construct new laws that did not detract from the rights and freedoms included in the Bill of Rights.

When the Bill of Rights was passed, it was an open question whether the courts would use its provisions to protect individual liberties that the federal government had infringed. The Bill of Rights was referenced in 35 court cases, the most notable being *R. v. Drybones*. The Supreme Court of Canada rendered a section of the Indian Act "inoperative" and no longer in effect because it violated the Canadian Bill of Rights that had guaranteed equality before the law. The case involved Joseph Drybones, an Indigenous man who was arrested in Yellowknife for violating a section of the Indian Act prohibiting Indigenous people from being intoxicated off reserve. His lawyers argued that it violated the Bill of Rights, as a non-Indigenous person could not have faced the same charge. The Supreme Court agreed, citing the Bill of Rights ban on punishing people based on race.

The courts used the Bill of Rights after an Ojibwe woman in 1970 married a non-Indigenous man and lost her Indian status and the status rights of her children. Men who remarried a non-status person did not lose their status. The petitioner, Jeannette Corbiere Lavell, won her case in the Federal Court of Appeal as the Indian Act was found to have discriminated based on sex. However, in a 5-4 decision, the Supreme Court of Canada ruled against Corbiere Lavell in 1973. A controversial and much-questioned decision found that the Bill of Rights did not invalidate the Indian Act. In his dissenting opinion, Justice Bora Laskin relied on the Drybones case and contended that the Canadian Bill of Rights took precedence over the provisions of a conflicting federal statute.

When confronted with unrest and the temptation to use the heavy hand of government, Diefenbaker demonstrated that it was not just words on paper but deeds that mattered. He recalled the episodes when Conservative prime ministers had reacted swiftly and aggressively to acts of protest, such as Meighen's response to the 1919 strike in Winnipeg or Bennett's determination to quell a protest march. These incidents made Tory leaders seem disconnected from the plight of ordinary citizens and more responsive to established sources of power and money. Diefenbaker contended those decisions would be more difficult to sustain when faced with Bill of Rights provisions.

Diefenbaker's mettle was tested when the Newfoundland government requested his government deploy the RCMP to deal with an International Woodworkers of America in Grand Falls strike that began on December 31, 1958. Despite the obligation to supply RCMP forces when requested by a province, Diefenbaker refused, saying, "It would be provocative and likely to cause further outbreaks of violence." This was more a question of security than of rights, although the Newfoundland premier, Joey Smallwood, likened the strike to the beginning of a civil war. But Diefenbaker went further. "Would Canada have been well served had every working man and woman come to regard the Royal Canadian Mounted Police as a strikebreaking force?" The pressing need for calm was made when St. John's Constable William Moss was hit over the head with a pulpwood club and died. Seven strikers were charged in the murder. But Diefenbaker held firm, as noted in his remarks to the House of Commons:

> The Premier of Newfoundland has greatly aggravated the present situation in that province by intervening in a labour dispute in a way which apparently goes beyond the usual role of government. The result, as might have been anticipated, has been a violent reaction on the part of the workers. Under the circumstances, we have concluded that it would be provocative and likely to cause further outbreaks of

> violence to authorize the sending of further members of the RCMP at this time.[7]

Diefenbaker said he would not sacrifice the reputation of the RCMP to save the interests of Joey Smallwood, or the profits of a corporation. Diefenbaker's failure to heed Newfoundland's requests for reinforcements led to the resignation of the commissioner of the RCMP.

It distressed the Newfoundland premier, who had staked his career on the benefits of Newfoundland joining Confederation. "Smallwood led us into Confederation with promises of what he could extract from Ottawa, such as access to the Baby Bonus or some other financial payment or service," said Newfoundland Senator David Wells. "That his request to Diefenbaker for RCMP support was rejected was a humiliation for Smallwood, who looked like a leader with little clout on the national stage." This was not Diefenbaker's only confrontation with Smallwood. When the Newfoundland premier requested $17 million in federal subsidies, Diefenbaker responded that this was not part of the deal signed in 1949. In protest, Smallwood ordered that public buildings be clad in black bunting to mark the 10th anniversary of provincehood.

Diefenbaker was animated by his experience as someone of German heritage, and it gave him sympathy for Canadians not part of the conception of Canada as a union of two founding peoples, English and French. He said it was his abiding purpose to see every Canadian secure in their liberty and with the knowledge of their fundamental rights and freedoms that no government could override regardless of their ancestry, including Indigenous Canadians who had not yet been granted the right to vote.

> It distressed me that those who were neither British nor French in origin were not treated with the regard that non-discrimination demands. I was even more distressed that many contended they would never become Canadians. My determination to see the Bill of Rights a reality was increased by experiences during and after the Second World War. Even now, I am still somewhat amazed at the opposition I encountered in trying to forward a Canadian Bill of Rights.

Despite the passage of the Bill of Rights, Diefenbaker was bothered that the War Measures Act could be invoked during times of peace. In March of 1946,

Diefenbaker stated in the House, "There is only one liberty, namely the liberty based on law and under law. So long as the War Measures Act is on the statute books, there is no reason why governments, if they so choose, might not create emergencies real or apprehended, thereby permitting them to commit arbitrary acts under its powers." Diefenbaker later proposed repealing the War Measures Act as it constituted a danger to society and an invitation to any government "to declare an emergency to the detriment to the rights of our people."

When Diefenbaker issued his warning, he foretold that the act could be used in times other than war. The temptation to unleash the power of the War Measures Act was so irresistible that Liberal Prime Minister Pierre Trudeau used it in October 1970 after a handful of ragtag terrorists dedicated to securing Quebec's separation from Canada by violent means instigated what became known as the "October Crisis." A crisis it was. A British diplomat was kidnapped, and a provincial cabinet minister was murdered. But Canada was not at war, and there was no insurrection. Under the powers of the War Measures Act, almost 500 Quebec citizens were arrested and detained; the overwhelming majority were never charged with a crime.

If Diefenbaker had had his way in 1946, a fearful federal government would not have been able to invoke the draconian measures that unleashed the might of the military and an unencumbered police force on the civilian population of Quebec that year, a power they had not requested. The blunt force was used to serve more as a political sledgehammer by Prime Minister Trudeau to the separatist cause than as a necessary power to constrain a small and disorganized group of violent radicals. In contrast, the Americans did not suspend their constitution when attacked by terrorists on September 11, 2001, causing the deaths of almost 3,000 people.

Diefenbaker did not speak out in 1970 when the War Measure Act was invoked, possibly because his name appeared on the assassination list of the Front de libération du Québec, the group that terrorized the nation. Diefenbaker was impressed at the hundreds of soldiers assigned to guard him during the crisis and humorously remarked that he had enough troops by his side to conquer Cuba. Some six years after the War Measures Act was invoked, Quebecers elected a provincial government whose primary purpose was to take their province out of Canada. Trudeau's political gamble had not paid off.

The Canadian Bill of Rights was a signature achievement for Diefenbaker. There is little doubt that it would not have been enacted without his vision and leadership. As a statement of values and aspirations, it was, at a minimum, a guide and point of reference for Parliamentarians and the judiciary. The extent of its capacity to constrain the federal government rests on the premise that it would be a transfer of power from parliamentarians to the judiciary and, effectively, the Americanization of Canada's political system. In the Drybones case, the court told the duly elected government that a law on the Canadian books was invalid.

Those with little faith in our politicians may see this development as progress. However, substituting judicial activism for government by elected officials creates its own set of problems. Few parliamentarians oppose individual rights and freedoms or favour an oppressive government. The critical question is, who is best placed to balance competing rights? Parliament, accountable to the people, made that call before the Bill of Rights and, subsequently, the Charter. Today, the judiciary has the final word, subject to the potential override held by Parliament. The check and balance on raw and unaccountable judicial power is the notwithstanding clauses that exist in Diefenbaker's Bill of Rights and Trudeau's Charter of Rights and Freedoms. Diefenbaker believed that Parliament was supreme, and his Bill of Rights conferred less power on the judiciary than Trudeau's Charter of Rights. In that sense, Trudeau's Charter took us closer to the American approach to constitution-making than the British traditions that Diefenbaker embraced.

Arguably, Diefenbaker's most remembered and eloquent statement came on Dominion Day, 1960, the month before his Bill of Rights passed the House of Commons on August 3, when he made this declaration to Canadians:

> I am a Canadian, a free Canadian, free to speak without fear, free to worship God in my own way, free to stand for what I think right, free to oppose what I believe wrong, free to choose those who shall govern my country. This heritage of freedom I pledge to uphold for myself, and all mankind.

When asked by a friend how long it took him to compose these words, Diefenbaker replied, "A lifetime."[8]

- 8 -

OUR HOME AND NATIVE LAND

In his epic 702-page, 1995 biography of John Diefenbaker, *Rogue Tory*, Denis Smith, has only one reference to Indigenous issues. It is a story of how Diefenbaker gave his brother money to buy cigars and pass them out as gifts on reserves. Yet, Diefenbaker frequently mentioned Indigenous people in the three volumes of his memoirs, and always with respect for their traditions, adherence to treaty rights, an end to discrimination, and the times when he was honoured by various tribes.

Growing up, Diefenbaker recalled how Indigenous people would drop by his family home. "They had tea with us and went their way. Our father would give them clothing. We liked them. One day, an Indian called Aaron Buffalo hit the jackpot. Father gave him the Prince Albert Coat he wore at his wedding."[1] Such was the affection and admiration Diefenbaker held for Indigenous Canadians throughout his life. Having felt the scourge of discrimination owing to his Germanic surname, Diefenbaker was sensitive to discrimination in any form, which, he noted, was systematically practised against Canada's Indigenous peoples throughout his life.

Diefenbaker had an affinity for and with Indigenous people: "Indian lore and Indian history, just as the story of the opening of the West, have always fascinated me," Diefenbaker wrote in his memoirs. He summed up his relationship with Canada's first peoples: "Over the years, I think the Indians have understood my feelings for them, and they have shown their reaction by making me chief of five or six tribes in Saskatchewan and Alberta."[2]

This did not mean Diefenbaker was on the side of every Indigenous or Métis cause. Louis Riel, who advocated for French language rights in western Canada and had engaged in battles with the RCMP at Batoche and Frog Lake in Saskatchewan in 1885, was not a man he held in the highest regard. "I do not consider Riel to be a martyr," wrote Diefenbaker. "Many who have united behind Riel have failed to recall that he regarded the Pope as anti-Christ and himself as the true viceroy of the Almighty on earth." Referring to Riel's offer to alter his demands in exchange for a suitable financial payment from the Canadian government, Diefenbaker cautioned, "If a man has principles, he does not put them up on the auction block."[3] After his government was defeated, Diefenbaker remarked that Riel should never have taken the stand and should have been found not guilty by reason of insanity.[4]

Diefenbaker acknowledged that the imposition of the death penalty on Riel while Macdonald was prime minister "resulted in serious damage to the fortunes of Conservatives in Quebec." Diefenbaker noted that the Liberals suffered no such consequence concerning the death of Kitchi-Manito-Waya, "Voice of the Great Spirit," who died in 1897 by shell splinters from a North West Mounted Police nine-pounder gun when Wilfrid Laurier was prime minister.

Diefenbaker has a long and continuous record of defending the rights and interests of Indigenous peoples as a lawyer, a backbench MP, and as prime minister. The earlier chapter on Diefenbaker's legal career cites numerous examples of defending treaty rights in the courts. In *Halfbreed*, written by Maria Campbell, the author wrote, "[Diefenbaker] would represent anyone, rich or poor, red or white. If they had a case and had no money, he would help.... Our people would come from miles in rain or snow to watch him. Then they would go home and repeat what happened, and by the second repetition, John was 10 feet taller. He helped us, and the important thing was that he did so when no one else would."[5]

In one of his early statements in the House of Commons in 1942, Diefenbaker paid tribute to the service of Indigenous men in the Second World War as he admonished the government for discriminatory treatment.

> If all the people of this country had enlisted as generally as have the Indians, there would have been no need for a plebiscite.... In western Canada, the reserves have been depleted of almost all the physically fit men. The Indians in service ask, 'Why are we discriminated against? Why are the ordinary rights to go to refreshment places and so on, which are allowed to other members of the army, denied to us? Why is it that as far as dependents' allowances are concerned, $35 is paid to the wives of other soldiers while the wife of the Indian receives $10 and $15 a month?' I ask the minister to give consideration to these Natives of our country who today are shouldering their responsibility in the armed forces as are those of no other race. They ask that the

> same consideration be given to their loved ones as is being given to the loved ones and dependents of the soldiers of other races.[6]

As the debate over recruitment and reinforcements arose on December 5, 1944, Diefenbaker again noted the contributions of native Canadians while highlighting the injustice that they were denied democratic rights at home:

> Let me tell you of one man in the Prime Minister's own constituency, an Indian by the name of Arcand, a man denied citizenship, but a man who has nine sons in the armed forces of this country, with one son who was turned down as unfit. The message of that man, *not a citizen, unable to vote, denied equality with the rest of us*, is: 'Won't you do something, you members of Parliament, to see that my boys overseas are assured of reinforcements?'

When not raising democratic and human rights, Diefenbaker frequently spoke of legal rights denied to Indigenous people. On October 14, 1949, he railed in the House of Commons that Status Indians were denied access to the courts where they could seek remedies for decisions made by the Crown regarding their welfare:

> Conditions existing on many of the reserves of this country require to be rectified, yet Indians residing on reserves find it impossible to commence an action against the Crown... The Indian operates under a handicap by reason of the fact that he is subject to control by and is a ward of the state, and whenever Indians feel there is an injustice, they should have a right of action against the Crown. I ask the minister the reason for continuing this anomaly of requiring a fiat from the Crown when a subject of His Majesty feels that he has been aggrieved.... Injustices that may exist on Indian reserves should not be permitted to continue simply because the state refuses to grant to the Aboriginal and the first subjects of the king the right to take action to have those injustices remedied.

On March 21, 1950, Diefenbaker asked the Indian affairs minister to invite representatives chosen by Indigenous chiefs of the tribes within each province to come to Ottawa, at government expense, to consult with them on proposed changes to the Indian Act. "That seems only fair," noted Diefenbaker, given that for two years, a parliamentary committee had considered changes to the Indian Act in their absence.

While Diefenbaker had become the representative of Indian chiefs on the committee, he believed this was not a substitute for hearing directly from the chiefs in Ottawa. As Diefenbaker noted:

> They believe that they occupy a position of secondary citizenship, and... there is no reason whatever why they should have an inferior citizenship. [Citizenship should have] no interference with, or abrogation or reduction of, their treaty rights under the several treaties made between successive sovereigns and their ancestors... and that those great rights which they cherish with such pride, and which were granted to them, particularly by Queen Victoria, shall not be diminished by the action of a parliament in which—and I say this advisedly—because of the fact they have no vote, they have no representation.

Diefenbaker continuously reminded parliamentarians that Indigenous people were not subject to conscription or military service in any way and yet signed up in large numbers: "When we were at war, members of the reserves in every part of Canada enlisted in numbers unexcelled by any other group in the Dominion."

Diefenbaker's devotion to civil rights for native Canadians was also complemented by his desire to preserve Indigenous history. For example, in June 1950, Diefenbaker sought to protect historic sites in Saskatchewan related to the rebellion of 1885 in remarks delivered in the House of Commons.

> These particular areas today are remembered by many as the scene of the last warfare that took place in Canada for the preservation and perpetuation of this union.... Today, all that remains to indicate that one of the most important battles of the rebellion was fought there are the trenches, which at this time are only six or seven inches deep, having been filled in by the erosion which has taken place over a period of sixty-five years. There and at Fish Creek, a number of volunteers lie buried, as well as numbers of Métis and Indians who fought in those two battles. There is nothing to indicate that these are two of the great

> historic sites in Saskatchewan, nothing other than a small monument erected on the banks of the Saskatchewan River at Batoche through private contributions.

While Diefenbaker was not a defender of Louis Riel, he wrote that many of the historical sites in which he was involved should be commemorated as this would help Canadians "relive the romance of the days of the fur trader, of the Métis, of Gabriel Dumont, the greatest Métis leader of his time and the greatest buffalo hunter of North America, not excepting Buffalo Bill." In that sense, Diefenbaker's advocacy for remembering 19th-century war sites was to remind Canadians how battles forge a nation. Similarly, Diefenbaker implored the government to maintain a Canadian tradition by remembering the country's history:

> In the years to come, Canadians will look at these sites as being places worthy of preservation because they represent battlefields, though they are small in comparison with modern battlefields, which are significant in that what occurred there contributed so much to the building of western Canada... If we are to build up a true Canadianism, if we are to have unity with no division because of race, colour or creed, nothing will contribute as much as the preservation of sites and areas which are so much a part of our history and tradition.

When amendments to the Indian Act were considered in Parliament on June 21, 1950, Diefenbaker opposed the Government's Bill in Parliament, which he said failed to reflect the committee's diligent work:

> I was one of those who believed that out of the Indian committee would indeed come a charter that would be beneficial to the Indians of Canada.... The chairman of the committee on Indian affairs... his observations and his conclusion regarding the bill... were a miracle in terminology (by saying) he believed that the minister had done as much as he could. Whatever he meant, one thing stands out, that he, as chairman of that committee, was disappointed with the bill. *It is a mirage*, Mr. Speaker. It is no charter. It is merely an alteration of some of the provisions of the Indian Act intensified in so far as administrative

> officials are concerned to make them more powerful than they have ever been before under the Indian Act as it has existed since 1880.

Diefenbaker reiterated his complaint that Indigenous people had no standing in the courts and were subject to the whims of the state and its administrative officials:

> The minister brings to the house a bill that is a negation of freedom, a denial of equality under the law. Indeed, it provides that Indians can have no recourse to the courts unless they have the permission of the minister to proceed. When I compare the report that the Special Committee on Indian Affairs made on June 22, 1948, with the bill now before the house, it is obvious that the master hands of the administrative officials of the Indian Affairs branch have wrought changes that Parliament never thought of. The bill, in its present form, simply places the Indian in a position where he will have no equality under the law, where he will be at the beck and control of officials on the various reserves. Rights? He cannot take a case to court when there is wrongdoing unless he has the permission of the minister.

One aspect of the bill that Diefenbaker found egregious was any appeals from the ruling of one departmental official were elevated to that person's supervisor, who lacked independence:

> He is a member of a government that brings before the House a bill that denies to the individual Indian that freedom and equality referred to by the Hon[ourable]. Member for Cariboo. When an Indian commits an offence under the proposed act or is alleged to have committed an offence, who tries him? Is it the ordinary courts of law? No; those who try him will be the Indian agent, or an official of the Indian department, or appointees of the minister who will act as justices of the peace. Why should an Indian be tried for a criminal offence before an appointee of the Department of Indian Affairs? Why should he not be tried by the ordinary courts of law? In its present form this bill is a travesty on the representations made by members of both Houses of Parliament.

Diefenbaker could not accept that Status Indians were denied the principles of equality that were foundational to Canada and accepted under international law or the Charter of the United Nations.

> As it is now drawn, this bill places these people in a position of wardship, making it impossible for the individual Indian to preserve and protect his rights against the tyranny of officials. Why not place the Indian in a position equal to that of other people in this land as far as the law is concerned? Why place him in the position that when he is charged with an offence, he must be tried by the person who prosecutes him?

The man who sought to be the voice of Indigenous peoples in Parliament and had actively sought legislative reform through the work in the House of Commons lambasted the government for a bill that fell short of his mark:

> I personally will not vote for the second reading of that bill. I will take no part in the passing of a bill that goes contrary to the desires, the wishes, and the recommendations of a committee of this Parliament.... There is a redrafting of some sections and a change in their numbers, but behind it all and through it all runs the thread of a subservience which I, for one, knowing Indians and having acted for them on several occasions, will not join in supporting in this house, no matter what other members may do.

The act was amended in 1950 to extend the federal franchise to Indians but only to those who waived their tax exemptions under the Indian Act respecting personal property. In other words, it was a hollow offering so the Liberal government could claim they were promoting equality. Meanwhile, Status Indians could not vote or sit on juries.

Diefenbaker raised the issue of applying income tax to Status Indians in the House of Commons for earnings outside of reserves on May 6, 1955. It had been in the previous years that the government had been imposing income tax on that basis, which caused Diefenbaker concern:

> It has been a cause of great alarm, if not indignation, amongst the Indians. They claim, and I think rightly, that under the law, tradition

> and history and the treaties of the past indicate that at no time was the Indian to be subject to taxation. This was the principle back in 1763, with the Royal Proclamation of that year, and it was followed year by year after the establishment of responsible government in Canada until very recently.

What Diefenbaker asked of the government was the legal foundation for the change in practice.

> At no time have successive ministers of Indian affairs been able to point out to [Indians] the legal justification for what is being done. I have the Indian Act before me, and I am familiar with the interpretation that has been placed thereon. I ask the minister if he will explain to the Indians, as clearly as he can, the legal justification in this instance, having regard to the original proclamation that was made immediately after the cessation of French rule in America and the subsequent treaties.

Diefenbaker wanted the matter settled by the courts. If the Supreme Court concluded that the law does permit the imposition of income tax on Indigenous people, Diefenbaker said, "That will be the end of it. But I believe that so long as the income tax is imposed there will be considerable ill feeling and remonstrance among the tribes."

A proposal Diefenbaker took to the government on July 2, 1956, was to place Indigenous people in positions of power within the administration of the Department of Indian and Northern Affairs as well as to appoint a Royal Commission on Indian affairs. "One of the things that might be achieved in that connection is to give more Indians an opportunity to be installed in administrative positions not only in the field in the reserves but in the administration of the department here in Ottawa.... All over the world, coloured races are demanding that they shall no longer be subservient to the white races. In our country, the major subject of complaint on the part of Indians is that they are placed in an inferior position."

He highlighted the discriminatory practice of a jail sentence of two months imposed on Indigenous people for the simple offence of being intoxicated. "I believe that in so far as these minor offences are concerned, such as are provided for in the Indian Act, a fine should be sufficient." It was something of a concession on Diefenbaker's part to allow a fine to be levied based on race and intoxication.

The suppression of liquor sales to native Canadians dated back to at least Confederation when an intoxicated Indigenous person could be imprisoned for up to one month, with fourteen days tacked on if the accused would not reveal the name of their supplier. The legal provisions were codified in the Indian Act (1876), which were expanded to simple possession in addition to intoxication, which was included in Treaties No. 1 to 6 to protect Indians "from the evil influence of intoxicating liquors."[7] The 1951 Indian Act restricted the possession and use of liquor by Indians off reserve and by any person on a reserve. The constitutionality of such an overtly discriminatory law was challenged in the Supreme Court in R. v. Drybones, which, as discussed in the previous chapter, held in 1970 that the off-reserve intoxication provision contravened Diefenbaker's Canadian Bill of Rights.

The injustices inflicted on Status Indians, which Diefenbaker characterized as tyranny under the Indian Act, required a broader and more fulsome assessment.

> Before the Indians in Canada can properly receive that consideration to which they should be entitled, the law should be brought up to date, and the Indian Act made an instrument of justice.... I believe the first thing that should be done is to appoint a Royal Commission, which would meet in all parts of Canada at appointed times and places so that the Indian's point of view might be placed before the Canadian people as a whole rather than through the narrow conduit pipe of the administrative services within the department itself. There are tremendous problems at stake in the administration of the Indian. These problems will never be met by a piecemeal haphazard amendment of the act from time to time. They can only be met by viewing the problem in the national sense through the medium of a royal commission of men and women who have some knowledge of Indian affairs so that recommendations may be made for the amendment of the act, which will remove many of the inequalities and injustices of the present.

Before Confederation and decades after, Status Indians across the land could not vote in Canadian elections. In 1885, Prime Minister John A. Macdonald was thwarted in his attempt to extend the vote to all Indigenous people without forging status or treaty provisions. One Liberal MP said it would be like bringing a scalping party to the poll; another that it was an insult to place white brethren "on a level with pagan and barbarian Indians." More than desiring a continuation of discriminatory practices, Liberals feared Macdonald would get most of the "Indian vote."[8] In 1885, Macdonald persuaded Parliament to at least grant the vote to Indigenous people living in the "older" provinces (those east of Manitoba). "Here are Indians," he told the Commons, "Aboriginal Indians, formerly the lords of the soil, formerly owning the whole of the country. Here they are, in their own land, prevented from either sitting in this House, or voting for men to come here and represent their interests."[9] This law that Macdonald championed was rescinded by the Liberal government of Sir Wilfrid Laurier in 1898.[10]

In the decades after that, politicians would respond that any Indian who gave up their status could gain the vote. Absent that acceptance, Status Indians were wards of the federal government with the same legal status as minors. Only a small number, estimated at 250, gave up their status and became vote-eligible after the First World War.[11]

Diefenbaker was determined to bring Canada's Indigenous population into the country's democratic and political processes without conditions. He had challenged the previous Liberal government in the House of Commons in 1955 to appoint an Indigenous senator: "They have no members in the House to speak for them. There are 160,000 of these first citizens of Canada, and I have often thought that one of the finest gestures this government could make would be to appoint a full-blooded Indian to the Senate of Canada in order that the views of the Indians might be expressed and Indians in general, would have an opportunity of having a spokesman in the Parliament of this country."[12] In his early days as prime minister, Diefenbaker reiterated his long-held position:

> Over the years, I have believed that the Indian population of Canada deserves representation in the Parliament of Canada.... While the time may come when one or more might be elected to the House of Commons, that time is still far distant. I want to see an appointment made (to the Senate) at the earliest possible date of a Native Indian so that representation in Parliament may be provided for these, our very first citizens.[13]

His point that it would take many years before a native Canadian would be elected to the House of Commons reflected the reality that they did not, as a people, hold sufficient numbers in any constituency to overcome entrenched societal prejudices. His immediate remedy was to send Chief James Gladstone to the Senate on January 31, 1958, who Diefenbaker called "an outstanding and devoted servant of his people."[14] Gladstone, of Cardston, Alberta, was known as Akaynamuka (Many Guns) in the Blood Tribe of the Blackfoot Nation.

An international example of the denial of rights also prompted Diefenbaker to urge that native Canadians be given full citizenship rights, including, obviously, the franchise. As it was, at Commonwealth meetings, Diefenbaker's criticism of South Africa's policies of apartheid was met with understandable claims that Canada was racist since Indigenous people were disenfranchised. In the 1960 Speech from The Throne, Diefenbaker sought to remedy that injustice:

> I say that so far as this long overdue measure (of extending voting rights) is concerned, it will remove everywhere in the world suggestion that colour or race places any citizen in our country in a lower category than the other citizens of our country. I say this to those of the Indian race, that in bringing forward this legislation, the Minister of Citizenship and Immigration (Mrs. Fairclough) will reassure, as she has assured to date, that existing rights and treaties, traditional or otherwise, possessed by the Indians shall not in any way be abrogated or diminished in consequence of having the right to vote.

The legislative change granting the right to vote was met with suspicion among Status Indians, as indicated in a letter to Diefenbaker dated January 20, 1960 (shown here with its various grammatical errors).

> Honourable Sir,
>
> I understand by the Throne Speech that you intend giving the Indians the right to vote I would like to know if the vote if it would take away some of our rights and Privileges: 1st Would we have to Pay Property and Lands Taxes; 2nd Would it mean We Would have no more Medical and Hospital care; 3rd Would we still be given relief.... I would like to State here, these Indians are very Illiterate,

> I must also State here, on this Reserve there are no Industries, and the Indians do not have sufficient land to make a livelihood. By voting, would we become enfranchised, most of the Indians here have no education if you take their rights away the majority would starve. We would be foolish to vote to change our treaties. We Indians are like the late Mr. Duplessis. We do not want you to change the British North American Act. I think that is why you was to pass a Bill of Rights. Trusting you will respect our rights, which We have enjoyed for so many years.
>
> Yours Very Respectfully, George A. Cree[15]

It was understandable that chiefs and other Indigenous leaders would reach out to Diefenbaker for advice and support. In May 1959, he was named Chief Walking Buffalo by Chief Little Crow of the Sioux Nation and asked to wear a full Indian Headdress. There are numerous pictures of Diefenbaker wearing a headdress when similarly honoured. It was not cultural appropriation but a gesture of respect and appreciation, grounded by the feeling that Diefenbaker was on the side of improving the lives of Indigenous peoples from a position of genuine admiration and respect.

The bill giving Indigenous Canadians the right to vote was passed in the House of Commons in March 1960, and it applied to any federal election held after July 1 of that year. This fulfilled the ambition that John A. Macdonald set 75 years earlier.

While Macdonald and all politicians in Canadian history up to the present can be rightly criticized for failures when it comes to the plight of Indigenous people, Canada's first prime minister was enlightened by the standards of his time, a fact often ignored today. He was in rare company in expressing sympathy for the Indigenous people: "We must remember that they are the original owners of the soil, of which they have been dispossessed by the covetousness or ambition of our ancestors... the Indians have been the great sufferers by the discovery of America and the transfer to it of a large white population."[16]

As Diefenbaker noted, Macdonald looked saintly compared with American leadership. Indeed, many Indigenous peoples migrated north, referring to the Canada-U.S. border as "The Medicine Line." South of the border, the commander of the U.S. Army in the West, Philip Henry Sheridan, was said to have remarked in 1869, "The only good Indians I ever saw were dead." Theodore Roosevelt, who himself and others might describe as progressive for that era, moderated that statement in 1886, but only slightly: "I don't go so far as to think that the only good Indians are dead Indians, but I believe nine out of every 10 are." Macdonald wanted to avoid an "Indian war" that had ravaged the United States, arguing it was better to feed them than to fight them.

Senator Gladstone offered a balanced analysis of the significance of Diefenbaker extending the vote to his people, commenting in a 1960 *Globe and Mail* column that many of the 60,000 newly eligible voters would choose not to cast a ballot over fears it would impact their status rights or ensnare them in the income tax system. But Gladstone predicted that over time, this would change, and participation would rise.

He did express hope it would accelerate the timetable when a native would be elected to the House of Commons.[17] There was a muted response, and the minimal press coverage of the change in voting status reflects that there was not a significant clamour for the vote by Status Indians and general indifference by voters at large. There was no celebration, and it did not evoke a feeling of emancipation. Extending the franchise would only be recognized in the decades that followed as a significant advancement in Indigenous rights.

Following Gladstone, however, there was a gap of 13 years before another Indigenous Canadian was appointed to the Senate. It was also why Diefenbaker was pleased when Leonard Marchand, the first MP with Indian Status, and Wally Firth, the first Indigenous MP from the North, were elected to the House of Commons in 1968 and 1972.

Diefenbaker understood that Indigenous people faced racism and economic hardship. As prime minister, he was determined to mandate legal equality, and offer opportunity and improve their quality of life wherever possible. He also knew that this mattered because they were growing in numbers. In the years around when Diefenbaker was prime minister the data showed the population of Indigenous people was on the rise from 151,558 in 1954 to 217,864 by 1965, a 44 percent rise in just those eleven years which roughly bracket the years just before and just after his term as prime minister.[18] This compares to a 28.5 percent increase in the Canadian population as a whole. Diefenbaker was also given data that the Indigenous population identified largely with Christian denominations. That meant Diefenbaker was given no reason to believe that the connection between Indigenous people and the dominant religion in the country was a concern. (In the 1959 census, 54 percent of aboriginals identified as Roman Catholic, 23 percent as Anglican, and 14 percent as United Church. Only 2.2 percent identified with traditional aboriginal faith with 2.1 percent stating no affiliation.)

Out of office, Diefenbaker consistently pressed the Liberal government on issues of concern to Indigenous peoples, although not always in words and tone that Canadians would find compassionate or empathic in 2025. In March of 1964, in what he believed to be a call for support, he referred to "Eskimos" as "primitive people," highlighting the responsibility of the federal government under law. In debate, he called out the federal government for transferring responsibility in some cases to the province of Quebec: "Eskimos are not serfs; they are not political captives or pawns to be shoved about at the will or the whim of a government or governments. They are Canadians." He continued:

> Can these people, who are within the sole jurisdiction of the federal Parliament, be transferred, bartered away, whatever the terms, to another legislative body? Where is the constitution of this country if this can be done? I am not resting it on the constitutional right of these people to have their rights respected by Parliament. How are we going to justify this? Today, we hear more and more, and in stronger terms than ever before, that the constitution must be maintained. Yet, at the very time this is going on, these poor people on the shores of the Arctic are being told that the Constitution belongs to others but not to them.

Such was Diefenbaker's concern for the plight of Indigenous Canadians that he made it an exception to his rule to support the government whenever it made investments to bolster their living standards, such as on July 7, 1964:

> Discrimination was removed in law through the Bill of Rights. Economic opportunity was provided through rising standards and the provision of technical schools for the Indian people who are, technologically, of a high standard of ability but who had not possessed an opportunity to advance and improve their position. I say to the minister that the action outlined in this statement will receive the full support of the opposition, for all of us are tremendously interested in assuring that the Indian population of our country shall attain the highest possible standards.

He went on to ask the responsible minister to establish an Indian claims commission "so that their historic rights, which too often over the years have been violated and diminished, shall be given the full consideration of a semi-judicial body where wrongs have taken place, rights will be substituted." He continued, "We were ready for the establishment of an Indian Claims Commission. We had the legislation ready at the time we were defeated.... Bring it in. It could have been brought in last session. Now, it is overdue."

On June 17, 1966, Diefenbaker rose in the House of Commons to support traditional Indigenous hunting rights. He remarked, with frustration, how he defended those rights as an attorney without success. He supported the idea that a day of honour should be set aside in 1967 in appreciation of the contribution of Indigenous people in times of war and peace. In wartime, he noted, they served Canada gallantly:

> They sacrificed and suffered as few other Canadians did, in proportion to the population. They made their contribution. They are still making it. I join with them in asking the Government of Canada to bring about the setting aside of one day in (our) Confederation Year, in which we can, as Canadians in every part of this nation, do honour to these people who, with their forebears, did so much for us.

In addition to the wars of the 20th century, Diefenbaker remarked on the critical contribution of Indigenous peoples to first, victories over France, and later, the Americans, and that Canada was forged, in part, because of native support on the battlefields: "Were it not for the contribution in 1812 and again, earlier, in 1775 and 1776, those portions of Canada under the British Crown might very well have been lost. They did their part, and we do them only appropriate honour by setting aside such a day for them.... Too often their contribution is forgotten." In addition to an Indian Day, Diefenbaker supported the construction of an Indian Pavilion at the site of Expo' 67.

As he did in Opposition before, and in power, and after the loss of office, Diefenbaker continued to press for memorializing important native sites. With the building of the Gardiner Dam in Saskatchewan, a rock of symbolic importance to the local tribes, "The Mistaseni Rock," was in the flood path and would be submerged by the rising waters. In 1966, Diefenbaker rose in the House of Commons to advocate for preserving the 400-tonne rock:

> I find it hard to understand the reason the historical society would hold the view that this rock is not of historical importance... in the 1600's, that rock was then a sacred place for Cree Indians. They regarded it as possessing particular magical qualities. That rock will be lost to all generations unless action is taken.... If the entire rock cannot be preserved, then at least a considerable portion of it can. This rock means much to the Cree people, and I make a special appeal that action be taken to preserve it for future generations. Few of our historical monuments have been preserved. We have been recreant in this regard. Let us not lose the one monument which the Indians have in what is now the province of Saskatchewan... which would permit this historic thing to be lost to people who, there, worship their manitou, their guiding spirit; and even those who have taken Christianity as their religion look upon this stone as something possessing those qualities which made their forebears famous for their warlike prowess.

Despite Diefenbaker's protests, the rock was blasted with 60 sticks of dynamite on December 1, 1966. Remnants were used in a memorial to Chief Poundmaker on the Poundmaker Cree Nation Reserve.[19]

On education, more generally, of the countless speeches and interventions in the House of Commons, Diefenbaker raised the issue of schooling for Indigenous people on only a few occasions. Typically, the content of statements referenced the need to continue federal investments in schools that most at the time believed were an investment in the education and welfare of Indigenous Canadians. On June 30, 1967, the Pearson government committed to keeping an "Eskimo School" open in Churchill, Manitoba, for three to five years. Diefenbaker responded, at the urging of Indigenous people, "Is the minister prepared to go a little further and say the three to five years will be extended? It would be most unjust to Churchill if this school were removed." It was a residential school, and according to the Truth and Reconciliation Commission, "the hostel associated with the school employed Roman Catholic and Anglican staff, and the students were segregated on the basis of denomination."[20] It was closed in 1973.

Diefenbaker, who boasted in the House of Commons that he was a quadruple Indian chief, asked the Liberal Minister of Indian and Northern Affairs and future prime minister, Jean Chrétien, about the reorganization of the Department of

Indian Affairs and whether he would put the project on hold to enable deeper consultation with the affected communities. Chrétien responded:

> As "Chief Gooslap," a title given to me recently, I am happy to answer. This reorganization.... has no other purpose than a more efficient administration of the department here in Ottawa. We have no intention of changing the situation in the reserves among Indian bands... as we had in Ottawa education services for Eskimos, education services for Indians, an engineering service for Indians and one for Eskimos, etc., in short, as there was a duplication of services, we decided to amalgamate them to enable Canada's Indians and Eskimos to be better served by headquarters in Ottawa.

The only time a question was raised by Diefenbaker in the House of Commons about malnutrition among Indigenous people was October 2, 1968. Diefenbaker asked Chrétien about the difficult winter conditions native Canadians in the La Biche area of Saskatchewan were experiencing. Chrétien responded that he had been informed that out of 800 people, 100 were registered Indians. "In December and January, the 45 Indian families received social welfare payments according to their needs," responded Chrétien. "Moreover, the department gave each of those families the necessary equipment for trapping and provided transportation for eight families to the working site. In addition, we established a special residential building program and gave special assistance to enable some Indians to do commercial fishing." Chrétien became Canada's longest-serving minister of Indian and Northern Affairs. When he was moved to a different portfolio, Indigenous leaders complained, arguing that it was "better that we deal with the devil they knew than someone they did not know."[21]

The final occasion when Diefenbaker raised the rights of Indians in the House of Commons was six months before his death, on February 22, 1979, on the issue of "sacred treaty rights." He referenced a court case won by natives in connection with migratory birds hunted outside the regular season. On this issue, Canada had entered a protocol with the United States, a country which, Diefenbaker said, in a supreme understatement, "has never been very considerate of Indian rights all through the years." When the judgment was set aside, Diefenbaker challenged the government, "You cannot take treaty rights and destroy them without the consent of the treaty nation concerned."

Diefenbaker added to his question: "Are you going to give them their rights, or will you deprive them of these sacred rights to which they are unquestionably entitled?" The Liberal minister replied that the matter had been dealt with and "This government has probably done more than any previous government to ensure the rights of the Indian and Inuit people." It was an opening Diefenbaker could not resist. "It was my government which gave them the vote that Liberal party governments denied them all through the years." As was recorded in Hansard, some MPs cheered "Hear, hear!"

Over Diefenbaker's 79 years, he consistently saw himself as a voice for equality and justice for Canada's Indigenous peoples, and by the reverence and honours they bestowed upon him, he was celebrated as the champion that he was. He consistently swept the polls on reserves by higher margins than he enjoyed elsewhere in the ridings he represented.[22] "When we campaigned among the natives on several reserves within the Prince Albert constituency," wrote Diefenbaker local campaign organizer Dick Spencer, "they were almost speechless in their awe of him."[23]

As a solicitor, Diefenbaker took up cases on a *pro bono* basis for Status Indians to advocate for treaty rights. For nearly 40 years in Parliament, both as a member of Parliament and prime minister, he was a steadfast defender of Indigenous communities and people based on the injustices of which he was aware.

Diefenbaker's legacy with Indigenous peoples was one of respecting treaties, enfranchisement without diminishing rights, honouring agreements and advancing a land claims process. He knew that it was common for Indigenous people to see themselves as a collective that was more important than the rights of the individual. Pierre Trudeau made that error with the release of a white paper on Indian policy in 1969 that advocated eliminating the Indian Act and assimilating Indigenous people. "Either we go on adding bricks of discrimination around the ghetto in which they live," noted Trudeau, "and at the same time perhaps helping them preserve certain cultural traits and certain ancestral rights. Or we can say—the time is now to decide whether the Indians will be a race apart in Canada or whether it (sic) will be Canadians of full status." Trudeau's desire was for natives to be equal under the law. "It's inconceivable, I think, that in a given society, one section of the society have a treaty with the other section of the society. We must be all equal under the laws and we must not sign treaties among ourselves." Many of these treaties, argued Trudeau, had little relevance in modern society.

Unlike Diefenbaker, Trudeau failed to appreciate that Indigenous leaders viewed the identity of their people in the collective sense, as tribes and nations, not as individuals. They do not individually own land on reserves; their territory is held in the collective. Ultimately, Trudeau abandoned his vision, and the Indian Act remained intact. He said that he would not force natives to do anything they did not want, adding, "We'll keep them in the ghetto as long as they want."

In his time, with what he observed and was told by many Indigenous leaders and others, John Diefenbaker was among the most sympathetic, compassionate and constructive leaders on Indigenous issues in Canada and around the world.

***

Over John Diefenbaker's 40 years in Parliament, residential schools for Indigenous youth was a topic that received little attention by any parliamentarian. When the subject was raised in the House of Commons by Diefenbaker, as per his 1967 comment in Parliament noted previously, it was often pleas to retain funding to keep residential schools from closing or to allocate new funds to expand the program that was initiated before confederation in 1831.[24]

Attendance at residential schools became mandatory for children between the ages of seven and 15 in 1920. The number of residential schools peaked in 1931. Due to costs, the system was ultimately shifted towards day schools and the compulsory attendance for residential schools was rescinded before Diefenbaker became prime minister. According to the Government of Canada 1964 Canada Year Book:

> On most reserves, day schools have been established to provide education for children who live at home. Residential schools are operated to care for orphaned children, children from broken homes, and for those who, because of isolation or other reasons, are unable to attend day schools. Seasonal schools have been established for the children of migratory families, particularly in the Far North.[25]

Of note, most Indigenous children did not attend residential schools. Of the 45,596 Indigenous youth attending schools in 1961, 20,896 were in day schools, 8,391 (or just under 19 percent) were in residential schools, 2,329 were at what were primarily residential schools but lived at home, and 14,241 were in either provincial or private day schools. At the time, three years before Canada's celebratory 1967 centennial year, government documents boasted of the investments made for the welfare and education of Indigenous youth.

A search of media stories, as well as government and church archives before and during Diefenbaker's years in Parliament (from 1940 to 1979), reveals less than a handful of stories about residential schools. However, there were exceptions. The most notable early warning about the hazards of residential schools was published in 1922 by Peter Henderson Bryce in the pamphlet *A National Crime: An Appeal for Justice to the Indians of Canada -The Wards of the Nation; Our Allies in the Revolutionary War; Our Brothers-in-Arms in the Great War*. Bryce had served as the chief medical officer of the Department of Indian Affairs. He provided data on the adverse outcomes on Indigenous peoples, mainly as it related to death from tuberculosis and the unsanitary conditions of residential schools. Bryce urged not closure but an investment and expansion of the schools to achieve better health outcomes.

In February 1944, near the end of the Second World War, in her testimony about postwar goals before the House of Commons Committee on Reconstruction and Re-Establishment (charged with looking into the nature of Canadian society after the war), Canadian Co-operative Commonwealth Saskatchewan MP Dorise Nielsen declared, "I do not like residential schools at all." In 1947, the United Church had publicly declared the schools should be shut down in favour of non-denominational day schools on reserves. In 1948, another federal committee recommended shutting them down completely.

Authorities were interested in closing schools for financial reasons, and they may have seen the benefit of having the children closer to their homes. However, there was some resistance to closing schools by Indigenous leaders. As was reported in *Maclean's* in 2003, "In the 1960s, when the churches and federal government wanted to close certain schools, some Indian bands pleaded to have them remain open... In communities where there was a lot of family breakdown, residential schools provided a much-needed social service." That's why the councillors of Alberta's Stoney band took legal action to stop the government from closing the Morley Residential School. As the legal counsel for the band pleaded, "The Indians are only asking for a halfway chance to educate their children."[26]

The newspaper accounts of the Indigenous experience that Diefenbaker may have seen when he was prime minister were limited and often positive. In 1958, the *Toronto Star* reported that other nations should be envious of the help given to Indigenous youth by the United Church of Canada.[27] A 1960 feature story titled "Indian Women on the Warpath," told the story of the Blackfoot of Alberta and the election of Mrs. Emily Duck Chief, to the ruling council. Other women were similarly profiled for taking leadership roles to serve their communities. Overcoming societal prejudice, a cause Diefenbaker held dear, was an obstacle the women sought to overcome. The women profiled said the greatest barrier to overcoming that barrier was giving Indigenous people formal education "at least comparable to, if not better than, a white girl's."[28] That was the context of residential schools in John Diefenbaker's era and for much later.

On Truth and Reconciliation Day, September 30, 2024, the *Globe and Mail* acknowledged its failure to report on residential schools and an editorial stance they now find lacking:

> Decade after decade, the *Globe* supported a policy of assimilation... From the beginning, the newspaper viewed the schools in a mostly positive light.... The Globe's centennial editorial in 1967 offered one of the first, albeit slight, indications the paper was starting to pay better attention to the many issues of assimilation and colonization facing Indigenous peoples, in spite of the slanted and sporadic coverage it had afforded since before Confederation.[29]

According to the Final Report of the Truth and Reconciliation Commission of Canada, it was not until October 30, 1990, when a CBC interview with Grand Chief of the Assembly of Manitoba Chiefs, Phil Fontaine, was aired that it "focused national attention on the extent and nature of abuse in residential schools in an unprecedented manner."[30] This came 27 years after Diefenbaker was prime minister.

Given Diefenbaker's affinity, connection, and persistent advocacy for Indigenous peoples, it is incomprehensible to believe that had he been made aware of abuses at residential schools, he would not have made it an urgent national priority to address. He made consultation with Indigenous people a priority and regularly met with and was honoured by Indian chiefs. During his time in office, there were no clear briefings or warnings of the harm that was inflicted on Indigenous youth and families.

In fact, it was fifty-five years after Diefenbaker's government enfranchised Indigenous Canadians, in June 2015, that the Truth and Reconciliation

Commission, launched in 2008 by another Conservative prime minister, Stephen Harper, made specific references to consultations with Indigenous people by the Diefenbaker government in its final report:

> The Conservative victory in the 1957 federal election set the stage for another Indian Affairs policy review. In 1959, Citizenship and Immigration Minister Ellen Fairclough established a new joint committee of the Senate and House of Commons to investigate Aboriginal issues. Before the committee finished its hearings, the government amended the Indian Act to allow people with Indian status to vote without having to surrender any of the benefits associated with their status. During the hearing, a variety of First Nations groups made presentations that emphasized their rights to sovereignty and self-government. There were variations and diverging opinions among Aboriginal presenters, but they did not support measures intended to erode their distinct status, or that would lead to the abolition of reserves. The hearings of 1959 to 1961 led to a government commitment to establish an Indian claims commission to deal primarily with treaty and land claims, and an amendment of the Indian Act that did away with the government's power to enfranchise a man without his consent.[31]

It was under Prime Minister Jean Chrétien that the last residential school was closed in 1996.[32] It is reasonable to conclude that had Diefenbaker been made aware of the abuses that were taking place at many residential schools, either because of representations made to him by Indigenous leaders, the parents of school children, the children themselves, or through journalistic or other investigations, that he would have responded promptly and decisively to address such horrific abuse.

- 9 -

THE AVRO ARROW

I knew that 10,000 men and women would be out of work ultimately by this decision. I knew that a great industry that had been established would be weakened. But it was right to end it.

The Avro Arrow has taken on myths of epic proportions since the Diefenbaker government scrapped its development in 1959. According to such folklore, the cancellation was the result of a deep conspiracy that scuttled superior Canadian technology at the behest of a jealous American military-industrial complex. If not that, it was a rookie Canadian prime minister in his early days in office buckling before an American political master who wanted to suppress Canadian ingenuity—this even though Diefenbaker's nationalist sentiments were hardly conducive to such imagined pressure.

Some 40 years after the ordeal, the CBC produced a four-hour television miniseries, "The Arrow," casting acclaimed actor Dan Aykroyd as the swashbuckling Avro company president, Crawford Gordon, whose dreams were dashed by a prime minister he thought had an inferiority complex. At the time, the CBC mini-series set viewership records for the network. When Canadians are asked about Diefenbaker, the cancellation of the Avro Arrow is often one of the first issues mentioned, even if they know little about the subject or the Chief's motivations.

The origin of the Avro Arrow dates back to 1952, when air force defence planners sought to construct a made-in-Canada airframe to be fitted out with British or American engines and systems. However, over time, and not as expected, it became a uniquely Canadian project as foreign suppliers abandoned the initiative. Canadian companies were happy to fill the void on the engine and other systems, with RCA Victor in Hamilton, Canadair in Montreal, and

Canadian Westinghouse earning lucrative contracts. Over 400 smaller Canadian companies became part of the supply chain.

In December 1953, the Royal Canadian Air Force had forecast it would need about five hundred planes, with a cost estimated at less than $2 million per plane. Four years later, that cost estimate increased by 500 percent, and the number of planes the air force needed dropped to about 100.

The Avro Arrow was an engineering marvel. Its speed matched the world record at twice the speed of sound. It flew as high as any other aircraft and, in theory, could defeat Soviet bombers that threatened North America if swooping in over the Arctic. However, difficulties with the Arrow were revealed as early as 1955 when the distressed Liberal "minister of everything," C.D. Howe, said, "I can say that now we have started on a program of development that gives me the shudders." Nonetheless, on October 4, 1957, the first Arrow prototype was displayed in a public relations triumph before 12,000 people at the Avro plant.

When Diefenbaker came into office in June 1957, the Royal Canadian Air Force had concluded that the Avro Arrow was not economically feasible or militarily desirable. In his memoir, Diefenbaker wrote, "I have it on unchallengeable authority that Mr. St. Laurent and Mr. C.D. Howe had decided that the Arrow was to be cancelled." Indeed, Canada's chief bureaucrat had independently studied the issue and concluded that the Avro Arrow had become a giant white elephant.[1]

Geopolitical risk mattered to this calculation. By 1958, it was more important to develop technology to counter a Russian buildup of intercontinental ballistic missiles, which was not within the capacity of fighter jets. An interceptor plane was heavily constrained by the distance it could cover. A briefing to cabinet delivered by Defence Minister George Pearkes indicated the changing nature of what was required to meet evolving threats and the mirroring defence requirements:

> The assessment of the threat to North America changed. In the 1960s, the main danger would probably be from ballistic missiles, with the manned bomber decreasing in importance after 1962–63.... The original requirements in 1953 for between 500 and 600 aircraft of the CF105 fighter had been drastically reduced. Finally, the cost of the CF105 program as a whole was now of such a magnitude that the chiefs of staff felt that, to meet the modest requirement of manned aircraft presently

> considered advisable, it would be more economical to procure a fully developed interceptor of comparable performance in the United States.[2]

The cabinet recommended cancelling further development of the Arrow and negotiating with the United States to share two Canadian Bomarc missile bases. Pearkes said the Bomarc was cheaper than the CF105 and likely more effective. The missiles could be fitted with an atomic warhead, which the Americans would likely provide. The military and financial implications pointed unequivocally to the termination of the Arrow. However, with 25,000 jobs at stake and potential technology transfers, it was as much a political as a military decision.

The country's top public servant, Robert Bryce, recommended cancellation and worked with the executive team at A.V. Roe, the designer of the Arrow, to minimize the economic and political fallout. Of note, Diefenbaker's Chief Government Whip John Pallett was the MP for Peel, the constituency most impacted by the termination of the Avro Arrow. Diefenbaker did not want to act abruptly, giving the company time to reorganize and redeploy its workforce. In the meantime, taxpayers' money continued to flow into the ill-fated Arrow. In other words, it was good money being invested for no purpose other than to ease the transition.

On September 23, 1958, Diefenbaker made an announcement that indicated the days of the Arrow were numbered. He was preparing the country and the company for a final decision that was not much in doubt:

> In view of the introduction of missiles into the Canadian air defence system and the reduction in the expected need for manned, supersonic, interceptor aircraft, the government has decided that it would not be advisable at this time to put the CF105 into production... the government has decided that the development program for the Arrow aircraft and the Iroquois engine should be continued until next March when the situation will be reviewed again in light of all the existing circumstances at that time.... Although both the Arrow aircraft and the Iroquois engine appear now to be better than any alternatives expected to be ready by 1961, it is questionable whether... their margin of superiority is worth a very high cost of producing them.[3]

The announcement was the equivalent of a severance package with six months' notice. Diefenbaker ultimately made what he thought was the responsible decision. He was not subjected to American influence; except they made it clear that they would not purchase the aircraft. The United States had its versions of the Arrow, such as the F-101B Voodoo and the F-106 Delta Dart, which were already in production and much cheaper than the Arrow. At the time, only five prototypes of the Arrow had been produced, none of which were equipped with munitions.

What Diefenbaker did not know was that a Soviet spy had infiltrated the Arrow team.[4] It's not clear the Americans knew about the espionage either, but procuring strategic military assets from a foreign source, including Canada, was a risk they assessed.

Diefenbaker would have liked nothing more than for Canadian talent to best its American counterparts. "I had listened to the views of various experts; I had read everything I could find on the subject; I thought about it constantly; and finally, I prayed for guidance. The buck stopped with me, and I had to decide." Diefenbaker set out his reasons in the House of Commons on February 20, 1959:

> The government has carefully examined and re-examined the probable need for the Arrow aircraft and Iroquois engine—known as the CF-105—the development of which has been continued pending a final decision. It has made a thorough examination in the light of all the information available concerning the probable nature of the threats to North America in future years, the alternative means of defence against such threats, and the estimated costs thereof. The conclusion arrived at is that the development of the Arrow aircraft and Iroquois engine should be terminated now.

The press was largely supportive. Pundits were impressed by Diefenbaker's decisiveness in the face of inevitable adverse political fallout. A *Globe and Mail* editorial called the decision "not only wise and courageous, but one which will save the taxpayers a good deal of money."[5] In *Maclean's* magazine, Blair Fraser wrote, "The plain truth is nobody thought the government would have the courage to make such a painful decision.... It meant an early end to more than twenty-thousand jobs, most of them in the very heartland of the Conservative Party... It disappointed a big Canadian industry with many Conservative shareholders.

In short, it was political poison of a kind to scare any politician out of a year's growth."[6] The *Saskatoon Star-Phoenix* commented the government acted "forthrightly and courageously."[7] Editorials aside, the A.V. Roe Company did not surrender and launched a powerful lobby to keep the project alive and to damage the government's reputation.

Diefenbaker's critics said he was slow to make decisions and routinely—even painstakingly—sought unanimity from his cabinet. However, there was little delay or lack of leadership for the Arrow: "We must not abdicate our responsibility to assure that the huge sums which it is our duty to ask Parliament to provide for defence are being expended in the most effective way to achieve that purpose." Diefenbaker reminded the company that he had the interests of 18 million "shareholders" to protect. It was an odd reference for Diefenbaker to make, as citizens are not shareholders, and he did not have a corporate mindset. However, he knew what it meant to send good money after bad. He understood there were no lobbyists for ordinary citizens, and his job was to represent them.

The company immediately laid off all staff working on the project and was not prepared to follow an orderly six-month shutdown as the contract with the government provided. Company president Crawford Gordon dramatically used the loudspeakers to tell workers on the production floor they had no jobs and to go home. Diefenbaker fought back. "Letting out thousands of workers... on Friday, was so cavalier, so unreasonable, that the only conclusion any fair-minded person can come to is that it was done for the purpose of embarrassing the government." And the government *was* embarrassed. Caught off guard, it had no plan to keep Canada's skilled workers and technology. Indeed, many laid-off workers ultimately emigrated to the United States, and NASA quickly picked up 32 engineers. The Diefenbaker government had lost its first major public relations battle.

It did not help that Crawford had been disrespectful to Diefenbaker. Crawford was a heavy drinker and chain smoker who blew smoke in Diefenbaker's direction to make a point. There is no evidence the personality clash and poor behaviour on Crawford's part impacted Diefenbaker's decision. However, some conspiracists who thought the prime minister was vindictive raised the possibility that the decision to cancel the Arrow was grounded in spite.

Much has been made of the decision to render the Arrow prototypes to scrap. Conspiracy theorists have suggested this was done to placate American interests, as they did not want any evidence of a superior Canadian product to exist. Diefenbaker insists he issued no such directive and was unaware that the pre-production models had been destroyed. While the decision became a political football, Diefenbaker took some consolation in a note from a Liberal Senator W. D. Euler, who had served in the Mackenzie King cabinet as the minister of trade and commerce:

> May I compliment you on your courage and common sense in "dropping the Arrow" despite the intense pressure, which will probably continue. The loss of employment is, of course, regrettable, but I hope we shall not adopt the philosophy which advocates useless and ruinous expenditures merely for the sake of providing employment. That must be dealt with in other ways.[8]

Liberals were critical, not of the decision, but of Diefenbaker's management of the file. There was no question that when the Liberals returned to power, the Arrow would never fly again. Out of office in 1964, Diefenbaker was asked by the CBC if he regretted cancelling the Arrow project:

> Wouldn't it have been much easier for me on behalf of the government to have continued with the Arrow. It was a beautiful aircraft. Wonderful. It didn't operate very far. But it was a fine example of workmanship. I had to make in the finality that decision for over every prime minister's desk hangs that motto that was referred to one time by President Truman, "The buck stops here." I realized what would happen in connection with the Arrow. When one is faced with a problem like this there is a higher source of strength. If one does not have that higher source of strength, he can never bear the attacks made on him.... He has to have that strength and that faith. He has to believe; he has to be assured that ultimately that right is going to triumph. This came to me. I knew that 10,000 men and women would be out of work ultimately by this decision. I knew that a great industry that had been established would be weakened. But it was right to end it.[9]

- 10 -

A DECLARATION OF COLD WAR INDEPENDENCE

They are not going to push me around.

Diefenbaker was not anti-American as much as he was pro-Canadian. However, he was not the first or last Canadian prime minister to seek political benefit by standing up to American power to demonstrate Canada's independence and strength. Whether that produces gain or harm depends on the players and how the game is played.

Diefenbaker greatly admired Canada's first nationalist prime minister, Sir John A. Macdonald. Canada was formed, in large part, through Macdonald's leadership to both reconcile French and English ambitions in the British colonies in North America and to thwart the continental pull of the United States with its "manifest destiny" impulse to have an American flag fly over the northern section of North America.

Diefenbaker frequently invoked Macdonald to get a laugh and make a point. He would tell stories of Macdonald on the campaign trail, such as when a heckler took on the first prime minister by saying, "I wouldn't vote for you if you were the Angel Gabriel," to which Macdonald replied, "My friend, you are so right. You would not be in my constituency."

Diefenbaker used the same inkwell as Macdonald, placed a life-sized sculpture of Canada's first prime minister in his office, hung a portrait of Macdonald above his desk, slept in the founder's bed (an extended version) and sat in Macdonald's chair. Every January 11, the first prime minister's birthday, Diefenbaker led a procession of Conservative MPs to lay a wreath at the foot of the statue of Macdonald on Parliament Hill. When troubled, Diefenbaker would read from Donald Creighton's 1952 and 1955 two-volume biographies of Macdonald.

Macdonald campaigned and governed under a national vision, which Diefenbaker evoked when speaking of his northern vision. He applauded Macdonald for heroically building east-west infrastructure, and for objecting to having even one inch of the transcontinental railway touching American soil—which it never did. This position significantly increased the cost and the time needed to complete the project. Thus, given his admiration for Macdonald's priorities, when campaigning, Diefenbaker stated his own objective was to "continue Macdonald's historic task of nation-building... see that Canadians are given a transcendent sense of national purpose, such as Macdonald gave in his day... to safeguard our independence, restore our unity." Diefenbaker believed that without Macdonald, there was no Canada. He described the first prime minister as "the indispensable, without whom Confederation would never have been possible. No one denies him the title of the great architect of Canadian Confederation."

While Canada was in its infancy, it was vulnerable to a pull by its southern neighbour, but as the nation matured, that risk was reduced. It helps explain why another Tory prime minister, three decades after Diefenbaker, sought closer economic ties to the Americans to protect Canadian industry from arbitrary trade sanctions. Brian Mulroney openly sought a close and productive relationship with the American presidents in power during his government. U.S. presidents Ronald Reagan and George H.W. Bush delivered monumental benefits to Canada in response to Mulroney's vision for free trade and clean air. It did not bother Mulroney that he was criticized for cozying up to his American counterparts, including singing "When Irish Eyes Are Smiling," with President Reagan on stage at a summit meeting in Quebec City. Both Mulroney and Reagan came from Irish stock.

Jean Chrétien, the Liberal prime minister from 1993 to 2003, took a different approach, more akin to Diefenbaker's. One of his top three priorities was to assert Canadian independence from America in the post-Mulroney era. However, in his unique style, he made every effort to amplify this sentiment as the public perception while privately establishing personal rapport and friendship with at least President Bill Clinton. "We can do more for you than even the CIA if we are not viewed as the 51st state," Chrétien told Clinton, a frequent golfing partner, in 1993.[1]

One cannot consider Canada's relationship with the United States under Diefenbaker without appreciating the tension between the U.S. and the U.S.S.R.

at that time. While Canada was an ally of the Soviet Union in the Second World War, that changed with the defeat of Germany and the surrender of Imperial Japan in 1945. Overnight, the U.S.S.R. went from ally to adversary. Canada and the United States were founding members of the North Atlantic Treaty Organization (NATO), which was established in 1949 to counter the threat to national security by the Warsaw Pact countries under Soviet domination.

For many, the beginning of the Cold War can be traced to Canada. It was from the Russian embassy in Ottawa on September 5, 1945, that Igor Gouzenko defected to Canada, bringing with him a trove of documents proving that Soviet spies had infiltrated several Canadian government departments, including the National Research Council, that had been conducting atomic weapons studies. Despite efforts of the Canadian government to keep the defection and the spy ring a secret, the FBI under J. Edgar Hoover wanted to stir public opinion and had the story leaked to an American newspaper columnist.[2] All was revealed in February 1946, with the Soviets uncharacteristically confirming the truth of their espionage. However, they downplayed the value of the information obtained by their covert activities, suggesting they had already achieved substantial technological progress in the areas to which Gouzenko had access.

On March 5, 1946, Sir Winston Churchill effectively issued a declaration of conflict in a speech he delivered at Westminster College in Fulton, Missouri, with President Truman at his side, declaring that an "Iron Curtain" had been erected across the continent of Europe:

> Behind that line lie all the capitals of the ancient states of Central and Eastern Europe. Warsaw, Berlin, Prague, Vienna, Budapest, Belgrade, Bucharest and Sofia; all these famous cities and the populations around them lie in what I must call the Soviet sphere, and all are subject, in one form or another, not only to Soviet influence but to a very high and in some cases increasing measure of control from Moscow.

While the United States was the first to develop nuclear weapons and then deploy them in 1945 in Japan to end the Second World War, it took just another four years before the U.S.S.R. developed a nuclear arsenal of its own. Both countries had the theoretical capacity to wipe out the other, if not the entire world, in what was described as a war that could never be fought.

In 1947, Truman signed the National Security Act, which substantially reorganized America's defence and intelligence infrastructure. This included establishing a Secretary of Defence as the head of the National Military Establishment, the National Security Council, and the Central Intelligence Agency. Truman had accepted Churchill's fundamental doctrine that the U.S.S.R. was the gravest threat to international security. He also considered that U.S. security was heavily dependent on its cooperation with Canada, as was noted in a 1950 Secret memo from the State Department:

> Our commitments and risks are so extensive and essential that Canada, in a military sense, must be considered as if it were an integral part of the United States. It is as important to our security to protect Canada as it is to protect California. Canada is the most logical avenue for a large-scale attack on the United States.[3]

It was not just Gouzenko that had raised national and international security concerns. In America, Julius and Ethel Rosenberg were convicted of spying for the Soviet Union after they shared nuclear weapon design secrets in 1951. Both were executed by electrocution in 1953. Klaus Fuchs, a German theoretical physicist who had worked in Los Alamos, New Mexico, on the Manhattan Project that developed the atomic bomb, confessed that he had passed information to the Soviets as early as 1942. He was sentenced to 14 years of imprisonment by a British court.

Communist-hunting and spy searches took on another level when Senator Joseph McCarthy of Wisconsin headed the Senate Permanent Subcommittee on Investigations in 1953 and 1954. Not only were government officials and the military put under scrutiny, but so was the entertainment industry, where suspected communists or friends of suspected communists were blacklisted and effectively banned from working. Some libraries burned books that did not conform with the committees' standards. President Eisenhower recoiled at the intrusion of civil liberties and public discourse through censorship. Nonetheless, McCarthy's committee then began an investigation into the United States Army. McCarthy overreached and was censured by the Senate. Yet McCarthy maintained a close relationship with the Kennedy family, including the future president, John. F. Kennedy. Of note, and this helps partly explain Diefenbaker's later antipathy to Kennedy, Diefenbaker's thinking was more in line with Eisenhower's than Kennedy's, believing McCarthy was "a destroyer of justice."[4]

***

While the Americans held numerical supremacy in nuclear weaponry, the Soviets developed an edge in space with the launch of the Sputnik satellite on October 4, 1957, just three months after Diefenbaker formed a minority government. At about the same time, the U.S.S.R. developed the capacity to deploy intercontinental ballistic missiles, which meant that every city in Canada and America was at risk.

All of this impacted public worry. Canadian and American children understood the world had changed when air-raid sirens were tested intermittingly. They practiced a "duck and cover" maneuver under their school desks should the alert sound that they would need to execute if bombs were headed their way. Backyard underground fallout shelters became a popular home renovation project, a place to stay for a few weeks while the radiation from a nuclear bomb dissipated. Diefenbaker wrote the foreword to a government pamphlet, "Survival in a Nuclear War," noting:

> It would be less than wise for the Canadian people or for people anywhere in the free world not to take those precautions which can be taken now. All of us pray that the occasion will never arise when Canada or those nations associated with her in the free world will ever be required to implement these plans of precaution.

The Diefenbaker government allocated $10 million to building bomb shelters, including a 100,000-square-foot facility where the prime minister could operate from just outside of Ottawa if the country were under attack. Today, it functions as a museum and is called the "Diefenbunker." While Diefenbaker gets the credit, or blame as the case may be, it was a project initiated by his predecessors.

The previous Liberal government had left much more than the Avro Arrow as unfinished military business heading into the 1957 election. Another sensitive issue was integrating Canadian and American defence forces for joint protection. On a visit to Canada in November of 1953, President Eisenhower articulated in the Canadian House of Commons that, "Defensively as well as geographically, we are joined together beyond any possibility of separation."

Prime Minister St. Laurent pulled a proposal on North American defence from a March 15, 1957 cabinet meeting, fearing a leak to the press. Diefenbaker concluded the highly consequential NORAD (North America Aerospace Defence Command) agreement that the Liberals had negotiated in their final years in office. In August, without much discussion, either with his cabinet or the Opposition in the House of Commons, Diefenbaker signed off on NORAD, hardly the act of someone who would later be accused of being anti-American. He expected little opposition from the Liberal front bench on defence issues since they would have been familiar with the intricacies of the file, which included U.S. overflights of Canada carrying atomic weapons and the conducting of American military exercises in Labrador. Without much analysis, Diefenbaker erroneously saw NORAD as an extension of Canada's NATO commitments with no substantial loss of sovereignty. However, NORAD had a completely different command structure than NATO.

NORAD committed the United States to defend Canada during war, as was the case under Article 5 of NATO. It also meant that U.S. military personnel could be deployed in Canada. Pearson, as leader of the Opposition, did not dispute the need for cooperation with the United States in these matters. However, he took the government to task for not bringing the international defence agreement to the cabinet for review and approval. Pearson accused Diefenbaker of hastily signing the agreement without adequate, consultation, or debate. In other words, it was process and not substance that he objected to, and he was likely driven by political exigency.

NORAD provided aerospace warning and air sovereignty to enhance protection for both countries, principally to counteract Soviet threats and incursions. NORAD is headquartered in the United States, with a U.S. commander and a Canadian vice commander. To Canada, NORAD was more than a treaty where one country backed up the other. It created an integrated and multi-pronged continental defence strategy and systems that included the Distant Early Warning Line (DEW), a string of radar stations in the Canadian Arctic and the Aleutian Islands of Alaska designed to detect Soviet bombers at the earliest opportunity.

After becoming prime minister, Diefenbaker's first public address on American soil occurred at Dartmouth College in New Hampshire on September 7, 1957. Much the same way that the U.S. Secretary of State John Dulles had said his responsibility was to "look out for the interests of the United States," Diefenbaker said he would do the same for Canada with a mindset of "common sense, frankness, absolute confidence and mutual trust."[5] In this posture, Diefenbaker was sensitive to military, economic and political integration with Canada's southern neighbours and strongest ally.

Diefenbaker expressed his concern that Canada was too dependent on trade with the United States and that he did not wish to have his country's economic or political affairs determined outside its borders. He signalled that this concern extended to large-scale and continued ownership of critical Canadian industries. "This has inherent danger to Canada," he said, "There is an intangible disquiet in Canada over the political implications of large-scale and continuing external ownership and control of Canadian industries." Despite the warnings by officials in the Department of External Affairs that these words would alarm American politicians, Diefenbaker was confident he could manage whatever consequences might arise. He described his relationship with President Dwight D. Eisenhower as "best of friends." From their first meeting, it was "Ike" and "John" between the leaders.

One sticking point was Diefenbaker's willingness to explore extending diplomatic relations with communist China. Eisenhower said he could not see the day when this would be possible and that if communist China were admitted to the United Nations, it would rupture the international body. He predicted Congress would call for a withdrawal from the U.N. and seek to terminate its presence in New York City if China became a member. The Americans were concerned with China's aggression in Korea and Vietnam, as well as the holding of American prisoners. The United States, Eisenhower communicated, was prepared to tolerate the sale of Canadian wheat to China provided that no American company or territory was party to the exchange. In time, Diefenbaker was proven correct with the People's Republic of China's entry into the U.N. in 1971 and the establishment of American diplomatic relations with mainland China following President Richard Nixon's historic visit in 1972.

***

Senator John F. Kennedy of Massachusetts visited Canada in October 1957, four months after Diefenbaker had become prime minister, to receive an honorary Doctor of Laws from the University of New Brunswick. Prematurely, but not inaccurately, he was introduced by the university chancellor as the next president of the United States. In his remarks, he dismissed Diefenbaker's attempt to divert trade away from the United States as "deluded," noting, "It would be a pity to rigidify the Canadian economy merely for the sake of breaking lances with a phantom American colonialism." These were harsh words, especially for an American politician to deliver on Canadian soil and an early indication of the difficulties he would encounter with Diefenbaker in matters of state and a personal relationship.

Impertinent comments by a then U.S. senator aside, President Eisenhower visited Ottawa in July of 1958, addressing the Canadian Parliament and meeting Diefenbaker at the prime minister's official residence at 24 Sussex Drive. Eisenhower's objective was to "discourage any trend towards a narrow position of Canadian nationalism."[6] In his address, Eisenhower declared "that we should talk frankly to each other. Frankness, in good spirit, is a measure of friendship." As a realist and optimist, Eisenhower added, "It is my conviction that for all our present problems and all our future ones, we will find acceptable solutions. It will take understanding, common sense and a willingness to give and take on both our parts. These qualities we have always found in our dealings with Canada. I hope that you have not found them lacking in us."

Refuting that Canada held fewer sovereign rights than the United States because of its dependence on its more powerful neighbour and ally," Eisenhower concluded, "The hallmark of freedom is the right to differ as well as the right to agree."

While in Ottawa, Eisenhower golfed at the Ottawa Hunt Club and shot 90 (winning $15.00 in a $5.00 Nassau, a friendly three-part wager on the front nine, back nine and combined score). George Hees, the Speaker of the Senate and the golf club president were in the group. There was a security threat, including a possible assassin, and Diefenbaker went to the course when they were on hole 14 to urge them to call off the game. Eisenhower, who got a mulligan on the first tee after hooking his ball into the woods, was up in his match, so they played on.[7]

Continuing in the spirit of cross-border comradery, the most notable Canada-U.S. venture that symbolized cooperation and economic linkages in the early days of the Diefenbaker government was the opening of the St. Lawrence Seaway by Queen Elizabeth and President Eisenhower on June 26, 1959. Diefenbaker was pleased to represent the Canadian government and graciously credited a former Liberal prime minister, Louis St. Laurent, for his leadership on the project. Similarly, at Eisenhower's invitation, Diefenbaker visited Washington, D.C., in June 1960.

While in Washington, Diefenbaker raised the issue of freedom of access to Berlin, then divided between the East (Communist East Germany) and the West (Democratic West Germany). Eisenhower was less concerned about Berlin, although Diefenbaker was prescient, given that the Berlin Wall was erected within three years. Despite this provocation from the U.S.S.R., Diefenbaker was steadfast in his view that West Berlin should under no circumstances be ceded to Soviet-controlled East Germany.

***

Canada could never protect its territory from Soviet invasion on its own. That was the role of NORAD and NATO. However, Canada's forces and military assets needed to be as modern and robust as possible so that its allies would take the nation seriously, giving Canada a voice at the table where critical decisions on defence were made. Canada also had a proud tradition, demonstrated through two world wars of carrying more than its fair share of what was required to keep the world safe and protect the nation's borders. When Diefenbaker became prime minister, the principal national security threat was bomber attacks from the Soviet Union. With the Cold War between the U.S.A. and the U.S.S.R. reaching a deep freeze and the emerging threat of intercontinental ballistic nuclear missiles preoccupying national security assessments, the Diefenbaker government had to decide how best to protect its population.

With Canada being no match for military superpowers, the critical decision was whether Canada would allow American nuclear warheads to be situated on and potentially deployed from Canadian soil. This reflected the reality that if nuclear missiles were fired from land by the U.S.S.R., they would likely cross Canadian territory before reaching their intended destination in America.

On September 23, 1958, Diefenbaker announced his government was considering the use of Bomarc ground-to-air missiles, which included an atomic capability. This would be a joint initiative with the United States, and discussions commenced within a few months "for the acquisition and storage of defensive nuclear weapons and warheads in Canada." Diefenbaker received advice from officials at the External Affairs department to reject the offer of allowing American missiles on Canadian soil. However, the department did not explain how this could be achieved while honouring Canada's commitments under NATO and NORAD. As historian John Boyko wrote in his seminal book, *Cold Fire*, on Canadian and American relations, "The decision to station American tactical nuclear weapons on Canadian soil would prove to be the most consequential of [Diefenbaker's] administration."[8] The following February, Diefenbaker informed the House of Commons of the conditions that needed to be met before the missiles could be stationed in Canada:

> We are confident that we shall be able to reach full agreement with the United States on appropriate means to serve the common objective. It will, of course, be some time before these weapons will be available for use by Canadian forces. The government, as soon as it is in a position to do so, will inform the House, within the limits of security, of the general terms of understanding which are reached between the two governments on this subject.

More specifically, the conditions he described included "Canadian custody" while the ownership of the warheads would remain "United States assets." The use or deployment of the warheads would be a joint responsibility of the two governments. Much needed to be discussed and then negotiated regarding these two principles, which Diefenbaker expected would take some years to conclude. This was not, Diefenbaker asserted, a matter of Canada adding some strategic launching pads for the U.S. military:

> Such weapons could only be used in Canadian territory or air space under conditions agreed to by Canada. The United States was able to exercise control over use by withholding presidential authority for the release of these weapons. Canada could exercise its share of responsibility only when the weapons were released. But, even so, the weapons could not be used if the Canadian government did not see fit to permit this. What we required amounted virtually to the power of a qualified veto. The close cooperation between Canada and the United States in defence matters would continue as long as we were mutually threatened.

Cooperating with the United States and other countries in NATO was, by definition, a "loss" of Canadian sovereignty to act independently. But then, so too is any agreement that allows a smaller power to bind a larger power to a rules-based international order, which matters much more for the minor power than the major power, the latter having much more room to maneuver given their size and capacity. And with such agreement comes responsibilities. For example, under Article 5 of the NATO treaty, Canada is obligated to defend a member country, as an attack on one is considered an attack on all. Such was the case on September 11, 2001, when Al-Qaeda terrorists attacked America.

With NATO and NORAD as a given, Diefenbaker was intent on retaining as much sovereignty and independence as possible, not just on military matters but also on the economic and cultural sway America held over Canada. Diefenbaker believed that preceding governments had not been mindful of the continental pressures exerted by the Americans. He did not want Canada to be seen as a satellite of the United States. Diefenbaker believed that Canada's ability to make consequential decisions on domestic and international matters without first having to check with an American administration would enhance Canada's credibility at the United Nations and the Commonwealth. Thus, a cabinet note was sent to the American State Department in March of 1960 that elaborated on three Canadian principles on American-owned nuclear weapons to be stationed in Canada:

1. Arrangements for storage would be the joint responsibility of the two governments;

2. The responsibility for the removal of these weapons from the base would be shared; and,

3. Responsibility would be shared for the use of the weapons.

Diefenbaker began to question the commitment of the Americans to the Bomarc program when it was revealed in March 1960 that the U.S. Department of Defense proposed to Congress that the planned expenditure on the program for the fiscal year 1961 was to be reduced by 90 percent and that the number of Bomarc sites be cut in half. The two proposed Canadian sites would be retained under this proposal. Diefenbaker concluded it was only a matter of time until the United States decided to scrap the program altogether, a prediction that would ultimately come to pass. On November 24, 1960, Diefenbaker elaborated his views at the Canadian Club of Ottawa:

> We have taken the stand that no decision will be required *while progress towards disarmament continues*. To do otherwise would be inconsistent. When and if such weapons are required, then we shall have to take the responsibility. The future of Canadians requires that we make that decision which, in the light of the best information we have, represents the maximum security for our country. We have made it equally clear that we shall not, in any event, consider nuclear weapons until, as a sovereign nation, we have equality in control—a joint control.

In this stance, Diefenbaker wanted to have it both ways. He desired a reduction in nuclear arms while also prohibiting countries from joining the nuclear club. At the same time, he agreed to certain conditions under which nuclear weaponry would be situated in Canada and under joint control, so we would be theoretically added to the club of nations that controlled nuclear weapons. Linking his decision to "progress on disarmament" allowed Diefenbaker to avoid deciding on nuclear weapons in the short term.

Eisenhower had termed out as president, and John F. Kennedy was sworn into office in January 1961, but Diefenbaker would have preferred Richard Nixon, Eisenhower's vice-president, as his counterpart. In 1958, Nixon had written to the recently elected Canadian prime minister: "I, personally, could not have been more pleased that you have now earned a majority from the Canadian people."[9] Diefenbaker not only liked Nixon but was skeptical of Kennedy, telling his ambassador to the United States, Richard B. Wigglesworth, a few months before the 1960 American election that the silver-spooned senator from Massachusetts was not ready for the job.[10]

In a conversation with Eisenhower, Diefenbaker suggested that Vice-President Nixon refuse a television debate with Kennedy, strategizing that "such a debate would only augment Kennedy's stature... [that] there was no advertising value in it for Nixon."[11] Diefenbaker was correct, as the debate with a younger "cool" and well-tanned Kennedy ready for the television age contrasted with what the public saw of Nixon: a five-o-clock shadow, beads of sweat, and eyes not accustomed to focusing on a camera and thus appeared shifty to a massive prime-time audience.

In subsequent years, Diefenbaker railed about Kennedy's unprecedented interference in Canadian elections to ensure that a Liberal government would be installed under Lester B. Pearson, motivated primarily to rid himself of having to deal with Diefenbaker. Hypocritically, Diefenbaker had no qualms about offering advice to his Republican brethren, limited as it was in the 1960 election. He later commented that without accepting the invitation to debate Kennedy, Nixon would have won the presidency on his first attempt. What was clear to Canadians was that while Diefenbaker was of the same generation as Eisenhower, he had little in common with Kennedy.

After the election, Diefenbaker sent Kennedy a congratulatory letter. When no response was forthcoming, the Canadian ambassador, Arnold Heeney, sought to confirm that the message had been received. The inquiry prompted a curt telegram in response, which Diefenbaker took as a personal insult. The slights continued, including Kennedy's persistent mispronunciation of the Canadian prime minister's Germanic surname. Some thought it was intentional or potentially due to his Boston Irish accent. What came out at a White House press conference on February 8, 1961, was "Diefenbawker." Canadian journalist and author Lawrence Martin interviewed the U.S. Secretary of State, Dean Rusk, about the incident, who took full blame. Despite Diefenbaker being in office for three years, a state department official advised Kennedy on the pronunciation. Nonetheless, Kennedy repeated the diplomatic blunder to Diefenbaker's irritation.

In preparation for Diefenbaker's three-hour visit to the White House on February 20, 1961, President Kennedy was briefed about Diefenbaker's nationalist sentiments. He was also told of a "Canadian inferiority complex" with a sensitivity to any actual or fancied slight to Canadian sovereignty and [that] the essential element in problems involving Canada tends to be psychological."[12] Thinking Diefenbaker was not anti-American but was keeping his distance from the Americans for political benefit, the concluding advice was to respect the Canadian prime minister and promise ongoing consultation, especially on matters related to national defence.

After Kennedy raised trade irritants involving Cuba, the more important topic of Canada accepting American nuclear weapons on Canadian soil was discussed. Diefenbaker affirmed that Canada would meet its responsibilities under NATO and NORAD. Still, it would not accept a policy "which will lay upon the United States a responsibility which we should carry upon ourselves."[13] There was no expectation that an agreement on the matter would be reached at the meeting.

More telling of how the relationship would evolve was a gratuitous comment from Diefenbaker about the paintings he observed in the Oval Office. Of one painting from the War of 1812, depicting an American triumph over British forces, Diefenbaker commented about British victories in the seas, of which Kennedy claimed something combining ignorance and disbelief. Diefenbaker said, "I'll show you," referring to the encounter between the American ship *Chesapeake* and the British frigate *Shannon* on June 1, 1813. Effectively, the question of who won the War of 1812 was being relitigated in a less-than-cordial manner and in a building the British had torched.

Diefenbaker then commented on the mounted stuffed sailfish that Kennedy had in his office that he had caught on his honeymoon. Diefenbaker claimed he caught a bigger fish the month before in Jamaica. Kennedy was skeptical. "You didn't catch it," said a dismissive Kennedy. "Yes I did," responded Diefenbaker emphatically. Then, the two contrasted how Kennedy won high office at an early age, and it took many tries before Diefenbaker won the top job at age 62. When Kennedy asked what Diefenbaker thought of his administration, the Canadian prime minister questioned Kennedy's choice of attorney general, his brother, Robert (Bobby) Kennedy. It was an unfortunate, inauspicious start. Diefenbaker did himself and Canada no favours by engaging in one-upmanship on fishing tales and insulting the new American president in the choice of his brother as attorney general, even though the appointment undermined the necessary independence of the role.

Private conversations and friction aside, departing Washington at 2:45 p.m. allowed Diefenbaker to report to the House of Commons and the Canadian public later that afternoon on his "positive" impressions of the young American president, genuine or not. Diefenbaker told the House of Commons that in their brief meeting, "The president… leaves upon one the impression of a person dedicated to peace, to the raising of economic standards not only in his country but in all countries, and to the achievement in his day of disarmament among all the nations of the world."

To his aides, President Kennedy found Diefenbaker untrustworthy and told his brother, Robert Kennedy, "I don't want to see that boring son of a bitch again."[14] Robert Kennedy elaborated on his brother's feelings about Diefenbaker much later in a conversation with Canadian journalist Knowlton Nash: "The president felt Diefenbaker was a grandstanding, insincere, sanctimonious bore. In time, he came to believe he was also a liar, a blackmailer, and a betrayer."[15] However, according to Lee Richardson, Diefenbaker's executive assistant during his later years in Parliament, Diefenbaker had no *personal* dislike of Kennedy and enjoyed being mentioned in the same breath.[16] He wanted to be treated as an equal and not a weak sister of a much larger neighbour. Nonetheless, that initial Washington D.C. meeting between the prime minister and the president set the tone for the executive relationship while both were in power.

Personal animus aside, the Canadian and American governments continued cooperating to protect the North American perimeter through NORAD. This was evident by an agreement that was signed between the two countries on March 28, 1961, where:

1. the United States would provide sixty-six F-IOIB interceptor aircraft for the RCAF squadrons assigned to NORAD;

2. the United States would procure from Canadian sources F-104G interceptor aircraft for NATO to the value of $150 million, with Canada contributing a further $50 million;

3. Canada would assume responsibility for the cost of manning Pine Tree radar installations now carried by the United States.

But any progress towards a resolution was quickly overshadowed by the American attempt to oust the revolutionary communist leader, Fidel Castro, from Cuba, who had violently overthrown the American-friendly government of Fulgencio Batista in 1959. Beginning on April 17, 1961, just three months after Kenney's inauguration, a military operation on the southwestern coast of Cuba at the Bay of Pigs led by the United States of America and the Cuban Democratic Revolutionary Front failed in spectacular fashion over three days of fighting. Kennedy was seriously damaged by the fiasco and his standing in America and around the world took a massive credibility hit.

Diefenbaker thought the invasion of Cuba had been a mistake, as did Kennedy, acknowledging that "victory has 100 fathers and defeat is an orphan." One lesson Diefenbaker learned from the fiasco was not to believe everything his generals were telling him about the dangers around the world and how best to manage them. Diefenbaker asked Kennedy why Canada, as a NORAD partner, was not consulted before the Cuban invasion was launched. Kennedy responded that he had no plans for another invasion unless provoked and promised, "We would talk with you before doing anything," a pledge he soon broke.[17]

With Kennedy, the Soviet Union sensed a weaker adversary than in Eisenhower. At their first meeting in June of 1961 in Vienna, the First Secretary of the Communist Party, Nikita Khrushchev, belittled Kennedy by referring to him as "the boy." This was not a literal stretch, as the then 44-year-old Kennedy was about the same age as Khrushchev's son. Kennedy described the encounter to a *New York Times* journalist as the "roughest thing in my life. He just beat the hell out of me." When the subject of a divided Berlin came up, Kennedy erred when not opposing the building of a barrier that would divide the city.

Kennedy soon found a more solid footing, at least rhetorically, after the Berlin Wall was erected a few months later. The president stood firm and said in a radio address from the Oval Office on July 25, 1961, "We cannot and will not permit the Communists to drive us out of Berlin, either gradually or by force."[18] With this stance, he had the full backing of Diefenbaker, and with NATO taking on a more important role than ever. But Khrushchev knew it was a point of vulnerability, recounting to an aide, "Berlin is the testicles of the West. Every time I want to make the West scream, I squeeze on Berlin."[19]

Kennedy's first foreign visit was to Canada in May 1961. He wanted to discuss Cuba, southeast Asia, and nuclear weapons. Going into the meeting, Diefenbaker believed Kennedy had been humiliated by the Bay of Pigs fiasco and was trying to regain his footing before a friendly foreign audience. Concurrently, though, and with the tragic irony of historical knowledge we now know about Kennedy's assassination in 1963, Diefenbaker recoiled at the proposed Secret Service security arrangements for the presidential visit. "They want to put men with guns all over the place," he remarked in reaction: "They are not going to push me around." However, the only injury on this trip came when President Kennedy attempted to plant a tree and reinjured his back. According to Kennedy's political pollster, Lou Harris, the president thought Diefenbaker orchestrated the event to throw the American president off his game.[20]

The tree-planting came after Kennedy had teased Diefenbaker publicly about his poor French. "I am somewhat encouraged to say a few words in French, having heard your Prime Minister." Another slight occurred at the State Dinner, where

Kennedy sought to renew his acquaintance with the Opposition leader, Lester Pearson, in a manner that visibly indicated he was ignoring the prime minister. There was also a dinner party at the residence of the American ambassador where a member of the U.S. diplomatic core remarked that Kennedy was "absolutely discourteous" to Diefenbaker while he joked around with Pearson.[21] Diefenbaker could often be over-sensitive to perceived slights. Still, on this occasion and others, Kennedy hardly helped the American-Canadian relationship or his own with Diefenbaker with such blatant public disdain for Canada's prime minister.

***

On Cuba, Diefenbaker said Canada would not, diplomatically or economically, disengage with the revolutionary republic. Oddly, for the staunch anti-communist that he was, the Diefenbaker government quickly recognized the provisional government of Fidel Castro on January 8, 1959, a mere eight days after the rebel forces overtook Havana. Two Canadian banks were permitted to remain open in Cuba, while other foreign banks had been nationalized. Diefenbaker's Cuba policy may have thus been part of his desire to demonstrate Canada's independence from the United States, even when Eisenhower was still in the White House. For good or ill, Castro maintained a particular affection for Canada throughout his life, famously serving as an honorary pallbearer at the funeral of Canada's 15th prime minister, Pierre Elliot Trudeau, who, unlike Diefenbaker, cultivated a personal relationship with the communist dictator.

After John F. Kennedy's ascension to president in January 1961, Diefenbaker assured him that the American embargo prohibiting trade with Cuba would not be circumvented by a trans-shipment of American goods through Canada. In a meeting at the prime minister's official residence, 24 Sussex Drive, during the same May 1961 visit, Kennedy asked Diefenbaker about Canada immediately joining the Organization of American States (OAS), which the president hoped would counter Castro's Cuba. Canadian diplomats reported that Canada was respected by Castro's revolutionary government, unlike the British and American governments, who were thought to be too cozy with the now-overthrown government led by Fulgencio Batista.

Diefenbaker was not inclined to do Kennedy any favours and certainly not to align with him after the disastrous Bay of Pigs attempted invasion. Diefenbaker responded that Canada would not be "tied up in" any OAS moves with respect to Cuba.[22] He said Canada would maintain its independence and not join but would send an observer to the organization's upcoming Economic and Social Committee meeting. In contrast, the Liberals thought joining the OAS was in Canada's interests. Canada eventually joined the organization in 1990.

Kennedy then advocated for the United Kingdom to join the European Common Market and asked Diefenbaker to support the initiative. Diefenbaker was opposed to the idea. It added tension to an already tense Canada-U.S. summit. Diefenbaker felt he was being bullied and responded by saying Canada was not Massachusetts or Boston.

A more controversial issue was whether Canada would accept American nuclear weapons on Canadian soil. All Diefenbaker would say was that Canada was open to negotiations. Diefenbaker was sensitive to not just sovereignty issues but public opinion on nuclear weapons being installed in Canada. The president thought this political calculation was superficial, telling Diefenbaker, "I could get a parade in Boston at any time on nuclear weapons, but it would not be serious."

Later that afternoon, Kennedy addressed Parliament and famously remarked, "Geography has made us neighbours. History has made us friends. Economics has made us partners. And necessity has made us allies. Those whom nature hath so joined together, let no man put asunder." With a veiled reference to troubles in Cuba and Central America, Kennedy said that it was fitting that his first foreign trip should be to Canada and across a border that knows neither guns nor guerrillas. Kennedy then spoke over Diefenbaker with language that he knew would provoke and irritate the prime minister:

> The Hemisphere is a family into which we were born—and we cannot turn our backs on it in times of trouble. Nor can we stand aside from its great adventure of development. I believe that all of the free members of the Organization of American States would be heartened and strengthened by any increase in your Hemispheric role. Your skills, your resources, your judicious perception at the council table—even when it differs from our own view—are all needed throughout the inter-American Community. Your country and mine are partners in North American affairs—can we not now become partners in inter-American affairs?[23]

On the very point where he had been rebuffed by Diefenbaker hours earlier, Kennedy made a direct pitch to parliamentarians and all Canadians. Kennedy then added nuclear weapons into the mix: "We must make certain that nuclear weapons will continue to be available for the defence of the entire (NATO) Treaty area, and that these weapons are at all times under close and flexible political control that meets the needs of all the NATO countries. We are prepared to join our Allies in working out suitable arrangements for this purpose."

After that speech, the Canadian foreign affairs minister, Howard Green, commented, "One of the least effective ways of persuading Canada to adopt a policy is for the president of another country to come here and tell us what we should do." After he met with Kennedy, Diefenbaker's assistant inadvertently discovered a briefing note prepared by the president's national security advisor, Walter Rostow, that had been tossed aside. It carried the title "What we want from the Ottawa trip" and contained four points:

1. To push the Canadians towards an increased role in Latin America,

2. To push the Canadians towards membership in the Organization of American States

3. To push Canadians towards a one percent foreign aid budget (an increase from $69 million to $360 million)

4. Canadian help for better monitoring of the Laotian–Vietnamese borders

The two leaders had discussed all four points. When he read the briefing note, however, Diefenbaker was incensed. No one, he thought, not even the president of the United States, was going to push him or Canada around. Of course, the proper response would have been to return the briefing note to the American embassy. But Diefenbaker was reluctant to give up any evidence illustrating American aggression and arrogance. As dangerous as it was, he held on to the note, possibly for future use to embarrass Kennedy and as a prop to demonstrate his ability and determination to stand up to the Americans and not have a lap dog in the prime minister's chair.

Not long after the summit meeting, Diefenbaker raised with Kennedy American actions restricting Canadian wheat sales to China. A few months earlier, the Canadian ambassador to the United States, Arnold Heeney, was instructed to inform American authorities that any efforts to impede the Canadian sale of wheat to communists would have serious consequences. Nonetheless, a problem was encountered in obtaining clearance for the sale of bunker oil to Norwegian and British ships hired to transport the grain. The U.S. Department of Trade and Commerce then held up the sale of American-manufactured grain unloaders. The equipment was delivered to the Canadian ports, but the American company was ordered to return it.

This was not the first time Canada faced restrictive trade practices of the United States. In 1958, the Eisenhower administration refused to allow the Ford Motor Company of Canada to fill an order for over one thousand vehicles to be shipped to China. Diefenbaker was not selling to communists just for the income. His belief was, "If the walls of suspicion and the difficulties are to be removed between nations, trade is one of the major methods to bring that about. When I say trade in so far as communist countries are concerned, I mean trading in not-strategic materials and in those things that ordinarily pass between trading nations."[24]

Diefenbaker informed Kennedy that unless the Ford equipment was released, he would go on national radio and television to tell the Canadian people that the American President was "attempting to run our country." Kennedy suggested that Canada apply for an exemption from U.S. Foreign Asset Control regulations, which Diefenbaker rejected, thinking it placed Canada in a subordinate position with the precedent that Canada had to go cap-in-hand asking permission from a big brother. Heated words were exchanged before U.S. sanctions were lifted. But as Diefenbaker wrote in his memoirs, "That was the end of any friendly personal relationship between myself and President Kennedy."[25] Diefenbaker may have been exaggerating. Kennedy had been in office for only five months, but the "relationship" had never been anything other than strained and even toxic.

- 11 -

THE COMMONWEALTH AND SOUTH AFRICA

South Africa's severance from the Commonwealth... we can have but genuine regret, assuaged by a faith that from all this, truly a watershed of history, justice and right will emerge in the end.

Diefenbaker was a monarchist and an admirer of most things British, especially the legacies of freedom bequeathed to Canada from England. Notably, these included reforms that protected individuals against the unchecked powers of a monarch and the state through the Magna Carta (1215), the Petition of Right (1628), and the Bill of Rights (1689). He was a great devotee of the British Commonwealth of Nations, established by treaty in 1921. "No other institution in the modern world," he said of the Commonwealth, "has the same global unity in the things of the spirit and the economic potential to preserve and defend the heritage of freedom."[1] Diefenbaker resisted anything that would weaken the Commonwealth: "I see the Commonwealth as a tremendous force for good in the world: for peace, progress, and stability in a world fraught with tension and on the brink of nuclear cataclysm."[2] On a personal note, he made a point of winter vacationing in Commonwealth countries, such as Bermuda and Caribbean nations.

He was not onside, however, when Great Britain applied to join the European Economic Community in 1961. He feared the move would diminish the relationship between Canada and Great Britain and spin Canada further into the grip of the United States. He went so far as to suggest the Americans were pushing Great Britain into closer ties with its European neighbours to the detriment of Canadian independence. Diefenbaker bellowed, "We have spent a hundred years resisting the magnetic pull of the United States. Now, this

British application will put us in danger of being sucked into their orbit." Lester Pearson believed greater cooperation within Europe was a net positive for the world and Canada. Diefenbaker was relieved when Charles de Gaulle vetoed the British EEC application in January 1963.

From its beginning with six members (Great Britain, Canada, South Africa, Australia, New Zealand, Ireland), the Balfour Declaration in 1926 made it clear that the United Kingdom had equal status to other members and in no way was one country subordinate to another. Diefenbaker said a virtue of the Commonwealth was that it had "no common political master and no common political denominator." The commonality was the attachment to each other and a history that involved the monarchy. After India and Pakistan joined in 1947, a principle was established that any dominion that became a republic had an automatic right to join the Commonwealth. When Diefenbaker became prime minister, the Commonwealth had expanded to over 30 members. While there was no attempt to establish standard policies, the Commonwealth did counter the spread of international communism.

Diefenbaker's proposal to lessen Canadian dependence on trade with the United States by expanding trade with Commonwealth countries resulted in the calling of a Commonwealth Trade Conference in Montreal in 1958. However, it produced few concrete results. A more pressing issue for Diefenbaker where he could gain traction was making the Commonwealth "colour blind," in that no member could have systemic discrimination on the basis of skin colour. This was not a view held by the government of Great Britain. Diefenbaker would note that Canada abolished slavery 40 years before the British, suggesting there were areas where Canada could lead on issues of conscience.

The membership of the apartheid regime of South Africa in the Commonwealth family of nations was abhorrent to Canada and other members from Asia and Africa. South Africa made international headlines in March 1960 after police fired upon non-violent protesters outside the Sharpeville municipal office, killing 69, including children. Blacks in South Africa were routinely assaulted physically by authorities and were restricted on where they could live. They were prohibited from holding elected office or voting in elections. America, not a Commonwealth member but a country of enormous influence, was coming to terms with its overt racial discrimination, particularly in southern states and had no moral authority to stand on regarding South Africa.

Canada made its position clear not just at the Commonwealth but also at the United Nations. In October 1960, the government of South Africa announced that after becoming a republic, it desired to retain its status as a member of the Commonwealth. Without the end of apartheid, Diefenbaker opposed the request. However, he did not believe then that prohibiting trade with South Africa would produce the desired reforms or lead to an end to the apartheid system.

When South African leaders ridiculed Diefenbaker for the absence of North American "Indians" in the Canadian Parliament, he noted that was an issue of demographics rather than discrimination since their numbers in any individual constituency were a small minority. Diefenbaker's rebuttal also referenced the voting rights that he had extended to "Indians" and that there was a native person in Parliament: Chief Gladstone, who Diefenbaker appointed to the Senate in 1958.

At a Commonwealth meeting in London in March 1961, the British government under Prime Minister Harold Macmillan supported South Africa's application to remain in the institution following its change in status to a republic. In opposition, Diefenbaker sought "uncompromising denunciations of apartheid." Canada stood with India and other Commonwealth members from Africa and against Britain, New Zealand and Australia. The U.K. High Commissioner to Canada, Joe Garner, told Macmillan that Diefenbaker would cause him grief: "John Diefenbaker is going to be troublesome about South Africa. He is taking a 'holier than thou' attitude, which may cause us infinite trouble. For if the 'whites" take an anti-South African line, how can we expect the browns and the blacks to be more tolerant?"[3]

Ultimately, rather than face continued denunciations, South Africa withdrew its application to remain in the Commonwealth. Diefenbaker told the House of Commons, "We tried to do whatever was humanly possible to avoid a break without sacrificing basic principles." His ultimate position was that the Commonwealth was stronger with South Africa expelled from the body than to have it remain as a source of division. At the annual meeting of the Conservative party at Ottawa's Chateau Laurier hotel that took place almost immediately after the Commonwealth conference, Diefenbaker expressed both regret and hope:

> To the people of South Africa, I say this. We were carrying out internationally within the Commonwealth the policies which we had adopted for Canada and represented our viewpoint in Canada culminating in the Bill of Rights. South Africa's severance from the

> Commonwealth, a self-imposed exile though it be, we can have but genuine regret, assuaged by a faith that from all this, truly a watershed of history, justice and right will emerge in the end.... My fervent hope is this, that they will return to the Commonwealth in due course, and for such a return there will always be a light in the Commonwealth window.[4]

A future prime minister, Brian Mulroney, met with Diefenbaker on his return from the decisive 1961 conference. Decades later when he became prime minister, in 1984, Mulroney took up Diefenbaker's battle against apartheid even though his advocacy went against the wishes of his good friends Ronald Reagan and Margaret Thatcher. (They too opposed apartheid but thought economic penalties would be ineffective and possibly damaging to the poorest South Africans, overwhelmingly if not exclusively black South Africans). Mulroney went further than Diefenbaker by imposing trade and other sanctions against South Africa, ones that remained in force until the apartheid regime was completely dismantled in 1994.

Mulroney has also been credited as the international leader who was most persuasive in securing Nelson Mandela's release from prison in 1990. When Mandela visited Canada in June 1990, his first international visit after being freed by the South African government, and addressed the House of Commons, he noted that Canada's struggle against apartheid had deep roots: "I would like to pay a special tribute to the prime minister of this country, Brian Mulroney, who has continued on the path charted by Prime Minister Diefenbaker because he knew that no person of conscience could stand aside as a crime against humanity was being committed." It would have pleased Diefenbaker to know that South Africa was readmitted to the Commonwealth in 1994—after the country's apartheid policies and laws were stripped from its books.

The Commonwealth ticked almost every box on Diefenbaker's list of what he wanted to represent and accomplish in world affairs. As Carleton University historian Norman Hillmer noted in his assessment of the Diefenbaker foreign policy record, "[The Commonwealth] was the institutional lens through which Diefenbaker most readily saw international affairs and his role in them. It was a link to the United Kingdom, a pathway to Africa and Asia, a bulwark of freedom against communism, and a counterweight to American power."[5]

- 12 -

FOREIGN AFFAIRS AND TAKING ON NIKITA KHRUSHCHEV

I ask this question: how many human beings have been liberated by the U.S.S.R.? Do we forget how one of the postwar colonies of the U.S.S.R. sought to liberate itself four years ago, and with what results?

After the 1958 election, Diefenbaker embarked on a six-week world tour with 30 stops that covered 56,000 kilometres. Diefenbaker saw himself as a man of peace, capable of influencing world events at a time when the Cold War was, as Diefenbaker described it, "a harsh reality" with nuclear weaponry that created a psychology of terror in Canada and around the world.

When meeting with the secretary general of the United Nations, Dag Hammarskjöld, in New York City, Diefenbaker discussed the impact of the diplomatic recognition of Communist China. Diefenbaker believed recognition was inevitable and that doing it sooner rather than later was better. In Paris, Diefenbaker met with General Charles de Gaulle, then prime minister of France, where the discussion focused on the role of NATO. De Gaulle wanted a small directorate of France, Great Britain, and the United States to address broad strategic questions. This would create an alliance *within* an alliance. The concept would have diminished Canada's voice, so Diefenbaker was strongly opposed. De Gaulle spoke of his worries about the potential for the reunification of Germany, fearing that it would fall more into the Soviet camp.

While meeting German Chancellor Konrad Adenauer, Diefenbaker was given every indication that a close bond with France would be the basis for a united Germany. They also agreed on the vital importance of keeping the United States firmly committed to NATO, so it did not slip back into isolationism, as was its stance in the 1930s and in the early years of the Second World War before the December 1941 Japanese attack on Pearl Harbor. De Gaulle was not naïve about what he could expect from the Americans. When former secretary of state Dean Acheson consulted him on an issue, the French president responded: "In order to get our roles clear, do I understand that you have come from the president to inform me of some decision taken by your president—or have you come to consult me about a decision which he should take?"[1]

For Diefenbaker, there was no better place to promote peace than at the Vatican, where the prime minister secured an audience with His Holiness Pope John XXIII. When asked if he was a Catholic, Diefenbaker replied that he was a Protestant Baptist. No matter, said the Pope, "We are all going to the same place." Sensing an opening for a lively conversation, Diefenbaker irreverently inquired, "How does it feel to be Pope anyhow?" The pontiff took it in stride: "Well, here I am near the end of the road and on top of the heap."[2]

Diefenbaker travelled to southeast Asia and, while in Pakistan, gained perspective on the limitations of democracy and the reasons why a military coup may not always be a tragedy. President Ayub Khan had been the head of the army when he told the country's elected prime minister that he, Khan, was taking over. Democracy, according to Kahn, was not producing results, and that unrest would have led to bloodshed. "We will not do anything improper or unjust," Kahn told Diefenbaker, a statement the prime minister left unchallenged.

Next door, diplomatic recognition of China came up during Diefenbaker's visit with Indian Prime Minister Jawaharlal Nehru in New Delhi. Nehru favoured such a move, citing China's infinite capacity for patience. In other words, they expected diplomatic recognition to be inevitable, and they just had to bide their time without the need to press their case. They then turned to a discussion of the U.S.S.R, where Nehru offered that Khrushchev felt vulnerable for having lived for 40 years in a state of "siege and encirclement," which caused him to overreact to provocation and interference.[3] Diefenbaker concluded that statements made in the United States about the dangers of communism created anger and fear in the Soviet Union. During meetings such as this, Diefenbaker developed an understanding of, and some sensitivity to, the dynamics and risks that were at the heart of the Cold War.

Further east, Malaysian Prime Minister Tunku Abdul Rahman was a strong opponent of the diplomatic recognition of China, fearing it would bolster its expansionist policies. This view, shared by Singapore and others in the region, ran counter to the view of Dag Hammarskjöld that Asians would sleep better at night if Communist China came under the umbrella of the United Nations. Diefenbaker believed that China's six hundred million people could not be ignored forever. However, he was prepared to wait for greater economic and political stabilization in non-communist Asia. China was admitted to the United Nations in 1971, as Diefenbaker foretold.

The six-week world tour was critical to forming Diefenbaker's view of how various countries worldwide perceived Canada, the United States, the Soviet Union and China. He was determined to develop a uniquely Canadian perspective on world affairs that respected Canada's allies and international treaties but was not necessarily in lockstep with American wishes and preferences. While Diefenbaker was willing to sell Canadian products to China, he remained a fervent anti-communist.

In July 1960, the Soviet military shot down an American reconnaissance plane. As tensions escalated between the two countries, British Prime Minister Harold Macmillan encouraged Diefenbaker to attend the United Nations General Assembly in a show of unity. With his travels behind him, Diefenbaker made what he and many others considered his most important foreign affairs statement at the U.N. a couple of months later, on September 26, 1960. International harmony was severely deteriorating, marked by what Diefenbaker saw as "extreme language, irritability, and rocket-rattling on the part of some countries."[4] By this, he meant the Americans and the Soviets.

Perhaps naïvely, at the September 1960 U.N. assembly, Diefenbaker hoped that the Soviet Union's Nikita Khrushchev would make meaningful steps towards de-escalation. Diefenbaker's immediate goal of the elimination of nuclear weapons, or at least halting the widespread possession of weapons beyond those who had already joined the nuclear club, also fell into this category. At the time, Canadian defence planning called for nuclear weapons to be "stationed" in Canada under a proposition that these were not "acquired" since the United States would "own" them.

Rather than reduce tensions while at the U.N., Khrushchev elevated the rhetoric. With a thinly veiled reference to the United States, Khrushchev remarked:

> We are all witnesses to the fact that many peoples are being continually subjected to hostile acts and crude pressure by a certain group of states

> which seek to set at naught the legitimate interests and rights of other countries. This is why the international situation is fraught with acute conflicts, the danger of which is intensified by the mounting arms race. It is quite evident that international relations cannot continue on such a basis, as that would mean a headlong descent into the abyss. It is the sacred duty of the United Nations to uphold the sovereign rights of states and to press for the re-establishment of international relations on a sound legal basis and for the ending of the arms race."[5]

Diefenbaker thought it offensive that the U.S.S.R. should advocate for the United Nations to uphold the sovereign rights of states, given how it had subjugated half of Europe during and after the Second World War, including the Baltic republics and central and eastern Europe. Despite that obvious imperial Soviet boot, Khrushchev then took rhetorical aim at the historical colonial practices of Great Britain and other aspirant nations.

> As regards the Soviet Union, I can say frankly that we are glad to see a great number of new states making their appearance in the United Nations. We have always opposed, and we shall continue to oppose, any curtailment of the rights of peoples who have won their national independence. We share with these states the desire to preserve and strengthen peace, to create on our planet conditions for the peaceful coexistence and cooperation of countries regardless of their political and social structure, in accordance with the peaceful principles proclaimed at the Conference of African and Asia States at Bandung. The facts show that the liberation of nations and peoples under colonial domination leads to an improvement in international relations, an increase in international cooperation and the reinforcement of world peace.

Diefenbaker was in the assembly when Khrushchev delivered his provocative speech and was the first Western leader to follow Khrushchev's 140-minute "tirade" to the podium. Ignoring the advice of bureaucrats at External Affairs who were advising Diefenbaker "to be kind to Khrushchev" and were inclined to "pussyfooting and dilly-dallying," Diefenbaker spoke boldly, provocatively, and instinctively in a speech he labelled "People Want Peace – Not Propaganda," delivered on September 26, 1960. He had never understood why Canada failed to criticize the Soviet Union when they held more than a million people in "slave camps." He was also frustrated that Canada responded to pleas for action from the Ukrainian Canadian Committee and the World Committee on Ukrainian Freedom with evasiveness and pretense. Despite his original intent to dial down the tension, Diefenbaker had been provoked. He did not hold back:

> I came here prepared to accept, to adopt and to agree with any good suggestion Khrushchev might offer, for I am of those who believe that his suggestions must not be rejected out of hand. I have been disappointed. Mr. Khrushchev, in a gigantic propaganda drama of destructive misrepresentation, launched a major offensive in the Cold War.

Diefenbaker countered Khruschev's contention of an American quest for imperial domination by the mere existence of Canada itself. He said Canada did not always agree with the United States. However, the fact that Canada had maintained its independence, with one-tenth of the population of the U.S. and possessing an abundance of natural resources, was proof that the propaganda that the United States had aggressive designs was false. Responding to Khrushchev's comments about the end of colonial regimes, obliquely aimed at the British Commonwealth and France, Diefenbaker took the offensive.

> Since the last war, 17 colonial areas and territories comprising more than 40 million people have been brought to complete freedom by France. In the same period 14 colonies and territories, comprising half a billion people, have achieved complete freedom within the Commonwealth.... Indeed, in this assembly the membership is composed in a very considerable measure of the graduates of empires, mandates and trusteeships of the United Kingdom, the Commonwealth, and other nations. I ask this question: how many human beings have been liberated by the U.S.S.R.? Do we forget how one of the postwar colonies of the U.S.S.R. sought to liberate itself four years ago and with what results? How are we to reconcile the tragedy of the Hungarian uprising in 1956 with Chairman Khruschev's confident assertion of a few days ago in this Assembly?

Diefenbaker concluded by challenging Khrushchev to make good on his stated intentions.

> What of Lithuania, Estonia, Latvia? What of the freedom-loving Ukrainians and many other Eastern European peoples, which I shall not name for fear of omitting some of them?... I ask the chairman of the Council of Ministers of the U.S.S.R. to give those nations under his domination the right of free elections—to give them the opportunity to determine the kind of government they want under genuinely free conditions.

To Diefenbaker's delight, the Soviet delegation in the chamber left halfway through his remarks, while delegates not operating under the thumb of the Kremlin rose to give the Canadian prime minister a standing ovation for his courage and oratory.

The speech was applauded at home and abroad in all democratic nations. Diefenbaker courageously confronted the Russian bear and triumphed on the world stage by standing up for the rights of all people to freedom and democracy. Diefenbaker was proud to be attacked on Radio Moscow, Izvestia, and Pravda for remarks they called "malicious and slandering." In contrast, the U.S. ambassador to Canada, Richard B. Wigglesworth, said Diefenbaker had been "truly magnificent."

Khrushchev became so annoyed by Diefenbaker and similar remarks by Senator Lorenzo Sumulong of the Philippines that he removed a shoe and slammed it on a desk at the United Nations in full view of the television cameras, which only added to the first secretary's growing reputation as a crude representative of his country. Meanwhile, reports of Diefenbaker's oratorical interventions were heard in Soviet prison camps, especially by those who had been defending the right of independence for Ukrainians. His 1960 speech would later lead in part to Diefenbaker's receiving of the Shevchenko Freedom Award in 1967 at the World Conference of Free Ukrainians, this for bringing world attention to the Soviet Union's denial of freedom to Ukraine and to the Baltic states.

- 13 -

THE JAMES COYNE AFFAIR

These letters reveal an attitude which, if accepted by the government, would result in two sovereignties in Canada, the Government of Canada and the Governor of the Bank of Canada, but not in that order.

The popular narrative from historians and commentators is that Diefenbaker was a big-spending prime minister who let deficits accumulate to the point that they imperiled government finances and took the country to the brink of financial disaster. This view is bolstered by the fact that the International Monetary Fund (IMF) was brought in to stop a run on the Canadian dollar. At the same time, the Canadian dollar was devalued, and the government felt compelled to impose deep spending cuts to restore creditor and investor confidence. To top it off, Diefenbaker sacked the governor of the Bank of Canada in a rather ham-handed manner. But was Diefenbaker reckless? Did his government deserve the condemnation it received?

While several biographies have covered Diefenbaker's record in government, none have provided an in-depth analysis of his government's economic and financial performance based on an analysis of audited public accounts and budget documentation over the six years that Diefenbaker held office.

On a personal level, Diefenbaker was a man of modest means with an aversion to debt. As a child, he witnessed the consequences of his family's increasing indebtedness, which became a severe burden and worry: "As a direct result... it became a fixed rule in our family that never again would we buy anything on credit."[1] To economize, his family ate largely out of their garden.[2] Because the water from their well had high alkalinity, a family member had to trek to a neighbouring farm twice a week to gather and then haul away a barrel of water on a stoneboat. When he rode a horse, it was bareback, as there was no money for a saddle.[3] In the winter, he would wake up to a wash basin with water that turned to ice in the night. Many long winter treks ended in disaster. On one occasion, he got lost and spent the night outdoors. His legs and feet were frozen solid, and ultimately, gangrene set in.

Growing up poor taught Diefenbaker never to waste money. Having experienced poverty, he saw his responsibility as prime minister to "bring about a higher standard of welfare for all Canadians, and in particular for those who because of age, disability, unemployment, or other causes would not normally enjoy a reasonable share of the good life." His goal was "fairness to each was fairness to all."[4]

His twin experiences of both debt and poverty meant Diefenbaker never saw his desire or his policies designed to help the poor as the opposite of fiscal prudence. He thought both were necessary and both possible. As a parliamentarian, he respected taxpayer dollars. He limited capital expenditures on 24 Sussex Drive, the official residency of the prime minister, to $18,000 during his six years in office. He paid the public treasury $5,000 per year in rent. He also paid for one-half the cost of the salary of the prime minister's driver. Diefenbaker undertook minor spending on the prime minister's summer residence at Harrington Lake, acquired by the government in 1951, rather than allowing it to be demolished as planned. Diefenbaker was satisfied that a small expenditure would make it livable but not extravagant. Diefenbaker latched on to the property to pursue his favourite hobby of fishing.

Diefenbaker was not personally motivated by money. He refused gifts and wanted obligations to no one. When a Montreal industrialist sent Diefenbaker a leather suitcase, he returned it, attaching a note that read, "with thanks for the courtesy of your gesture." When he became prime minister, to be personally and financially responsible, he rented out his home in Prince Albert. When his government cut back spending in 1962, he initiated a reduction in the operating costs of 24 Sussex Drive, including a 10 percent reduction in the food budget. After his death, it was revealed that a trust fund was established in his name in 1960 by unnamed domestic sources friendly to the Conservative party to ensure he would never have to worry about finances. The fund was never touched.

***

Diefenbaker came to government without a clear vision of where he wanted to take the economy other than to advance the nation's welfare for the benefit of all Canadians. But when the economy slowed, he was determined to respond more rapidly and compassionately than had the last Conservative prime minister, R.B. Bennett, in the early 1930s at the outset of the Great Depression. Unlike Bennett, Diefenbaker signalled his intention that a recession would not burden the disadvantaged and that the unemployed would not suffer. Diefenbaker would always side with workers when given the immediate choice of fighting the deficit or unemployment.

Like most western politicians of his era, Diefenbaker thought it appropriate for the government to run deficits to stabilize the economy during a recession and help those suffering from an economic downturn. During Diefenbaker's time in office, his government faced two economic recessions, one in 1957 to 1958 that he inherited from the Liberals and another in 1960 to 1961 that followed the American experience but was exacerbated by flawed monetary policies of the Bank of Canada.

Diefenbaker had no inkling that the economy was in recession when campaigning in the June 10, 1957, election. Upon becoming prime minister, he rebuked the Opposition Liberals for deliberately withholding that fact from the Canadian people and for timing the election to avoid accountability for the tough times ahead. Following Diefenbaker's surprise election victory, his finance minister, Donald Fleming, delivered the first economic statement by a Conservative in the House of Commons in over 20 years on December 6, 1957.

Following up on the election promises, Fleming announced that the low tax rate for small business corporations would apply to the first $25,000 in profits, an increase from the existing limit of $20,000. The excise tax on automobiles was reduced from 10 to 7.5 percent. The personal income tax deduction for dependents was increased by $100. Tax rates were substantially decreased for low to modest-income individuals, benefitting 70 percent of Canadian families. When Fleming was pressed about offsetting spending reductions, he emphasized that he was not presenting a full budget as the government was still studying the country's accounts.[5] The government's economic statement was modestly stimulative in that it left more money in the hands of Canadians to spend to counter the adverse consequences of a recession. In essence, this was a "supply-side" approach to combatting a weak economy and unemployment: make it easier for businesses to thrive and hire, and for consumers to spend—the "rising tide lifts all boats" strategy. This approach was to be popularized decades later by University of Chicago economist Milton Friedman and put into policy under Ronald Reagan in the United States after his 1981 ascension to the presidency.

The government's first complete budget was tabled on June 17, 1958. The minister reported that a decline in economic activity was partly caused by diminished business capital investment in resource industries. At the same time, the labour force increased at about double the average annual rate of the preceding five years due to an unusually high rate of immigration and an increase in the proportion of the population, especially women, seeking jobs. Employment was higher through 1957, but so was unemployment. The economic downturn led to a decline in the value of the Canadian dollar relative to the U.S. buck, from a high of $1.06 in August 1957 to a low of $1.01 in January 1958.

The deficit was projected at $40 million for 1957-58, rising to a peacetime record of $648 million for 1958-59. When the numbers were tallied, the deficit for 1958 came in at 1.9 percent of GNP.[a] The recession and the government's tax relief caused a 5.8 percent decline in revenues in 1958 and a 5.4 percent rise in spending. This was to be expected when the economy was in recession, which marked the period from March 1957 to January 1958.

It is worth noting that since 1945, the country began paying off borrowings that accumulated during the Second World War when debt peaked at almost 100 percent of GNP, and the annual deficit was nearly 25 percent of GNP. Over Diefenbaker's time in government, the relative debt burden barely budged, beginning at 34.8 percent relative to the size of the economy when he became prime minister, peaking at 35.5 percent, before declining to 34.5 percent by the time the Liberals took over. On a per capita basis, the debt load was flat.[6] Net public debt charges varied little, from 1.2 to 1.4 percent of GNP. With rising interest rates, the debt charge on a per capita basis rose slightly.

While investors and currency traders consider trends, Diefenbaker's policies did not alter the fundamentals of the government's financial position. While government spending rose from 16 percent of GNP to 16.3 percent while in office, there was a noticeable decline in the burden of taxation, falling from

---

a GNP or Gross National Product was used as the relevant measure of economic activity at that time and has since been replaced in government documents by GDP or Gross Domestic Product. The differences are not material. GNP considers the market value of goods and services produced by all citizens both domestically and abroad. GNP does not include the output of foreign residents.

16.7 percent to 14.6 percent of GNP, suggesting a growing economy made up for falling revenue. In other words, the "supply side" approach of expanding the economy through reduced taxes was working to do just that.

Of note, more spending was dedicated to programs that helped individuals. For example, federal hospital spending increased from $28 million in 1958 to $260 million in 1961. Spending on family allowances rose from $437 million in 1958 to $521 million in 1962.[7] Old Age Security rose from $473 million in 1958 to $625 million in 1962.[8] Allowance for people with disabilities increased from $11 million in 1958 to $16 million in 1962.[9] Unemployment Insurance benefits were enhanced and rose from $11 million in 1958 to $87 million in 1962. In summary, federal expenditures on health and welfare for Canadians rose about 60 percent in nominal terms during the years Diefenbaker was in power.[10] The proportion of the overall budget spent on national defence, however, declined from 36.3 percent to 25.1 percent during Diefenbaker's time in office, still substantially higher than defence spending in recent decades. (In 2023, defence consumed only 7.1 percent of government spending, less than one-third in relative terms of what the nation spent over 60 years ago).

In his April 1959 budget, Fleming had better news to share with Canadians. The recession was over, and the economy was growing. Fleming claimed the government's stimulus did its job. "The most important forces stemming the decline in business activity during 1958 were to be found in the fiscal policy and position of the federal government—lower tax rates and revenues, higher expenditures and increased cash disbursements, particularly in housing loans."[11] The minister also noted that the deficit was related to capital investments (the government did not then distinguish between capital and operating expenditures in the deficit calculation) with the development of Canada's natural resources, the building of the Trans Canada Highway, the St. Lawrence Seaway, railways, and housing projects. In other words, the stimulus was not more public servants and administrative costs but lower taxes and capital expenditures to enhance the nation's infrastructure.

Concern over inflation was noted, with consumer prices rising modestly but sufficient to gain the government's attention. "This tendency toward rising prices, particularly in a period of recession," noted the minister in his budget speech, "is a matter for concern.... To argue that inflation is inevitable is a reflection upon, indeed, an insult to the intelligence and the moral fibre of free peoples." However, inflation during Diefenbaker's time in office did not vary materially from the level experienced in the United States and remained near or below two percent. The Canadian rate was lower than almost every other developed nation.[12]

While his previous budget lowered taxes, the government responsibly followed the principle that debts should be paid down when the economy grew. This led to higher sin taxes (on alcohol and cigarettes) and increased income taxes in the 1959 budget. When Diefenbaker declared he wanted the deficit reduced, the Liberal finance critic howled at the change in the government's direction: "It appears the electorate voted for cake, but now they find the cake has to be paid for. I suspect the timing of the taxes is the utmost in political cynicism."[13] Labour leaders called it a "pedestrian, orthodox budget."[14] Business leaders from the Canadian Manufactures Association commented, "The chickens of excessive government spending have come home to roost... to remind the average Canadian of the simple economic fact that as the government spends, so must it tax, and so must the citizen pay."[15]

While the deficit declined in 1960, from $610 million the prior year to $413 million, it remained in a territory that left the government feeling the need to restrain spending so long as the economy grew. However, heading into 1961, there were signs that the economy was weakening. In an unusual move, Fleming introduced a supplementary or "baby" budget, as it was termed, on December 20, 1960. The decline in economic activity worldwide, particularly in the United States, caused the finance minister to introduce tax measures that he argued would stimulate domestic capital investment in Canada and provide modest tax relief, just as the government had instituted a few years earlier at the outset of a recession.

The government also signalled that it wanted Canadians and Canadian pension funds to invest in their own country. It adopted policies that discouraged foreign investment in Canada by increasing the withholding tax on investors from abroad from between zero and five percent to 15 percent. It was a strongly nationalist sentiment that countered conventional free-market economic thinking. However, the nationalist policies expected of Canada in Washington were less punitive than forecast.[16]

From the very early days in office, the Diefenbaker government was at odds with the governor of the Bank of Canada. James Coyne became governor on January 1, 1955, an appointment of the Liberal government headed by Louis St. Laurent. Coyne was a lawyer and not an economist. He most recently served as the deputy governor under his predecessor, Graham Towers. A more qualified candidate, Louis Rasminsky, a trained economist with a strong international reputation, was passed over by the St. Laurent government because of his religion. Rasminsky was Jewish.[17] Coyne was an ardent nationalist who ultimately engaged in political commentary critical of Diefenbaker's fiscal policies. This placed him well outside of the mandate of the Bank of Canada and the role expected of its governor.

When Coyne was appointed governor, it was not a particularly demanding job. The bank's overnight lending rate had held steady without change between 1950 and 1954 at two percent before briefly falling to 1.5 percent in 1955. With Coyne at the helm, the bank rate was set on a rollercoaster ride. Under Coyne, the Bank of Canada raised the rate from just above one percent in 1958 to 6.4 percent within one year, then reduced it to two percent before sending it upward again to near six percent in 1962.[18] In these years, Canadian interest rates were erratic, making business planning and investment decisions difficult.

As an example of the chaos caused by gyrating rates and other policy, when the central bank rate was increased to 5.72 percent in July 1959, a sharp contrast from 1.97 percent 13 months earlier in June 1958, that spike wreaked havoc with the bond market. The interest cost on short-term securities generally increases the risk on investment decisions and the operation of capital markets. To give context to the unusual nature of these interest rate gyrations, consider how the bank rate had remained low and consistent in the years before Diefenbaker came to power. For a stretch between 1950 and 1954, the rate went unchanged. The fluctuations began in 1955, the same year Coyne was appointed governor.

For much of the 1950s and into the 1960s, the Canadian bank rate exceeded its U.S. counterpart, although that differential sharply peaked in 1959 and 1960 at over 200 basis points, or two percent. In both countries, inflation was relatively low, which made Coyne's actions to precipitously lift the bank rate more puzzling.

Another problem that countered attempts to boost the economy was that before and during the years Diefenbaker was in power, Canadian chartered banks were prohibited from charging an interest rate above six percent. This meant funds they borrowed from the Bank of Canada when rates were high could only be lent out at a loss, which effectively froze many credit markets, which in turn weakened the economy at the very time tax relief and spending were designed to expand it. To market watchers who predicted interest rates as well as the value of the dollar to manage risk, it was a turbulent period.

On the positive side, in the early days of the Diefenbaker government, Coyne successfully navigated the restructuring of Canada's national debt holdings. It came from a suggestion made by investment dealers concerned that a significant portion of the government's debt was coming due simultaneously. This program converted 90 percent of maturing debt, roughly 40 percent of Canada's total debt, into longer-term bonds. Locking in interest rates on long-term bonds was a solid risk management policy, making the government less susceptible to a rise in interest rates or needing to renew a significant portion of its debt at a moment in time. The Bank of Canada modestly enhanced the bond interest rate to entice conversions. However, not long after that, interest rates rose dramatically and unexpectedly by the Bank of Canada under Coyne's leadership. Government finances were partially shielded from the rise in interest rates due to the recent conversion to long-term debt at a fixed interest rate. Bondholders, however, were unhappy after the value of their investments declined when the returns shrunk in value, as bond prices dropped when interest rates rose.

When the Bank of Canada began to tighten monetary policy in 1957, there were voices in cabinet who thought it was going overboard. The minister of finance was officially tasked in cabinet minutes to speak with Coyne and "to impress upon him the necessity of taking measures to relax the present tight monetary policy and to remove credit restrictions."[19] Coyne denied that he was pursuing a "tight monetary policy," and in his 1957 annual report, inappropriately released during the 1958 election period when such reports are to be withheld to avoid political controversy, posited that he was following a "sound monetary policy." In Donald Fleming's memoirs, Diefenbaker's finance minister thought the report was a blatant attempt to "sabotage the Conservatives."[20] Diefenbaker called Coyne "an unregenerate Git."

Some background here helps explain both the Diefenbaker government's frustration and that of James Coyne. By design, the governor of the Bank of Canada operates with some independence from the government of the day but is expected to stay in the monetary policy "lane." Not long after it was established in 1935, Liberal Finance Minister Charles Dunning said the Bank of Canada should not be a department of the government and should have "sufficient independence of judgment to be able at all times to talk in equal terms to the government of the day with respect to matters that came under its jurisdiction." However, under no circumstances did this include commenting on the government's fiscal policies—the Bank of Canada governor is not the auditor general or the leader of the Opposition. That was the practice generally followed by Coyne's predecessor.

Also, the governor did not report to the government of the day but to Parliament. The appointment continued "during good behaviour" and not "at pleasure." This meant a governor could only be dismissed by legislation and not by an order-in-council of the cabinet. When appearing before the House Standing Committee on Banking and Commerce in 1956, Coyne said, "If the government were sufficiently displeased with the bank or the management of the bank... if the government were so determined to make a real issue of it, a public issue presumably, the governor would have to resign."[21] That was his view before a crisis emerged, but it did not hold when a disagreement was evident.

Coyne began speaking publicly about what he thought was the government's economic mismanagement in 1959. In a January 1960 speech in Winnipeg, Coyne argued that Canada's economic woes were due to overspending and high borrowing levels by the Diefenbaker government. A nationalist at heart, Coyne also said that Canada was at risk of losing its economic independence and should cease immediately to borrow on foreign markets "as would any country that had reached a level of economic maturity." Coyne proposed that Canada "live within its means":

> We must realize that [this] would have meant that we would have built fewer homes and perhaps lower-cost houses... smaller expenditures on streets, sewers, etc. by municipalities... fewer miles of high-cost highways... somewhat less in the way of natural resource development... somewhat less on public buildings and other public facilities.

Coyne's commentary on the government's fiscal policies was demonstrably outside the legitimate purview of the Bank of Canada. He had repudiated Diefenbaker's nation-building investments in natural resource and infrastructure projects as it was implementing policies on which they held a mandate from Canadian voters. Coyne doubled down in a speech in Hamilton not long after his Winnipeg incursion, claiming that Canada's future as a sovereign nation should not be taken for granted:

> Rapidly growing foreign debt must ultimately lead to the loss of any capacity to be masters in our own house. If we do not effectively

> change the trends of the past, we shall drift into an irreversible form of integration with a much larger and more powerful neighbour. I do not believe this is what Canadians want, for it means surrendering the very idea of Canadianism... which gripped the imagination of... John A. Macdonald and George Etienne Cartier.

Coyne had not only drifted further into fiscal policy but became an interpreter of Canadian public opinion. He had left the confines of monetary policy in his dust and had entered the political realm, particularly by invoking Diefenbaker's lifelong heroes—Macdonald and Cartier, to bolster his position. Coyne had to know this would raise Diefenbaker's ire. Addressing a crowd in Calgary in October 1960, Coyne argued for an increase in import tariffs as a "nation cannot truly call itself a nation or provide a satisfying way of life to the many people within its boundaries unless it can achieve full diversification of its economic activities."

The press gave him a nickname consistent with his self-appointed status: "Jesus E. Coyne."[22] In May 1960, Coyne took on the role of prognosticator and talked down the prospects for the Canadian economy: "I shall probably not make myself popular by remarking that all is not gold that glitters. It is not a pleasant task to talk about economic problems rather than success. Canadians had for at least five years been living beyond our means on a grand scale." This was close to the same period that the Diefenbaker government had been in power. He said he was trying to "save the country from economic ruin," a task that was not justified by the underlying economic data.

Investors disagreed with Coyne's view that the Canadian economy was in a perilous position. Over the years that Diefenbaker was in power, the Toronto Stock Exchange fluctuated but generally moved in a positive direction.[23]

Diefenbaker and his finance minister took Coyne to task for his impertinent remarks. In December 1960, in his supplementary budget, Finance Minister Fleming remarked, "The result of blocking our foreign investors would be to produce a *little Canada*." Fleming felt compelled to visit New York City to reassure investors that the country remained open for business despite the Bank of Canada's warnings. Officials at the Department of Finance, who typically offer restrained language in written communication, were uncharacteristically blunt. In a memo to Deputy Minister of Finance Kenneth Taylor, his senior officials within the Finance Department took a run at the Bank's governor:

> Mr. Coyne appears to be not only an ardent nationalist but also an interventionist and protectionist. One is driven to the conclusion, not because he advocates intervention and protection explicitly but because one cannot imagine how the extensive and, in some cases, extreme changes which he advocates could be attempted, let alone attained, in any other way. There is a fundamental economic misconception underlying his speeches. This is the misconception that Canada itself provides a market big enough.[24]

Finance officials added that Canada's high living standards relative to most other countries were based on its abundant natural resources, which needed large amounts of capital and technology to be developed.

Coyne understood both the Department of Finance and the Diefenbaker cabinet believed that his speeches were inappropriate, his conclusions were erroneous, and that he had ventured well outside the bank's mandate. For its part, the press enjoyed the copy generated by the feud and, if anything, was sympathetic to the governor's nationalist urgings. Fleming rose in the House of Commons to say, "Mr. Speaker, may I say that I have no right of censorship over the speeches of the governor of the Bank of Canada. He does not refer them to me.... He makes his own speeches and chooses his own themes.... I trust I am not to be held responsible for what may be said.... The governor of the Bank of Canada does not speak for the government."[25]

Conservative MPs noted the close friendship between Coyne and Liberal MP and party strategist Jack Pickersgill. Coyne was less than clear about how Liberals may have influenced his public statements when asked about his possible political connections.[26] Meanwhile, Diefenbaker was hearing credible criticisms that the bank governor was indifferent to the plight of individual Canadians and wrongheaded on the fundamentals of monetary policy. "Coyne," wrote Diefenbaker, "seemed to develop an obsession with his own infallibility."[27] After Coyne met with the president of the conglomerate Procter & Gamble, the business leader told a public audience, "I'm not saying he is a nut, but he's the most illogical person I have run into."[28]

In frustration, the premier of Ontario, Leslie Frost, wrote to Diefenbaker: "Should the whole economy of this country be dependent upon the unrestricted and uncontrolled decision of one man?" In a cabinet meeting on March 21, 1961, Fleming expressed his frustration with Coyne, which followed a meeting he had held with the Bank of Canada governor on March 18. Fleming told Coyne that his speeches, of which he had delivered 14, should be restricted to monetary policy. Fleming also made it clear that Coyne's public statements had caused damage to the government while creating the impression of a division of opinion between the government and the Bank of Canada. That was harmful to both the bank as an institution and the government, which had a mandate from voters. Fleming sensed that Coyne had lost the confidence of the bank's directors, and he knew the government would not reappoint him. Fleming told Coyne he had been authorized to tell Coyne that the government preferred that he resign or retire "at this time... for health or other reason."

The Coyne-Diefenbaker dispute was no mere quibble over the intricacies of economic policy. That was important, but just as critical, the public falling out was an argument about the proper role of the Bank of Canada and its governor's public musings. A significant collection of Canadian economists and academics addressed both elements when they publicly concluded that Coyne was damaging the economy by his actions in 1960 and 1961. This was expressed in a letter to the finance minister that started with two signatories and grew to 29, calling for the end of Coyne's tenure at the bank. The letter's signatories were all economists from Canadian university faculties engaged independently in economic research. They went to great lengths to demonstrate how unprecedented their intervention was, noting that "Economists have very rarely made joint representation to the Government, and we do not profess a professional association":

> We send this letter to you with considerable regret that we have felt it necessary to abandon the individuality which our profession cherishes, protects and promotes.... The undersigned economists... have lost confidence in the ability of the Bank of Canada under its present management to play its proper role... Recent public statements by the governor of the Bank of Canada have seriously shaken our faith in the wisdom and competence of the Bank's management. As professional economists, we are both puzzled and distressed by the economic reasoning contained in these public statements.[29]

Economists said that Coyne had become an autocrat and was blind to the hazards of unemployment and the benefits of capital expenditures. The restrictions on foreign investment in Canada that Coyne advanced were, in their opinion, "muddled economics and nonsensical." Even staff within the research department of the Bank of Canada believed that Coyne had gone rogue and warned him that statements he wanted to make in the bank's 1960 annual report could not be defended, and at least one resignation was offered.[30] To say that Coyne was dogmatic about inflation was an understatement. "I don't even like to think of inflation at the rate of 1% a year," offered Coyne, "because after 30 years, what have you got? Savings are cut in half if you had any savings."[31]

While Coyne's future as Bank of Canada governor was in serious doubt, his public standing was further damaged when the government was informed that Coyne's pension arrangement had been dramatically enhanced to provide $25,000 per year, regardless of age. The most recently retired governor's pension was $13,750, and the bank's board advisor had recommended a pension of $19,000. Fleming said he only learned of the pension after the board had approved it. Diefenbaker thought it was outrageous that Coyne did not use his power to veto the board's decision, which had not been published in the Canada Gazette. Diefenbaker said that Coyne "sat, knew, listened, and took." It was, for Diefenbaker, the proverbial "last straw." Fleming told Coyne he was guilty of a dereliction of his duty, which justified his removal from office.

The government concluded Coyne was incompetent in monetary policy, reckless and out of bounds in his public commentary, and unethical in how he bolstered his pension without full transparency. However, Fleming and Diefenbaker did not realize they had given Coyne a lifeline to keep his job. So long as his integrity was attacked over the pension issue—a minor issue and not worthy of the government's attention when more important matters were at stake—Coyne claimed he could not accede to the government's wishes. Coyne's statement to the press went further in criticizing the government:

> On Tuesday, May 30, the Minister of Finance, on behalf of the government, requested that I resign at once as governor of the Bank of Canada without waiting for the end of my present seven-year term of office, which expires December 31 this year. To aid me in my consideration of this matter, he said the cabinet were upset by the fact that the bank's board of directors had taken action in February 1960 to improve the conditions of the pension, which, according to the rules of the bank's pension fund had always been provided immediately on the

> termination of service of a governor or deputy governor.... The cabinet was of the view that I had failed to discharge the responsibilities of my office in allowing the board of directors to take the action they did take unanimously and after a thorough consideration in amending the pension fund rules, an action which the Department of Justice had said was entirely within the powers of the board.

This was Coyne's version of the facts the government used against him. Yet, the primary, if not exclusive, concern was over the highly restrictive monetary policy that was thwarting Canada's economic recovery. But that was not the debate Coyne wanted in the public square, which he had lost badly. Coyne took on the role of a victim of government oppression:

> The slander upon my integrity I cannot ignore or accept. It appears to be another element in the general campaign of injury and defamation directed against crown corporations, their chief executive officers and other public servants. I cannot and will not resign quietly under such circumstances.

Later, Coyne added the following point of principle: "The governor should not, however, resign merely because he is asked to do so." This reversed the position he had taken a few years earlier. It was not only Diefenbaker who wanted Coyne out. The bank's board of directors had a change of heart and voted nine to one on a resolution "that it is in the best interests of the Bank of Canada that the governor do immediately tender his resignation." Coyne had lost the confidence of the government, some provincial premiers, the bank's board of directors and a significant collection of academic economists.

The government did not have the authority to fire Coyne. That authority lay with Parliament. A simple one-sentence bill was introduced on June 20: "The office of Governor of the Bank of Canada shall be deemed to have become vacant immediately upon the coming into force of this act." In a bloodless and unemotional verdict, the bond market reacted strongly and positively to the news that the bank governor was on his way out.

Pearson did not want to be seen defending the policies of the unpopular governor but was quick to disparage the government for mismanaging the dismissal. Specifically, he criticized the lack of due process in that Coyne was given no official opportunity to defend himself. All the while, Diefenbaker and Coyne engaged in a personal and vindictive public dialogue. Coyne wrote, "Mr. Diefenbaker has been the evil genius behind this whole matter. It was his unbridled malice and vindictiveness which seized on the Bank of Canada's pension fund provisions... as a clever stick with which to beat me and intimidate me." Diefenbaker countered that this correspondence from Coyne confirmed he was unfit to run the Bank. "These letters reveal an attitude which, if accepted by the government, would result in two sovereignties in Canada, the Government of Canada and the Governor of the Bank of Canada, but not in that order."

When Pearson questioned Diefenbaker in the House of Commons, Diefenbaker replied: "Does the honourable member think $25,000 a year is a fair pension?" The amount, Diefenbaker pointed out, was greater than that due to a retiring prime minister. The pension of the recently retired Louis St. Laurent, for example, was just $3,000 annually.

The one-line bill deeming the office of the governor of the Bank of Canada vacant passed the House of Commons. Coyne decried that he could not defend himself before a committee of the House. In a letter to Fleming, he wrote, "Behind the shelter of Parliamentary immunity (you) have brought serious charges against me.... The use of smear tactics, and the attempt to intimidate public servants with the idea that smear tactics will be used against them in public if they do not bow to improper suggestion from the government, should not be allowed to go on."[32] Liberal MP Paul Martin said that even Adolf Eichmann, a key architect of the Holocaust, had his day in court. But this was not Nazi Germany, and Parliament was not a court of law.

When the bill was discussed in the Senate at a committee of Liberal-dominated appointees, Senator Adrian Hugesson, appointed by Mackenzie King in 1937, spoke for many:

> Yes, Coyne must go.... He will leave behind him two things: first, a tarnished Minister of Finance, a negligent administrator of his department, an inept bungler in the matter of the pension with, I am afraid I must add, a reputation for telling the whole truth, which leaves a good deal to be desired. The second thing... a discredited government, stumbling aimlessly along from blunder to blunder and from crisis to crisis.[33]

In hushed tones, Coyne told senators on July 13 that passing the bill was tantamount to a guilty verdict. "I shall be marked for life as a man... unfit to hold a high office in Parliament.... A verdict of not guilty... will permit me to retire honourably." After three days of lengthy testimony and with a clear promise that his resignation was forthcoming, the Senate defeated the government bill by a vote of 33 to 16. Coyne claimed vindication, then resigned ten minutes after the vote was recorded.

In replacing Coyne, Diefenbaker was not looking for a malleable top banker. His choice, Louis Rasminsky, had significant credibility as one of the architects of the 1944 Breton Woods agreement and the International Monetary Fund. Rasminsky had joined the Bank of Canada in 1940, served as executive assistant to the governor in 1943, and was the deputy governor of the Bank of Canada under Coyne from 1955. There was no question that Rasminsky was his own man and would not follow the government's dictates. According to Diefenbaker's memoirs, he should have been appointed to the position in 1955, but the St. Laurent government decided that "under no circumstances could they consider appointing a Jew to head the bank."[34] He insisted on running the bank without government interference and cautioned he would resign should there be a persistent conflict between the government and the bank over monetary policy. With provisions for a more modest pension than his predecessor, Rasminsky held the position until February 1973.

Diefenbaker spent a considerable chunk of his political capital in the Coyne affair, which left the impression of general incompetence over his tactics. Any gains were likely negligible—reducing by only a few months the term of an unpopular governor. Diefenbaker turned an outspoken purveyor of recklessly high interest rates into a folk hero who would be remembered for protecting the independence of the Bank of Canada by not following the government's wishes that Coyne resign.

The Porter Royal Commission on Banking and Finance was struck to clarify the bank governor's power and recommend how disputes with the government should be handled. The principle that the government had directive power over the bank was established, but should it invoke such power, it would be seen as a loss of confidence in the governor, and a resignation should result. The successor Liberal administration passed legislation in 1967 requiring the government to approve the bank governor's pension arrangement.[35]

In a largely sympathetic assessment of Coyne's legacy, author James Powell concluded that the governor had elevated the bank's command of monetary policy.[36] Still, Powell concluded Coyne's actions or lack thereof, exacerbated the 1960-61 recession, caused an over-valuation of the Canadian dollar and misjudged the causes of Canadian unemployment. Coyne's belief that high interest rates would reduce foreign borrowing was judged to be erroneous.

Coyne collected the elevated pension, but his ignoble dispatch as Bank governor did not foreclose other earning opportunities. He took a position with a Toronto-based law firm and offered financial consulting services. Next, he became chairman of York Savings and Trust and then president of the Bank of Western Canada. The bank never became operational, and the board of directors asked for his resignation. After he refused to comply, he was fired.[37] To the Diefenbaker loyalists, this was evidence that Coyne would never have quit as governor when his resignation was requested.

The episode stained the Bank of Canada, the minister of finance and Prime Minister Diefenbaker. While dismissing the governor six months before his term was scheduled to end may have ceased the harm he was inflicting on the Canadian economy, it left a scar on the Diefenbaker government. Diefenbaker tried to make it known that Coyne's resignation coincided with the recession's end in Canada.[38]

- 14 -

THE "DIEFENDOLLAR"

If I didn't have the name I have, I don't know what the Liberal party would do.... The playing with my name [Diefendollar] indicates what they think of those of non-French and non-English origin.

In a nearly three-hour budget speech on June 20, 1961, Finance Minister Donald Fleming moved away from previous concerns about a balanced budget and instead turned his attention to unemployment. Rather than an expected surplus, the minister recast his projections towards a deficit of nearly $300 million. "There is more unemployment and unused capacity in our industries than we can possibly accept.... We do not intend to let events take an unguided course in the hope that these problems will solve themselves," noted Fleming. "In the circumstances confronting Canada today, it is appropriate, indeed desirable, that the federal government should, by incurring a sizeable deficit, help to stimulate the economy."

The government hoped to increase exports and reduce imports to strengthen the economy. The policy the minister outlined in the House of Commons was, in his words, "more significant, more powerful, and more pervasive than anything that could be implemented in the way of subsidies and controls. Moreover, it is free from the arbitrary decisions and the bureaucratic delays that always attend incursions by the government into the affairs of private industry." This policy was a modest downward adjustment in the value of the Canadian dollar, which had been trading at a premium to its U.S. counterpart, partly from relatively high interest rates. It would help exports and would be a boom for Canada's tourist industry, which was seeking to host foreign visitors.

One way to bring the dollar down was to lower interest rates, which Coyne had resisted. The new Bank of Canada governor, Louis Rasminsky, was open to a "nudge" from the finance minister. "Interest rates in Canada," noted Fleming, "are out of line with those in the United States and some of the European capital-exporting countries.... High interest rates are a double drag, at times like these, on our economic activity and expansion. We should like to see these spreads narrowed."

The 1961 budget repealed the 7.5 percent excise tax on automobiles, which served as a precursor to the 1965 Canada-U.S. Auto Pact, which created an integrated North American automobile industry. Another equally forward-looking policy permitted scientific research expenditures to be fully deductible in the year incurred. While the government was pulling on major policy levers, it signalled that it did not have all the answers and that more fundamental reforms were needed in the post-Coyne era of monetary policymaking.

> It has become almost trite to say that the economic environment of the sixties will be different from that of the fifties....We have, however, become aware of the need for a broader, fuller survey than is possible under the pressures of day-to-day government decisions.... The last major study was made by the MacMillan Commission in 1933.... Having in mind the length of time which has elapsed since this last review of our financial framework, and having in mind also the fact that the Bank Act must undergo its regular decennial review in 1964, the government has decided to appoint a royal commission to examine Canada's financial structure and institutions.

The measures that the government had introduced were working as planned and hoped for: Employment and GDP were rising and the final Diefenbaker government budget was delivered on April 10, 1962, just two months before an anticipated June election. With the optimistic tone expected to encourage voters to re-elect Conservatives, the finance minister said he was happy to report that "the circumstances attending this Canadian budget are rising prosperity, more jobs, greater opportunities, and rapid economic growth. The policy expressed in this budget will continue to be expansionist, suited to our national economic circumstances."

The *Globe and Mail* congratulated the government for not using the budget to buy votes for the upcoming election and that its relative fiscal restraint in a challenging circumstance was evidence of prudence.[1] It assessed the budget as a sound, pro-investment, pro-small-business, pro-resource exploration plan with tax measures designed to encourage capital expenditures to ramp up the capacity of Canadian industry. Since deficits were projected to continue, opposition politicians slammed the budget for offering a "Vote now, Pay Later" regime.

Diefenbaker entered the June 18, 1962, election with confidence that the fundamentals of the Canadian economy were strong. Indeed, there was no hint that when Canada's 24th Parliament was dissolved, an economic crisis was about to rock his government to its core.

Ten days after the parliamentary dissolution, Diefenbaker was informed by the secretary to the cabinet, Robert Bryce, of a looming fiscal crisis and a run on the Canadian dollar. Bank of Canada reserves used to maintain the Canadian dollar's value were being rapidly depleted. Diefenbaker said it was the first time there was any indication of difficulties, and the timing, politically, could not have been worse. Finance officials were concerned that currency speculators would exploit the weakness of a central bank without adequate reserves.

> The government was presented with four options by officials:
>
> One: Support the Canadian dollar at the current rate of 95 cents to the U.S. dollar.
>
> Two: Support the Canadian dollar within a range of 93 to 97 cents to the U.S. dollar.
>
> Three: Fix the Canadian dollar at 95 cents to the U.S. dollar with the agreement and support of the International Monetary Fund (IMF).
>
> Four: Fix the par value of the Canadian dollar at 90 cents to the U.S. dollar.

That the International Monetary Fund (IMF) was not only a consideration but an integral component of executing Canadian monetary policy spoke to the weakness at the Bank of Canada and the loss of confidence that markets attached to the ability of the Canadian government to sustain the value of its currency on the open markets.

However, as with how a falling stock price reflects poorly on a company, a devaluation under almost any circumstances indicates a weakening of a country's economy. Diefenbaker remained flummoxed as to why this crisis came about without warning. He was told that markets had lacked confidence in Canada because of a worry that fiscal and trade deficits would persist. While the numbers were not always produced on a timely basis, under Diefenbaker, the balance of trade deficit declined and went into surplus by 1962. Canada's number one export that year was newsprint, followed by wheat and lumber. Its chief imports were machinery, automotive parts and electrical appliances.[2] But there were no dramatic shifts in trade.

Diefenbaker was left to wonder how an otherwise strong and growing economy was suddenly judged to be in peril and why the dollar was under pressure. With the support of the International Monetary Fund, in early May 1962, just six weeks before the election, the government was determined to peg the dollar at 92.5 cents U.S. It was a steep drop, given that the Canadian "buck" had traded above par the previous year. While a lower dollar helps exporters, it raises the price of imports, resulting in a one-time increase in inflation. Problematically, this was not part of the recently submitted budget plan. Diefenbaker told his finance minister that the embarrassment of a devalued dollar would "cost us the election."

The Liberals, the media, and ordinary Canadians began to refer to the cheaper dollar as the "Diefendollar" or "Diefenbuck." Mock "Diefendollars" were circulated by Liberals across the country issued by the "Bunk of Canada," signed by James Coyne with the promise "Will pay to the bearer on demand... More or Less."[3] Diefenbaker responded to the jabs alternately with humour and accusations of intolerance. "If I didn't have the name I have, I don't know what the Liberal party would do.... The playing with my name indicates what they think of those of non-French and non-English origin." These names were to be added to a long list, including "Diefendumb," "Diefenbubble," and "Diefenbunker."

Pearson ridiculed the government for its economic mismanagement, saying it would inevitably lead to higher prices and a lower standard of living. Throwing aside his mantra of free enterprise, Diefenbaker promised to defend the consumer at all costs: "I don't want any group or corporation in this country, no matter how successful they may be, to take advantage of this situation. I serve notice here and now that if, in the next few days, (price gouging) is going on, there will be action as effective as it is drastic."

The underlying fundamentals were not as severe as the markets had suggested. The Minister of Finance explained in a letter to Diefenbaker on May 28, 1962, that the issue was not economic fundamentals but *market sentiment*.

> The announcement, on the night of May 2, that the value of the Canadian dollar was to be fixed forthwith at 92.5 in terms of U.S. currency and that Canada was thus, once again after nearly twelve years, in full conformity with the articles of agreement of the International Monetary Fund, has achieved its immediate objective.
>
> But the situation remains precarious, and this carries implications regarding the nature of forthcoming policy pronouncements. The most immediate objective of the announcement of May 2 was to staunch the outflow of our international reserves.... While the (decline in the dollar) has been checked, confidence has not been restored. Reports have come in from many quarters, both in Canada and abroad, of widespread nervousness that exists in business and financial circles. This is focused on the Canadian exchange rate. Thus, the foreign exchange situation remains precarious....
>
> While the causes of nervousness and lack of confidence are explained and rationalized in many ways, the question most frequently asked is whether the Canadian government is really concerned about balancing its budget. People are, rightly or wrongly, wisely or unwisely, putting or keeping their funds abroad because they fear lest the basic value and integrity of the Canadian dollar may be continuously eroded by continuing massive government deficits in good times as well as bad.[4]

In his memoirs, Diefenbaker expressed regret that his government succumbed to the will of the markets and the bearish, if not self-affirming, sentiments of market speculators who sensed weakness and an opportunity to exploit a country with weak defences.

> I must wonder if official advice given [to] me in 1962 was entirely free from partisan consideration. If I had stood my ground, we would have continued to buy Canadian dollars with our gold and foreign reserves,

> thereby maintaining the desired value of the Canadian dollar until after the election campaign. We could then have moved to a fixed rate of exchange in the first budget following the election. Quite probably, speculative pressure against the dollar would have diminished quickly in the face of a determined effort by the government to maintain its value.

It bothered Diefenbaker that his finance minister seemed helpless and unaware that a crisis was about to unfold at the most unfortunate moment possible. His Liberal opponent used this fresh ammunition to attack the government's basic competence while all eyes were on the government amid an election campaign. It was not uncharacteristic, but not entirely unfounded, for Diefenbaker to sense a conspiracy was in play. The only explanation of the 1962 financial crisis that made sense to Diefenbaker was that "It was orchestrated for political reasons. Its object was to get rid of my government.... The crisis began with a 'spooking' of the New York money market. I believe that it is more than possible, indeed highly probable, that the administration of President Kennedy used its influence to bring this about."

It is true that Diefenbaker believed in borrowing and investing to build a national infrastructure to support economic development in the regions and took on debt to finance significant capital investments while stimulating economic activity during periods of high unemployment. He completed the Trans-Canada Highway; funds were allocated to provide a floodway to protect Winnipeg from the flooding of the Red and Assiniboine Rivers; the Fortress of Louisbourg was reconstructed on Nova Scotia's Cape Breton Island; roads to the Far North were constructed; the federal government agreed to finance up to two-thirds of the cost of municipal sewage treatment plants; a fund was established to promote physical fitness and amateur sports; and grants to universities were doubled.

It was not just one-off projects. The federal government also enhanced financial support to the provinces with lower fiscal capacity than the more revenue-rich provinces via equalization payments. Over the years, it became a program where the "haves" contribute to the "have not" provinces, entirely consistent with Diefenbaker's sensitivity to regions or provinces that were struggling. He said he would never consign any province to a "permanently inferior position in relation to the rest of the population and provinces." Yet, overall, government spending as a size of the economy had not significantly changed over Diefenbaker's tenure.

While Diefenbaker made specific spending promises in the 1962 election campaign, they were tempered by measures designed to balance the books. These included temporary tariff surcharges on approximately half of Canada's imports and temporary graduated surcharges on all imports except essential goods, reduced duty exemptions for tourists returning from the United States, and a $250 million reduction in government expenditures.

***

But how could a loose connection of currency speculators overtake the financial markets and the power of a sovereign government? While the fundamentals of the government's financial condition had not changed to any material degree, Diefenbaker's strategy to boost exports and reduce imports could not alter those forces that sensed the Canadian dollar was bound to fall.

The market questioned the government's capacity to maintain the value of the Canadian dollar at 92.5 cents to the U.S. dollar. Diefenbaker took some blame for not being more decisive when the currency crisis became apparent:

> In retrospect, the party did poorly during the election campaign in capitalizing on the benefits that would (and did) accrue from devaluation. We stood on our record and did not adapt sufficiently to meet the challenge of the Liberal attack. The final phase of the exchange crisis had come upon us so suddenly that there was no opportunity to fully consult the entire Cabinet before its first post-election meeting.[5]

Ultimately, Diefenbaker's Tories lost their majority in the 1962 vote, but retained power. The currency crisis was a blow to the government but did not cause its downfall, the reason for which is explained in the following chapter.

However, post-election, the crisis for the Canadian dollar continued. In the weeks following the campaign, the Bank of Canada was forced to deplete its reserves to dangerously low levels to stop a run on the dollar. The government had to persuade financial markets that it would do what was necessary to manage the economy and reduce the deficit. Diefenbaker had no choice but to put the brakes on his plans for investments in social and infrastructure developments. Instead, his new policies included increased tariffs and duties and across-the-board cuts in government spending. The crisis was quickly but painfully overcome. But the financial limitations were akin to fiscal handcuffs for Diefenbaker: They limited his options for programs he wanted to enhance or implement.

In hindsight, Canadians can look longingly at the strength of the Canadian dollar under the Diefenbaker government. Over the generation that followed Diefenbaker, the Canadian dollar declined, deeply. Far from trading near par or even 92 cents to the American dollar, in many of the following years and decades, Americans could buy up Canadian dollars for less than 70 U.S. cents.

Diefenbaker's House, Prince Albert, 1957.

Diefenbaker's arrival for Commonwealth Conference, 1957

Talking to newsmen, 1957.

Campaign photo in New Brunswick, 1958.

Diefenbaker, 1958.

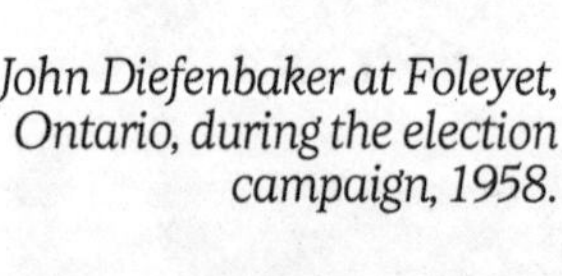

John Diefenbaker at Foleyet, Ontario, during the election campaign, 1958.

John Diefenbaker and Sir Winston Churchill stand on sidewalk peering into entranceway of Churchills' Hyde Park Gate house, London, England, 12 May, 1960.

Mary, John, Olive, and Elmer Diefenbaker at Christmas Saskatoon, 1960.

Diefenbaker and JFK, 1961.

Diefenbaker and the flag, elements of which he fought to keep.

Diefenbaker birthday, 1967.

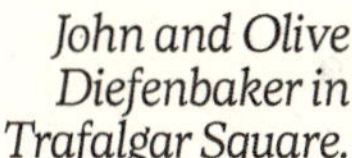

John and Olive Diefenbaker in Trafalgar Square.

Diefenbaker's funeral Ottawa, August 19, 1979

FIGHTS WITH FRIENDS AND FOES

- 15 -

1962: MAJORITY TO MINORITY

I am the only leader capable of preventing United States domination of Canada.

Senator John F. Kennedy of Massachusetts had little contact with Diefenbaker before he became prime minister. But he did take note of Lester B. Pearson when he became leader of the Liberal party, and thus Opposition leader, in January 1958. Following lectures that Pearson delivered at Boston's Tufts University in October of that year, Kennedy described Pearson as a man full of vigour and Canada's chief architect of Canadian foreign policy over his years of service in the diplomatic core. Kennedy said Pearson's contributions to NATO and the United Nations were "brilliant" and that he was a "superb interlocuter" combining scholarship and statesmanship.[1] There was little doubt that Kennedy was a cheerleader for Pearson as these words fell outside diplomatic discourse among politicians from different countries, especially for an American senator with presidential ambitions. Diefenbaker correctly assumed Kennedy had taken sides and would do what he could to help Pearson.

Heading into the 1962 election, the Diefenbaker government continued to pursue its reform agenda. It had already narrowed the list of crimes subject to the death penalty, established the National Parole Board and the Farm Credit Corporation, extended the vote to native Canadians, completed the Trans Canada Highway and provided greater flexibility to provinces in taxation. While the list of reforms was long and impressive, the great "northern vision" promised in 1958 remained a work in progress, that included over 6,000 kilometres of new roads built in northern Canada.

Politically, the landscape in Quebec had become riskier for Diefenbaker. The Tory-friendly Union Nationale became a shadow of its former self following the death of Maurice Duplessis in 1959. (Of note, Diefenbaker was an honorary pallbearer at the funeral.) In the 1960 provincial election, the Liberals under Jean Lesage formed government. Without the levers of power and patronage that had worked for Diefenbaker in Quebec in 1958 and without a political machine, most of his Quebec seats won in 1958 were vulnerable. Outside Quebec, the Tories took comfort in winning three out of four by-elections spread across four provinces in May 1961. However, as the traditional four-year term of government was near, the Tories were bound to lose seats if not the government itself.

Diefenbaker went into the June 1962 election campaign behind in the public opinion polls. The magic spell he had cast over the nation four years before had been broken by a performance that fell short of its high expectations. Diefenbaker tried to turn the election into a referendum on free enterprise versus socialism. However, this was not a battle over economic policy. To Diefenbaker, socialism was a euphemism for communism, which, in the context of the Cold War, was a source of general anxiety in the nation. Diefenbaker reminded voters that Canada had stood tough against Nikita Khrushchev at the United Nations under his leadership.

It was a danger for Diefenbaker to rely on conservative ideology in an election campaign focused on small government and laissez-faire capitalism rather than his personal qualities of leadership and attachment to the plight of ordinary Canadians. As he was advised by Leslie Frost, the premier of Ontario, "There are not enough Tories... to elect a Conservative government (in Canada)," and that victory requires the politically and ideologically unaligned to come onside. Besides, populism rather than ideology was Diefenbaker's brand. To gain voter interest, Frost proposed tax reductions and a comprehensive review of the tax system to rid the system of policies hurting employment, wages and economic growth.

Diefenbaker was not only fighting a resurgent Liberal party in the election but a popular U.S. president. Kennedy's ambassador to Canada, Livingston Merchant, privately wrote to the U.S. secretary of state to complain that Diefenbaker's views on nuclear weapons were dismaying and "probably stem from compound of ignorance of complex subject and profound reluctance (to) face up to a disagreeable subject."[2] These sentiments appeared in pointed questions in the House of Commons from the Liberal front bench. Diefenbaker assumed Pearson had a direct line to Kennedy officials, and there was evidence that American military officials were loose-lipped and that the leaks were intended to become fodder for Diefenbaker's opponent.

Domestically, a Canadian official in the External Affairs Department fed the Liberals with inside information.[3] Diefenbaker had long been wary of any advice from a department that revered Lester Pearson as one of its most successful diplomats. In his memoirs, one of those diplomats, George Ignatieff, who named his son Michael after Pearson's commonly used nickname given to him by his First World War flying instructor, took pride in being labelled what Diefenbaker called a "Pearsonality."[4] According to his associate minister of national defence, Diefenbaker "never concealed his conviction that top diplomats were either pompous bores or expensive parasites."[5]

It distressed Diefenbaker that President Kennedy included Liberal Leader Lester B. Pearson when he hosted Nobel Prize winners at the White House on April 29, 1962, just 19 days before the Canadian election. The event was for American laureates, but Kennedy added Pearson to the list to elevate his stature. When Pearson expressed concern that it might look like election interference, Kennedy arranged for Canada's Opposition leader to receive an honorary degree from Boston College, providing another excuse for making the trip to America. Unlike the other Nobel laureates, Kennedy invited Pearson to meet with him in the family residence, and the two men entered the event together and stood beside each other whenever possible. Maryon Pearson sat at the president's table, and Lester Pearson sat with Mrs. Kennedy. The president opened his remarks by saluting Pearson. To highlight the calibre of his guests, Kennedy declared that those assembled "represented the most extraordinary collection of talent, of human knowledge, that had ever been gathered at the White House," humorously adding, "with the possible exception of when Thomas Jefferson dined here alone."

Diefenbaker fumed at the diplomatic transgression but did not publicize his distress, fearing he would appear petty. However, to his aides, he called it a direct and blatant intervention by the American president in a Canadian election. And it was. However, the only thing Kennedy feared was that his bias would be so apparent that it could be used against Pearson.

Saying that Canada-U.S. relations would be a critical issue in the election, Diefenbaker considered revealing the contents of the president's confidential briefing memorandum that had accidentally been left behind during an official state visit. However, despite showing Kennedy's intentions to influence

Diefenbaker and "push Canada," the disclosure came with serious risks. Diplomatic protocol called for the note's return, and the likely consequence of such a breach of practice would be a public rupture in relations with Ottawa's most trusted ally.

At a Saturday evening meeting at 24 Sussex Drive, Diefenbaker advised Ambassador Merchant that he had the president's briefing memo. The prime minister told the ambassador he intended to use the note in the election to demonstrate that "[I am] the only leader capable of preventing United States domination of Canada." Merchant told Diefenbaker he had not yet informed the president of the prime minister's intent, which may not have been true. Nonetheless, he warned that the consequences would be "catastrophic" for Canada-U.S. relations. He urged Diefenbaker to abandon the idea. Merchant downplayed the words "push Canada," which were integral to the briefing note, as not being aggressive but equating it to "press" or "seek to persuade."

It was rumoured that Kennedy had written the letters "S.O.B." on the briefing note, referring to his opinion of Diefenbaker's character. Theodore C. Sorenson, in a biography of Kennedy, said that was impossible since Kennedy had not yet formed his opinion of Diefenbaker. "I didn't know he was an S.O.B.," remarked Kennedy to Sorenson, "*at that time.*" It was suggested by those close to the president that S.O.B. was more likely O.A.S., the acronym for the Organization of American States, which the president wanted Canada to join, and that Kennedy was known to make indecipherable scribbles.[6] When Kennedy was told that Diefenbaker threatened to release the memo, he told his secretary of state that the Canadian prime minister was a "prick" who should have his "balls cut off."[7] Kennedy was determined never to speak to Diefenbaker again, although events concerning Cuba after the election would make that impossible.

A weak economy, high unemployment, and a diminished Canadian dollar worked against Diefenbaker in the campaign. As described in the preceding chapter, the Liberals took full advantage of a lack of confidence in the Canadian dollar's plunging value, blaming the entire mess on Diefenbaker's economic mismanagement. The Liberal campaign team created the "Diefendollar" moniker to ensure the responsibility for the fiasco was placed at the feet of the prime minister. Taking the offensive the Liberals launched a "Truth Squad" to follow Diefenbaker on the campaign trail. The leading member of the squad was MP Judy LaMarsh, who made herself conspicuous at Diefenbaker events. In this, Diefenbaker sensed an opportunity where he would invite LaMarsh to the stage and make her the subject of ridicule. The Liberal tactic flamed out badly against a clever and opportunistic opponent.

Diefenbaker gamely fought back. He effectively cast the Liberals as communist-loving friends of big business; quite the contradiction, but devastating, nonetheless. He warned they would make Canada beholden to American interests. The Liberals adopted the slogan "Take a stand for tomorrow." But Pearson was a poor campaigner and appeared meek compared with Diefenbaker.

Diefenbaker not only had to deal with a stronger Liberal party but also with a phoenix-like Social Credit party that was wiped out in the 1958 Tory sweep. It was not just the traditional western wing of Socred, then under the leadership of Robert Thompson, that would take votes but its populist leader from Quebec, Réal Caouette, who captured hearts and minds in rural areas by advocating a bizarre policy on expanding the money supply that would grow the economy simply by putting cash in people's bank accounts to spend.

A fast talker with charisma to burn, Caouette was never pinned down on how his approach would inevitably lead to rampant inflation that would only hurt the people Caouette claimed he wanted to help. Certainly, Diefenbaker could not expose the flaws of the Socred funny-money theory in French. The new provincial Liberal government in Quebec was not taking sides, and Lester Pearson was not an attractive candidate for rural Francophones. This left a wide opening for Caouette to capture unaligned voters as the only French-speaking leader.

While Canadians were not warming up to Pearson as a politician, the Liberal brain trust determined to follow a strategy that had helped Kennedy win in 1960. With Kennedy's blessing, his chief pollster, Lou Harris, was dispatched to Ottawa to give Pearson a hand. Previously, Kennedy was asked to lend Harris to a British campaign and had refused.[8] Harris took on his wife's maiden name, "Smith," to camouflage his presence and operation. Remarkably, the U.S. state department issued him a phony passport to assist in the covert mission.[9] When asked if Kennedy personally intervened with the state department to provide the fake document, Harris responded, "I'd rather not get into that."[10]

Harris kept away from Parliament Hill in Ottawa to avoid being recognized by the press or Conservatives. His official meetings were private and held at Stornoway, the residence of the official Opposition leader. Reporters traced down a rumour that Harris was helping the Liberals, which they denied.[11]

Harris introduced issue-based micro-polling to Canadian politics—on policy, regional issues, and even the style and dress of the leader. The American pollster refined his craft after learning the lessons from the 1948 U.S. election when experts wrongly predicted the winner. Decisions were driven by what the randomized polls indicated would resonate with voters. The initial Harris poll was not good news for Liberals, where it was ascertained that Canadians found Diefenbaker to be "honest, sincere, straightforward," while Pearson was seen as a "diplomat" aspiring to be prime minister.

On a more practical level, the polls led to Pearson scrapping his bow ties which had reinforced his image as anything but an ordinary Canadian. He was also given a low profile, with the Liberal team taking more of the stage. Kennedy followed the campaign closely, receiving regular updates from Harris to feed his curiosity. "He was all but shouting from the sidelines," said Harris, adding, "He hated Diefenbaker.... He obviously couldn't say anything publicly. But every day or two he would want to know how the election was going."[12]

Evoking the importance of the 1960 presidential debate between John Kennedy and Richard Nixon, Lou Harris advised Pearson to challenge Diefenbaker to a televised debate. While Diefenbaker was a great debater, he refused as he believed it would give "free advertising" to his opponent.

Diefenbaker remained as forceful on the campaign trail as he did in a court of law. Portraying himself not as prime minister but as a lawyer for the defence, he told voters four days before the election that he always thought of these contests as a trial, "in which the electorate listens to and weighs the evidence."[13] In the two prior elections, he prosecuted Liberal arrogance and incompetence, but in this election, he had to defend his record, flaws and all.

Diefenbaker accused Pearson of being a weak leader who was soft on communism. This sentiment was reinforced by Pearson's response to a question from journalist Pierre Berton about what he would rather face: life under communist Khrushchev or nuclear war. "I'd rather be red than dead," Pearson replied. Diefenbaker called it a policy of defeatism. He countered the public view that the Nobel prize-winning Pearson was a great diplomat, charging that he said nothing at the United Nations for twelve years while the Soviets inflicted suffering on the people it subjugated through tyranny.[14] He claimed he won the Nobel prize because he sided with the communists and against the interests of France and Britain. The election was a choice, Diefenbaker said in hyperbolic terms, "between free enterprise and the slavery of socialism, which has destroyed every country it entered."

At the outset of the campaign the Liberals were heavily favoured to win a majority government. With a few weeks to go, the Grit lead in the Gallup poll had shrunk to two percentage points. Then Diefenbaker opened the spending taps that had been shut due to recurring deficits. This included promises for a major capital investment in the Welland Canal, which surprised the St. Lawrence Seaway Authority that operated the locks. Contrary to the engineering studies, Diefenbaker claimed he would proceed with a causeway linking Jourimain Island in New Brunswick and Borden Point in Prince Edward Island. He made promises he knew he could not keep.

The Tory government was returned but with a minority of the seats in the House of Commons. The Tory caucus was almost halved: from 208 to 116 seats. While the Liberal share of the popular vote increased by only 3.6 percentage points, the party doubled its seat count to 99. Social Credit picked up an astonishing 30 seats, 26 of which had been held by Tories. Of their 30 seats, 26 were in Quebec, mainly attributed to its dynamic leader, Réal Caouette. The New Democratic Party, renamed from the Co-operative Commonwealth Federation in 1961, gained 11 seats to hold 19 after the 1962 campaign.

Given his weak poll position before the writ was dropped, a minority government was good news for Diefenbaker: The Tories had just won their third successive victory. They were only 17 seats short of a majority in Parliament, but few expected his government to last very long. Pearson interpreted the results as something of a triumph and said, "It is clear that the Tory government has been decisively rejected." On election night, Diefenbaker accepted the result graciously:

> While I am disappointed of the fact that the government has not an overall majority, nonetheless the present situation is not without precedent.... Elections under our system are the embodiment and the essence of democracy. What happened today is simply the people speaking... being a democracy, let us uphold it strongly.[15]

Currency speculators saw the election results as another opportunity to short the Canadian dollar. Short of a firm declaration that the government would restrain its spending and curtail deficits, the Bank of Canada and the IMF could not hold the dollar's pegged value against international market forces that sensed weakness and were driving it down contrary to underlying economic conditions. It was a game of economic and political chicken.

Diefenbaker felt he had little choice but to implement emergency measures. Otherwise, the dollar would be left exclusively to the vagaries of the day-to-day sentiments of the markets. The measures hastily imposed included tariff surcharges on about one-half of Canada's imports and a massive reduction in planned spending. It also meant the end of Donald Fleming, who had held the post of finance minister since the 1957 Diefenbaker victory. It would not take long before the markets forgot the crisis as interest rates began to fall and the import charges were removed. The speed of the reversal of economic fortunes underscored Diefenbaker's contention that the crisis had been concocted by speculators at President Kennedy's behest to drive him from office.

- 16 -

THE CUBAN MISSILE CRISIS

Our duty, as I see it, is not to fan the flames of fear but to do our part to bring about relief from the tensions, the great tensions, of the hour.

On October 14, 1962, U.S. reconnaissance planes took photographs of what appeared to be missile bases being built in Cuba, 90 miles from American territory. Eight days later, President Kennedy addressed his nation and the world to reveal what became known as the Cuban Missile Crisis.

During those eight days, Kennedy and his team gamed out various scenarios behind closed doors. On day one, they concluded that they would not consult or inform their allies, including their closest defence partners in NATO or their NORAD partner, Canada. As a matter of strategy, everything they knew and planned to do remained a secret until they had decided on a course of action.

While Kennedy and his team explored options on Cuba, the president engaged Diefenbaker on another issue. Two days before the Cuban Missile Crisis became public, Kennedy wrote to Diefenbaker to express his displeasure about Canadian attempts to lead on the issue of nuclear disarmament. On October 20, 1962, Kennedy wrote to the prime minister:

> To my distress, I have learned that your government intends to support in the General Assembly this year a resolution cosponsored by the eight new members of the 18 Nation Disarmament Conference and others and calling for an unverified moratorium on nuclear weapons tests. As I wrote you on last April 13, I am convinced that there is no safety in such a proposal, and it leads away from the only honest and workable road to arms limitation.

> Should Canada cast its vote in favour of a moratorium this year, it will be tantamount to Canada's abandoning the Western position at Geneva on this issue. This will be seen by the Soviet Union as a successful breach of the Western position. In this event, what hope can we hold for pressure on the Soviet Union to take the extremely reasonable step we have proposed? Or to agree even to the limited treaty covering the testing environments of greatest concern. Mr. Prime Minister, I cannot overemphasize my concern in this matter, and for the reasons I have advanced above, and in the interest of vital Western solidarity on this testing issue, I hope you will reconsider this decision to cast an affirmative vote for a resolution which can only damage, and damage seriously, the Western position on an essential issue of Western security.

If Kennedy had a reason not to bring Diefenbaker into his planning circle, this letter provides a strong clue as to why. A mere hours before Kennedy's fateful speech from the Oval Office on October 22, Diefenbaker was officially informed by Livingston Merchant, the recently retired U.S. Ambassador to Canada, of the events leading up to the presidential address. In Washington, Canada's ambassador to the United States, Charles Ritchie, was briefed just one hour before Kennedy informed the world that we were on the brink of nuclear war.

Unknown to the Americans, however, Diefenbaker, through the work of Canadian intelligence officials, had been made aware just two days after the United States first obtained photographic evidence that offensive ballistic missiles had been installed by the Soviet Union in Cuba. Given the defence agreements between Canada and the United States and the explicit requirement for consultation, the prime minister was displeased not to have been briefed directly by the president as events unfolded.

Not knowing the full extent of the threat, Diefenbaker nonetheless acted by sending a diplomatic message to Khrushchev banning Soviet airplanes from Canadian air space. Planes from other Warsaw Pact countries that landed in Canada were searched for weapons.

Canada's military also had some forewarning of a pending U.S. action at four in the morning on October 22 when the U.S. government requested that Canada temporarily prohibit transit stops or overflights of Czechoslovakian and Cuban aircraft at Gander, Newfoundland. It took little speculation on Diefenbaker's part to figure out that a blockade, bombing, or invasion of Cuba was in the works. He was worried about what this would mean for the encircled city of West Berlin and the possibility that this crisis could escalate into a global war. Canada could not avoid this conflict as a member of NATO and NORAD. If America was at risk of war, we were bound to be with them. For Diefenbaker, that's why Canada, at a minimum, should have been consulted before the president made consequential decisions that could impact its allies.

While Kennedy was determined not to inform American allies of their plans, he made an exception for British Prime Minister Harold Macmillan, who had been briefed on the crisis three days before the American ambassador informed Diefenbaker.[1] Given the threat was more relevant to Canada than the British, this was further evidence that Kennedy did not trust Diefenbaker. While Kennedy did not like Diefenbaker, there was no reason to believe the Canadian prime minister was untrustworthy or had any sympathy for the Soviet Union. Diefenbaker had demonstrated at the United Nations that he did not fear the Soviets and used strong language to highlight the subjugation of neighbouring countries.

Canada's Department of External Affairs suggested to Diefenbaker that Canada could play a neutral peacemaking role at the United Nations rather than stand foursquare behind its American ally. Diefenbaker, usually suspicious of advice offered by bureaucrats from External Affairs, had already adopted that position.[a] Though the United States wanted to control matters on its terms, as the crisis unfolded, the exchanges at the U.N. were clearly favourable to the Americans. However, Kennedy did not want to go to the U.N. to negotiate with the Soviet Union or reach some form of compromise. They used the U.N. to pin down and embarrass the Soviet's U.N. ambassador and to cast blame where they thought it belonged.

Diefenbaker wanted cool heads to prevail. He thought that Kennedy was still smarting over the failed U.S.-sanctioned invasion of the Bay of Pigs in Cuba in 1961 and a subsequent exchange with U.S.S.R. leader Nikita Khrushchev in Vienna, which had destabilized the American president. Earlier in the year,

---

a Thirty years later, Brian Mulroney would react differently when the Soviet Union's president, Mikhail Gorbachev, was removed from office in a military coup in 1991. Mulroney received the same sort of cautious advice from External Affairs and its minister, Barbara McDougal: "Let the issue play out . . . don't take a strong position . . . don't take sides . . . keep your options open." But he rejected it and took a firm stand: the safety of Gorbachev and his family was of paramount importance, and he should be returned to office forthwith.

Diefenbaker told a journalist that Kennedy was a "hothead," warning, "He's a fool, too young, too brash, too inexperienced, and a boastful son of a bitch.... Mark my words; he'll get us all into trouble with his arrogance and his presumptions."[2]

Diefenbaker's thinking was to have the Security Council of the United Nations engage a group of "neutral" nations to "conduct an onsite investigation in Cuba of whether that country had permitted the installation on its territory of offensive nuclear missiles." This underscored a fundamental mistrust that Diefenbaker held about Kennedy. His efforts were designed, as he wrote in his prime ministerial memoirs, "to prevent any rash and hasty decision by the United States in this crisis. I considered that [Kennedy] was perfectly capable of taking the world to the brink of thermonuclear destruction to prove himself the man for our times, a courageous champion of Western democracy."[3] In other words, it was a test of the president's ego.

Merchant briefed Diefenbaker at 5:00 p.m. on October 22 with a request that Canada support the United States in whatever actions it took to defuse the crisis. Merchant read the text of the planned presidential remarks on which Diefenbaker suggested toning down the language where the Soviet foreign minister was called dishonest and dishonourable. Better, thought Diefenbaker, not to insult the person with whom you need to negotiate with. Diefenbaker's suggestion was relayed to Kennedy, and the line was deleted. In Merchant's note, the American president promised, "We should all keep in close touch.... I will do all I can to keep you informed."[4] It was a commitment Kennedy had no intention of keeping.

In the House of Commons, Diefenbaker made public declarations of support for the United States and expressed outrage that the Soviets had chosen to destabilize the world with an initiative that brought us closer to war. However, he also used the occasion to advance his idea of having the United Nations investigate the facts on the ground through an independent inspection. It was reminiscent of an offer Diefenbaker made to Khrushchev in his speech at the U.N. General Assembly on September 26, 1960, where he said he would open the Canadian Arctic for international inspection provided there was a comparable concession on the of the part of the U.S.S.R. "They say that we prepare, in cooperation with the USA in our Arctic areas, to attack. I gave them the opportunity now to have an answer to their fears."

This left open the implicit question from Diefenbaker about which nation could be trusted: the Americans, who claimed to have irrefutable proof that nuclear weapons had been planted in Cuba, or the Russians, who denied the allegation. It was only through the U.N., Diefenbaker told reporters, that "the truth will be revealed."[5]

Diefenbaker understood an inherent weakness in the American position. As he told his cabinet colleagues, "Some years ago when the U.S.S.R. had complained about the establishment of U.S. bases ringing the Soviet territory, the U.S. had responded that they had been invited to establish these bases by the countries concerned. The U.S.S.R. could now use a similar argument to justify the establishment of bases in Cuba.... [I have] discussed the situation with the U.K. High Commissioner, who had pointed out that it was difficult to classify weapons strictly as offensive or defensive."

"Our duty as I see it," Diefenbaker said as the crisis was evolving, "is not to fan the flames of fear but to do our part to bring about relief from the tensions, the great tensions, of the hour." The U.S. administration informed Canadian officials in Washington that Diefenbaker's remarks "had pained and dismayed everyone."[6]

When briefing Diefenbaker, former ambassador Merchant requested that Canada place its NORAD component on a higher alert level. Just before Kennedy's Oval Office address, the Americans raised their alert level to DEFCON 3, meaning an attack could be launched within 15 minutes. Given the lack of official notice of the events that led to this request, Diefenbaker refused. In the House of Commons, Diefenbaker said, "This is a time for calmness," so not a time to signal escalation in preparation for armed conflict. "Above all, it is a time when each of us must endeavour to do his part to assure the preservation of peace, not only in this hemisphere but everywhere in the world."

As Diefenbaker observed in his memoirs, Canada was "not a satellite state at the beck and call of an imperial master." Yet because of the integration of the Canadian and American military operations under NORAD, it was impractical, if not impossible, for the two nations to operate at different readiness levels when the continent was under threat. However, that agreement specifically referenced "the fullest possible consultation on all matters affecting the joint defence of North America." When put to the test, Kennedy did not consult with the Canadian prime minister about the threat and did not inform Diefenbaker of measures the Americans had already planned to take until after the fact. That Diefenbaker was annoyed should come as no surprise. Referring to Kennedy, he told his associate minister of National Defence, "That young man has got to learn that he is not running the Canadian government."

Canada's defence minister, Douglass Harkness, a hawk in times of peace and war, pleaded with Diefenbaker to issue the order to put Canadian troops at the same level of readiness as the Americans, but he was rebuffed. At cabinet, Diefenbaker remarked: "Canadian mothers do not want their sons to be killed in any foreign war, and the Cuban business is no affair of Canada's."[7] This ignored the fact that many Canadian soldiers in the 20th century *had* died in foreign wars, and Canada's national security was directly threatened by what was transpiring in Cuba. Diefenbaker did not respond to the American request immediately, partly to register his disapproval of Kennedy's decision not to consult with Canada as promised and stipulated under the NORAD framework.

The level of readiness was raised on October 25 to DEFCON 3, but it was after the American military had elevated their readiness to DEFCON 2, a level implying an enemy attack was imminent. As to Canada, there is a debate about whether Ottawa went to DEFCON 3 on October 22 on an order Harkness gave rather than the prime minister as was required. Diefenbaker told Harkness he wanted to discuss the matter with his cabinet before an order was issued. When cabinet met, Diefenbaker argued for further delay and recommended moving to a higher state of alert only "if the situation deteriorated." According to Peter T. Haydon, a senior research fellow with the Centre for Foreign Policy Studies at Dalhousie University in Halifax, Harkness preempted the Prime Minister and cabinet and issued the order unilaterally.[8] Professor Asa McKercher of the Royal Military College stated the reality this way: "As Canadian ships patrolled for Soviet submarines in the North Atlantic, Royal Canadian Air Force pilots readied themselves to defend North American airspace... Canada was thus the only U.S. ally to take on an active military role during the October crisis."[9]

In his memoirs, Diefenbaker dismissed the claim that his defence minister jumped the gun and exceeded his authority. However, that statement might have been offered only to show that a member of his cabinet had not undermined him. (In a similar move, Henry Kissinger, as Secretary of State, raised the U.S. level of military readiness on October 24, 1973, during the Yom Kippur War in the Middle East, while Richard Nixon, then embroiled in the Watergate scandal, was in bed for the night.[10])

Diefenbaker told Kennedy's emissary that Canadian defence forces would be ready if a "real crisis" developed but also that he did not believe that Khrushchev would allow the issue to escalate to the stage where a maximum military defence posture would be required. When Kennedy pressed directly to raise the alert level on a phone call, the conversation became heated. Diefenbaker pressed Kennedy on not being consulted on the initial American response to the intelligence findings of Russian military assets and personnel on Cuban soil. "When were we consulted?" Diefenbaker challenged Kennedy. "You weren't," was Kennedy's dismissive reply. Days later, Robert Kennedy sarcastically remarked, "Canada offers all aid short of help." [11]

Diefenbaker made it clear that he would not defer to Kennedy's judgment and would not do the bidding of an American president. Ultimately, Canada officially raised the state of readiness of its armed forces and ensured that Canadian air space was not used to transport arms to Soviet bases in Cuba. However, Diefenbaker did not want to be seen as standing shoulder-to-shoulder with the United States as they navigated the crisis. He reported to the House of Commons on October 25 the position of the Canadian government:

> The free world as a whole cannot afford to permit its essential security to be endangered by offensive weapons mounted on bases adjacent to North America... (and) we take encouragement from the restraint being exercised at the moment. However, it would be dangerously premature to assume that the critical phase of the current situation has passed. I think members of the House are in agreement that the greatest hope of finding such a solution lies in the United Nations.

In the House of Commons, Diefenbaker also clarified that supporting the United Nations did not mean distancing ourselves from the Americans. On October 25, he reported the Canadian position: "We intend to support the United States and our allies in this situation."

Standing by the U.S. meant a declaration that the quarantine imposed by the Americans on Russian shipments to Cuba was justified and legal. As Diefenbaker noted in the House of Commons, all action is justified when the national security of Canada was imperilled:

> There is a debate going on throughout the world regarding the legality of the quarantine measures which the United States has imposed. To my mind such arguments are largely sterile and irrelevant. We have a situation to face. Legalistic arguments, whatever they may be, cannot

> erase the fact that the Soviet Union has posed a new and immediate threat to the security not only of the United States but of Canada as well.

After the Soviet missiles were removed from Cuba, Diefenbaker boasted that Canada "was the first nation to stop overflights of Soviet aircraft so as to prevent war material being carried to Cuba." The cabinet knew that was not the whole story, especially regarding raising Canada's level of defence readiness. In fact, as Diefenbaker's shifting public and private positions, foot-dragging on readiness, and preference for a U.N.-brokered end all showed, Diefenbaker had been moralizing in part because of his disdain for Kennedy, as well as his desire to be engaged on matters on national and international security. Those impulses were hazardous during an international crisis. Even Diefenbaker's most loyal ministers questioned his leadership. Gordon Churchill, who was later appointed defence minister, remarked, "The country just could not afford to have the prime minister in that position at a time of crisis—he refused to act when action was absolutely necessary."[12] The American ambassador to Canada concurred with Churchill's assessment. "I didn't think Canada had earned... the right to the extreme intimacy of relations which had existed in years past." This was an astonishing statement, given the sacrifices made by the Canadian people over two world wars. Diefenbaker made that point in 1936 when speaking of the vital role Canada played in the First World War: "[We] ensured liberty instead of autocracy such as prevails in Germany today where free speech, a free press, and the right to freedom of association ceased to exist, and there is no longer equality of all peoples, irrespective of race and creed, before the law."[13]

When the crisis ended on October 28, after Khruschev relented, President Kennedy was given high praise for the removal of the Soviet weaponry 90 miles from U.S. shores. Diefenbaker was less generous and was not particularly discrete when expressing his views about Kennedy to other world leaders. When he attended a meeting in Bermuda with President Kennedy and British Prime Minister Harold Macmillan in December 1962, he noted to his British counterpart that Kennedy's lack of assuredness in world affairs may have precipitated the Cuban Missile Crisis. To bring Macmillan to his side, he indiscreetly shared what the president had said privately about the United Kingdom: that it was a "spent force."

What Diefenbaker could not deny was that Kennedy was enormously popular in Canada. A Gallup poll indicated Kennedy had the support of 80 percent of Canadians for his conduct during the Cuban Missile Crisis.[14] Diefenbaker was given little credit for asserting an independent Canadian foreign policy and much derision for being seen as less than a true friend and ally. A rift in Diefenbaker's cabinet was revealed to the nation, with some remaining loyal to the prime minister and others beginning to question his leadership. In a crunch, one where nuclear missiles were in play and might have launched, most ministers took national security more seriously than any concerns that Canadian sovereignty was at stake.

1963: THE NUCLEAR ELECTION

There are powerful interests working against us, national and international. Everyone is against me, but the people.

When Parliament opened on September 27, 1962, the government's agenda included the patriation of the constitution of Canada (the British North America Act was a law of the British Parliament), consultation on a new national flag, a commission on land claims made by various tribes and bands, and establishing a national economic development advisory board. The Diefenbaker government's agenda also included exploring a national system of contributory old age pensions with disability and survivor benefits, which required provincial concurrence and an amendment to the British North America Act.

Just before the parliamentary session, Diefenbaker launched a Royal Commission on Taxation, typically known as the Carter Commission for its chair, Kenneth Carter.[1] In addition to accountants and lawyers, the commission members included a farmer and the treasurer of the National Council of Women. The mandate was to examine the distribution of the tax burden, the effects of the system on employment and the economy, anomalies or inequities in the system, the impact on the Canadian ownership of domestic industries, and general simplification and ease of administration. The committee did not issue its final report until 1966, but its recommendations were profound and led to a significant redesign of Canada's tax system. Carter is most often remembered for the quip, "A buck is a buck is a buck," which led to the taxation of one-half of capital gains. The tax system the committee recommended meant that taxes for about 50 percent of Canadians declined while wealthier Canadians paid more.

Lester Pearson dealt with the Carter Commission report in 1966. But in the fall of 1962, he was determined to thwart the government's overall program. He instructed the Liberals in the Senate, who held a majority of seats in the Red Chamber, to defeat bills that passed the House of Commons that Liberal MPs had opposed. As a result, the Diefenbaker minority government was on a short leash, and an election was imminent.

Diefenbaker had a more powerful cadre of political opponents to deal with than the Liberals. In the aftermath of the Cuban Missile Crisis, a national vice-president of the Progressive Conservative party, George Hogan, advocated that Canada break off diplomatic relations with Cuba and suspend all trade with the country Kennedy had called "that imprisoned island." He urged Diefenbaker to have Canada immediately acquire defensive nuclear weapons and that senior Canadian officers at NORAD should have carte blanche to raise the readiness of Canadian air defence forces. "I believe we must either honour the NORAD agreement or withdraw from it. To withdraw from it is unthinkable," wrote Hogan. To ensure there was no confusion about where he stood, Hogan circulated his views to the press. Hogan charged, "[Diefenbaker] has done, and is still doing more damage than any other single thing that has happened since we came into power. I gather from the press that the Cabinet is not solidly behind this policy. I profoundly hope so because I believe we are in real trouble unless it is changed."[2]

To Diefenbaker, the policy issue went beyond national defence; it was about whether Canada would continue as a sovereign state or, as he put it, "whether Canadian policies would be made in Canada by Canadians, or by the United States."[3] Diefenbaker called Hogan the day he read his remarks in the newspaper and accused him of betraying his duty for having "done a complete job against the federal Conservative Party." Diefenbaker dismissed Hogan in the House of Commons as speaking only for himself and not for the party. (Hogan would later run in the 1963 and 1965 elections under Diefenbaker's leadership, failing both times to win a seat.)

Despite U.S. President Kennedy telling his staff that he wanted nothing to do with Diefenbaker, British Prime Minister Harold Macmillan made that desire awkward to fulfill. In December 1962, Macmillan met Kennedy in the Bahamas to resolve a dispute on missile deployments and to establish a ballistic missile submarine base near Glasgow, Scotland. It was customary that when a British Prime Minister came to America or met with its president, he would also visit the

Canadian prime minister before or after the visit. However, Macmillan wanted to directly return to Great Britain after the Bahamas, so he invited Diefenbaker to join him after his business with Kennedy concluded. Macmillan's meetings with Kennedy took longer than anticipated, leaving an overlap between the time Diefenbaker arrived and the time the American president returned to Washington. Macmillan suggested the three leaders get together over lunch. At first, Kennedy refused the offer but relented so long as he was never left alone with Diefenbaker.

Kennedy was late for lunch, and when he arrived, Diefenbaker did not say hello but began, "Well, Mr. President, what are we going to do about the North American unemployment problem."[4] It was an awkward beginning that Kennedy shrugged off. Diefenbaker implied to journalists that he was involved in resolving the dispute between the Americans and the British on military matters, but at best, he was briefed on the decisions taken.

The issue that vexed Kennedy and Diefenbaker was the question of American nuclear warheads on Canadian soil. Kennedy's view was shared by many members of Diefenbaker's cabinet. Some ministers threatened to resign if Diefenbaker did not clearly and decisively accept American weaponry. At the Progressive Conservative party's annual meeting in January 1963, a resolution on nuclear warheads was put forward despite Diefenbaker's attempt to remove it from the agenda. It was an indication that Diefenbaker had lost control over the party apparatus. Diefenbaker pleaded with delegates, "Give us the benefit of your ideas. But in the face of changing circumstances, do not bind in any way to things which in the light of events in the next few months may be ill-advised or premature."[5] Do not tie my hands in the quest for peace, was Diefenbaker's plea. He embodied the Macdonald maxim: "Precipitous action does not always result in wise decisions." In the end, delegates approved a motion that urged the government to decide on a clear course of action. But Diefenbaker was not ready to make a choice. He suggested Canada wait until May when the next NATO meetings were scheduled. He told the House of Commons that when the history books were written, they would say that his government "refused to be stampeded" and that his government's position would be judged to have "led to the achievement of peace." To many in Diefenbaker's cabinet, this was simply another excuse to delay making a decision.

As NATO and NORAD allies, Canada and the United States maintained close contact on issues of military procurement and the strategic positioning of troops.

Going back to September 1961, President Kennedy stated that his government would prohibit the transfer of control over nuclear weapons to states that do not now own them. Diefenbaker was asked by the press what this meant to nuclear weapons that may end up in Canada. Did that not mean the Canadian government had no control over them? To this, Diefenbaker replied:

> We believe that the spread of nuclear weapons to an ever-increasing number of countries would pose a threat to mankind. We consider that the only satisfactory way to dispel the dangers inherent in the possibility is through international agreement on a comprehensive and carefully verified system of disarmament. Consistent with this policy, the Secretary of State for External Affairs and all Canadian representatives have worked for the recognition of the importance of including measures to prohibit the spread of these weapons as part of a disarmament programme. I am glad that they form part of these new proposals.

Diefenbaker thought that Kennedy was undermining the commitment he had made for joint control of nuclear weapons on Canadian soil. "I considered that it effectively ended the prospect of joint control and with it the prospect of nuclear weapons in Canada, unless there was war." It was possible to argue that the "ownership" of the weapons would remain with the U.S. and would not constitute an extension of the nuclear club. But Diefenbaker thought this was a weak argument and a play on words.

Many in cabinet had become less preoccupied with nuclear warheads and more interested in how to get rid of Diefenbaker. The Prime Minister stared down his opponents in cabinet meetings, threatening an election or resignation. Diefenbaker sometimes mollified them and pledged support for their views on the nuclear warhead issue, only to later change his mind.

Defence Minister Douglas Harkness seized on one of Diefenbaker's pledges of support and issued a press release stating the government had chosen "a definite policy for the acquisition of nuclear arms." Diefenbaker summoned his minister for a dressing down. "This is terrible. You've ruined everything. Why did you do it?... You had no right to make such a statement. You have put me in an impossible situation." Harkness offered to resign, a safe move because Harkness knew that Diefenbaker wanted to suppress any talk of cabinet divisions. Harkness was not as concerned about being fired as he was determined not to remain defence minister in a government that did not follow a course he deemed was fundamental to national security. He was not bluffing.

Diefenbaker sought to forge a consensus among competing visions in his cabinet. On one side was Harkness, his defence minister, who wanted Canada protected by having American nuclear weapons stationed in Canada. On the other was the External Affairs Minister Harold Green, who preferred keeping nuclear weapons out of Canada but with a plan to bring them across the border in the case of an emergency. Most of the cabinet had aligned with Harkness, while Diefenbaker wanted to keep his options open. Based on the correspondence he received, Diefenbaker claimed the Canadian public was against accepting nuclear weapons by a margin of three-to-one.[6]

On January 3, 1963, the retiring supreme allied commander of NATO, U.S. General Lauris Norstad, visited Canada as part of his tour of NATO capital cities. His meetings with the Governor General, defence minister, and various military leaders highlighted the significance of his visit. Oddly, Diefenbaker cancelled a meeting that was scheduled with Norstad.

Gen. Norstad then held a press conference, which was not standard protocol for a military commander. Appreciating the sensitivities within the Diefenbaker government on nuclear weapons, reporters pursued the general on whether Canada was fulfilling its NATO commitments. Norstad bluntly said Canada was not: "She would be meeting it in force but not under the terms of the requirements that have been established by NATO," adding, "We are depending upon Canada to produce some of the tactical atomic strike forces." This contradicted what Diefenbaker had been saying to Canadians and MPs in the House of Commons. Newspaper editorialists admired the general for his forthrightness and condemned Diefenbaker for indecision and equivocation. According to the *Toronto Telegram*, "The Government of Canada must now face up to its responsibilities in the field or be prepared to accept the judgment of Canadians generally that it is incapable of decision in the most important single area of Canada's role in international affairs."[7] The ***Globe and Mail***, well-known for being resistant to Canadian forces' involvement in the deployment of American nuclear weapons, declared that Canada should either honour the provisions of the NATO and NORAD treaties or withdraw from the agreements. A spokesperson for the Progressive Conservative Party ridiculously attempted to downplay the remarks, telling reporters that Norstad had "no more official standing than any other American tourist."[8]

The following week, President Kennedy summoned Norstad to the White House to bestow the Distinguished Service Medal. In his remarks, Kennedy noted that Norstad held the confidence of America's allies in Europe and its partner to the north.

In the following days, Lester Pearson flipped his position on nuclear weapons. Pearson claimed this was no longer a moral decision for Liberals but a national security issue: "[The Canadian government] should end at once its evasion of responsibility by discharging the commitments it has already accepted for Canada. It can only do this by accepting nuclear warheads." Any other position, he argued, would betray our allies. This starkly contrasted with what he had said during the 1962 election about Canada not becoming a nuclear power. In his correspondence to voters that year, he wrote, "Canada should stay out of the nuclear club."[9]

In August of 1960, Pearson suggested that Canada should withdraw from a direct form of continental defence that involved the Bomarc program: "It seems to me that our experience in the last three years has shown that in attempting to participate in continental defence in the way we have, we are becoming nothing more than just the last two knots on the Bomarc tail of the defence kite." But the political calculus had changed. The majority of Canadians in a post-Cuban missile crisis world were supportive of our military possessing nuclear weapons to counter the Soviet threat. It was the moment that Pearson admitted that he had gone from being a diplomat to a politician.

Diefenbaker received the news of Pearson's flip-flop with glee. Diefenbaker would hold the ground of protecting Canadian independence and sovereignty, while Pearson would have to explain why he sold out his principles to the Americans. "Never since Saul at his conversion on the Road to Damascus," bellowed Diefenbaker in his speeches, "had there been such a change in the thinking in one person." However, Pearson had the advantage of being in sync with public opinion, which Kennedy's pollster, Lou Harris, had confirmed.

President Kennedy took notice of Pearson's conversion. So did the new U.S. Ambassador to Canada, William Walton Butterworth. A foreign diplomat rarely exchanges correspondence with opposition politicians to rebuke a sitting duly elected government. But, a possible exception was made in a letter from Butterworth to Pearson on January 14, a copy of which allegedly had been mailed to Canada's High Commissioner to the United Kingdom, George Drew, and was included in Diefenbaker's memoirs:

> Please accept my sincere congratulations on the excellent and logical speech you made at the Liberal Party conference on nuclear weapons on January 12th. We appreciated your statement, which indicated that the points of view expressed by the Liberal Party and my government are identical. As a result of your address, no other Canadian politician on record has gained as many devoted friends in my country as you have. I was delighted with the timing, which I considered perfect, announcing the stand taken by the party. The Conservatives will be forced to repeat what you have already stated. It will be quite evident to the electorate that the policy of the Conservatives is narrow-minded and that they are unfit to continue governing the country. At the first opportune moment, I would like to discuss with you how we could be useful to you in the future. You can always count on our support.

The authenticity of the correspondence was disputed, causing Diefenbaker to launch an investigation to satisfy himself of its legitimacy. Given the potential fallout to Canadian-American relations, Diefenbaker chose not to release the letter during the 1963 election campaign, a decision he would ultimately regret. Had the evidence confirming the legitimacy of the correspondence been more compelling, Diefenbaker would have made a different choice. In his memoirs Diefenbaker outlined the evidence that convinced him it was authentic.

For his part, Butterworth regularly interacted with opposition politicians and members of the Canadian press. He routinely fed them stories critical of Diefenbaker based on information officials from across the American administration gave him.[10] There were also "background" briefings to members of the parliamentary press gallery, 20 at a time, held in the basement recreation room of the house occupied by the counsellor of the U.S. embassy.[11] The Americans crossed the international diplomatic and political lines on more than one occasion with Canada in multiple ways, the January 1963 letter being only one glaring example. They were about to do so again in an even more dramatic way.

For Diefenbaker, it was not the case that he would never have accepted nuclear missiles on Canadian soil. It was a question of the conditions: who would control their deployment, and under what circumstances would they be used? He was prepared to negotiate with the United States on all matters subject to respecting certain vital principles. In whatever arrangements were made, he did not want Canada to be seen as limiting any progress on disarmament by expanding the number of countries in the nuclear club. It is likely, however, that his conditions and desires were irreconcilable and could never be met and that Diefenbaker was using the prospect of disarmament as a stalling tactic.

Initial questions about the early January Butterworth letter aside, there was no disputing the authenticity of the U.S. State Department's position after it issued an unprecedented press release on January 30, 1963, regarding the statements made by Diefenbaker, his ministers, and other parliamentarians over the preceding weeks in the House of Commons. It was a shot across the prime minister's political bow if not a direct broadside hit:

> The Department has received a number of inquiries concerning the disclosure during a recent debate in the Canadian House of Commons regarding negotiations over the past two or three months between the United States and Canadian Governments relating to nuclear weapons for Canadian armed forces. In 1958, the Canadian Government decided to adopt the BOMARC-B weapons systems. Accordingly, two BOMARC-B squadrons were deployed to Canada, where they would serve the double purpose of protecting Montreal and Toronto as well as the U.S. deterrent force. The BOMARC-B was not designed to carry any *conventional* warhead. The matter of making available a nuclear warhead for it and for other nuclear-capable weapons systems acquired by Canada has been the subject of inconclusive discussions between the two governments. The installation of the two BOMARC-B batteries in Canada without nuclear warheads was completed in 1962.

Moving beyond a statement of what the U.S. government believed were facts, the press release ventured into political territory:

> Shortly after the Cuban crisis in October 1962, the Canadian Government proposed confidential discussions concerning circumstances under which there might be provision of nuclear weapons for Canadian armed forces in Canada and Europe. These discussions have been exploratory in nature; the Canadian

> Government has not as yet proposed any arrangement sufficiently practical to contribute effectively to North American defence.
>
> Reference was also made in the debate to the need of NATO for increased conventional forces. A flexible and balanced defence requires increased conventional forces, but conventional forces are not an alternative to effective NATO or NORAD defence arrangements using nuclear-capable weapons systems. NORAD is designed to defend the North American continent against air attack. The Soviet bomber fleet will remain, at least throughout this decade, a significant element in the Soviet strike force. An effective continental defence against this common threat is necessary. The provision of nuclear weapons to Canadian forces would not involve an expansion of independent nuclear capability or an increase in the "nuclear club."
>
> As in the case of other allies, custody of U.S. nuclear weapons would remain with the U.S. Joint control fully consistent with national sovereignty can be worked out to cover the use of such weapons by Canadian forces.

Diefenbaker viewed this statement as a violation of Canadian sovereignty and a demonstration of "American cultural imperialism." He believed there was an attempt to portray him as leading a "crypto anti-Yankee government" with a thinly veiled message that it ought to be replaced by a régime which promised to be faithful to the concept of "Canadian-American interdependence." Even the leader of the NDP, Tommy Douglas, found the American critique of a Canadian prime minister to be unconscionable: "I think the Government of the United States should know from this Parliament that they are not dealing with Guatemala,"[12] a reference to the well-known tendency of a variety of American administrations to upend governments in third-world states they thought inimical to American interests.

Kennedy attempted to distance himself from the official statement of his State Department. Still, the evidence indicates he was informed of its contents before it was released and planned to identify a scapegoat should the provocation backfire. When the secretary of state was called before a Senate Committee to explain the diplomatic transgression, he responded with details he could only have known with inside information about the discord within the Diefenbaker cabinet. Knowing about the rift among Conservative cabinet ministers emboldened the American administration to speak out on matters where they would normally be reserved. In evidence provided to the committee, the communiqué from the American ambassador to Canada to his State Department officials provides a clear indication of their thinking and plan:

> We should not be unduly disturbed at the steam of resentment which first blew off upon publication of the Department's release. Diefenbaker's reaction was expected. He is undependable, unscrupulous political animal at bay and we are ones who boxed him in. Pearson and other party leaders could not permit him pose as sole spokesman for Canadian nationalism; hence they had to protect their flanks and join chorus of protest at our "intrusion." Let us also face fact that we are forcing Pearson to go faster and further than he desires in the direction we favor.
>
> We have reached point where our relations must be based on something more solid than accommodation to neurotic Canadian view of us and world. We should be less the accoucheur of Canada's illusions. I recommend, therefore, that the Department and all other agencies concerned continue to stand politely but firmly behind the January 30 release and that nothing be said or done to indicate any doubt whatsoever that the time for hard decisions has come.[13]

The Senate hearing aside, the American government was weary of Canadian dithering. The Canadian ambassador to the United States, Charles Ritchie, was summoned to the State Department so the contents of the communiqué could be reiterated to him. The prime minister countered by recalling his ambassador for "consultation." Diefenbaker addressed the House of Commons on January 31, 1963, and called the American statements an "unprecedented and unwarranted intrusion in Canadian affairs.... Canada will not be pushed around or accept external domination or interference in the making of its decisions. Canada is determined to remain a firm ally, but that does not mean she should be a satellite."

For Diefenbaker, matters came to a head on Sunday, February 3, when the cabinet, absent Ellen Fairclough for an unexplained reason, met informally at 24 Sussex from 9 a.m. until 2 p.m. Diefenbaker had been warned that his defence minister, Douglas Harkness, was going to resign and proceeded with caution: "I did not know whether this actually would happen or, if it did happen, whether he would be acting alone," he wrote in his memoirs. Diefenbaker began the meeting by proposing that Parliament be dissolved to prevent a defeat in the House of Commons. Everyone in the room wanted to avoid an election, but the anti-Diefenbaker ministers did not want to defer the real issue at hand, which was the prime minister's leadership.

The defence minister offered a blunt assessment at the meeting: "You might as well know that the people of Canada have lost confidence in you, the party has lost confidence in you, and the cabinet has lost confidence in you. It is time you went." Diefenbaker fumed and challenged his cabinet colleagues. "I did not ask for this job; I don't want it, and if I am not wanted, I'll go." Only part of that statement was true. "Those who are with me stand up; those against remain seated." The tally was 11 to nine against the prime minister. He immediately offered his resignation. "I propose that Donald Fleming be named prime minister. I will leave you to discuss the proposal. I will be in the library."

Ministers supporting Diefenbaker called the dissidents a "nest of traitors," the exact phrase Tory leader Mackenzie Bowell had used for dissident ministers in 1896. Agriculture Minister Alvin Hamilton took the lead: "You treacherous bastards. No Prime Minister has ever had to deal with so many sons of bitches." The cabinet also feared that replacing the prime minister would cause the minority government to fall, and they believed an election would be disastrous for the party.

With one exception, the call for Diefenbaker's resignation was abandoned. Instead, the cabinet passed a resolution solely to avoid triggering an election. But the resolution was favourable to Diefenbaker: "The Cabinet expresses its loyalty to the Prime Minister and its willingness to continue to give him full support. Without in any way imposing any condition in respect of the foregoing resolution, Cabinet is of the opinion that immediate dissolution is most undesirable and that we should meet at the House of Commons tomorrow and seek by every means to avoid defeat."

The statement carried the scent of desperation. The actual plan among the majority of cabinet who wanted Diefenbaker to resign was improvised and lacked a solid foundation. The haphazard nature of the scheme was evident by the fact that it was pinned on the hope that Diefenbaker would be appointed chief justice of the Supreme Court, presumably by Diefenbaker's successor.

The sitting chief justice, Patrick Kerwin, had died on February 2, the day before the confrontation at 24 Sussex Drive. The ministers who headed the dissidents learned of the death on February 3 while on their way to 24 Sussex Drive to meet Diefenbaker, where they settled on their scheme.

Diefenbaker thought the plan was pure lunacy. "They appeared not to know that the appointment of the Chief Justice of the Supreme Court of Canada, the position that was to be my 'reward,' is a prerogative power of the Prime Minister; they were, in fact, offering me what only I could give," he wrote in his memoirs. But the plan was not entirely slapdash. Tory Senator Wallace McCutcheon had discussed the idea with the other justices who did not oppose it conceptually. McCutcheon had told Olive Diefenbaker, "Your husband will be the first man who has occupied both positions in this country, and only one other person in a democracy will have done the same. Taft was President of the United States and also Chief Justice of the United States." Public Works Minister Davie Fulton told Diefenbaker it was best for the party and the country.

With Diefenbaker still at the helm, Harkness resigned as defence minister. Several ministers asked Harkness to tone down his letter of resignation, which he limited to a disagreement over a matter of policy.

> My Dear Prime Minister:
>
> For over two years, you have been aware that I believe nuclear warheads should be supplied to the four weapons systems we have acquired, which are adapted to their use. Throughout this period, I believed that they would be authorized at the appropriate time. During the past two weeks particularly, I have made absolutely clear what I considered the minimum position I could accept, and several times have offered to resign unless it was agreed to. It has become quite obvious during the last few days that your views and mine as to the course we should pursue for the acquisition of nuclear weapons for our armed forces are not capable of reconciliation, thus it is with a great deal of regret that I now find I must tender my resignation as Minister of National Defence.
>
> Yours regretfully,
>
> Douglas Harkness

Diefenbaker did not view the resignation as fatal or even consequential, as indicated in his reply:

> My Dear Mr. Harkness:
>
> I am naturally very much disappointed that you have taken the course of action set out in your letter of the 3rd instant, and frankly, I find it difficult to understand your decision. Following lengthy discussions with our colleagues, in which you participated fully, a decision was reached which is embodied in the statement on policy I made, as reported at page 3136 of Hansard for January 25, 1963. When I concluded my speech, you shook my hand and expressed your approval. From the position I took in the House of Commons on that day, I have not deviated. Since you approved it then, and since you later made it clear in your speech of January 31st, as reported in Hansard at page 3322 and following pages, that you supported my stand, I am at a loss to understand your suggestion now that your views and mine are not in agreement. We were on January 25th and January 31st. My views have not changed. Between then and Sunday, you must have changed yours. Much as I regret your decision, I can do no other than accept your resignation. At the same time, I wish to thank you for your service in the Cabinet, which was at all times most cooperative. I wish you well in the days ahead.
>
> I am,
>
> Yours sincerely,
>
> John G. Diefenbaker

Addressing the House of Commons, Harkness said he resigned on principle: "The point was finally reached when I considered that my honour and integrity required that I take this step." Pearson pounced on the divisions within the government and introduced a motion of non-confidence on February 4: "This government, because of lack of leadership, the breakdown of unity in the

Cabinet, and confusion and indecision in dealing with national and international problems, does not have the confidence of the Canadian people."

Diefenbaker turned to his justice minister, Donald Fleming, and said, "You are going to be prime minister before this day is over.... You and I are going to see the Governor General this afternoon," suggesting that he would resign and that an election was inevitable.

The government was on the precipice of being defeated, either in the House of Commons or from an internal revolt. Diefenbaker thought that if his caucus was with him, he could count on the votes of Social Credit members in the House of Commons to defeat a Liberal motion of non-confidence. The Quebec wing leader of the Socreds, Réal Caouette, was travelling, and Robert Thompson, the official party leader, listened to the Liberals' arguments. As Joe Clark discovered in 1979, when his short-lived government was defeated after believing Social Credit votes were his for the taking, Diefenbaker could not assume Socred support. But he still made his pitch in the House of Commons to avoid defeat:

> Mr. Speaker, I ask this house for a vote of confidence, for the opportunity to do the things we want to do and have been denied the opportunity of doing. The other day, I saw the benefits of calling an election, thinking only of the political consequences in our favour. But I asked, 'What will its effects be on a rising economy in the years ahead and the months ahead unless we get those things on the statute books that would continue the upsurge of the economy of Canada?' I now ask for a vote of confidence from all honourable members in the house.

In the years before his death, Dalton Camp told CBC reporter Keith Boag that the Diefenbaker minority government was being kept alive by Social Credit MPs because it was receiving regular cheques out of Tory coffers. Camp ended the payments, which contributed to the government's defeat. Camp told Boag that he intended to reveal the tawdry dealings in his memoirs, but his passing prevented the story from coming to light.[14]

Brian Mulroney, then deeply involved in the Tory backrooms, noted that because Diefenbaker had failed to build personal relationships with his cabinet colleagues and MPs, he was ill-equipped to deal with dissension when it surfaced. "Strains of disloyalty (existed) among people who wanted nothing more than to be sought out, flattered, thanked, and encouraged.... At the very moment he should have stepped up these contacts, Diefenbaker withdrew." When he became prime minister, Mulroney learned from Diefenbaker's missteps and took the opposite approach to caucus management.[15]

As his cabinet was disintegrating, Diefenbaker needed the support of Social Credit to continue governing. Leader Robert Thompson wanted to avoid an election and offered to support the government if it agreed to four conditions, mostly related to the budget and a clear commitment on nuclear weapons. Diefenbaker would have none of it. Rebuffing the Social Credit leader, Diefenbaker stated, "Thompson never loses a chance to humiliate me... let Thompson know I will not be kicked around."

The Social Credit premier from Alberta, Ernest Manning, pressured Thompson to remove Diefenbaker. Manning wanted Diefenbaker out because he believed Social Credit's prospects of gaining more seats in the Prairies would be lower so long as an MP from Saskatchewan held the prime minister's chair.[16] Thompson told a few Tory cabinet ministers that he would abandon his four conditions and oppose the non-confidence motion if the prime minister resigned.

Diefenbaker turned to the 30 Social Credit MPs in the House of Commons and, without referring to any offer they had made, effectively responded to three of their four conditions. He ridiculed a possible alliance between Social Credit and the Liberals, claiming, "Pearson loves thee, but he loved you not until yesterday." But it was too little and too late for Social Credit to back Diefenbaker. Only his resignation would have prevented his government's defeat in the House.

After a vote of 142 to 111 on February 5 ended his government (Harkness and another Conservative MP did not vote, another Tory abstained, and two NDP members voted to sustain the government), Diefenbaker told his secretary of state for external affairs, Howard Green, that he was resigning as party leader. "Like hell you are," Green responded. "You can't give in to those bird-brained bastards." Canada's twenty-fifth Parliament was dissolved by proclamation of the Governor General on February 6. Diefenbaker determined he would put his leadership in the hands of his caucus.

With Harkness out, the dissidents designated Trade Minister George Hees to take Diefenbaker down. According to Diefenbaker, Hees "presented in detail to caucus" cabinet deliberations on the nuclear weapons question, "something that his oath as a Privy Councillor forbade him to do." The meeting, held on February 6, was designed, as Diefenbaker recalled in his memoirs, to "foil the plans of the cabal in cabinet who, after months of clandestine meetings, had finally come up with an agreed plan to force me out." Nine ministers threatened to resign and told the caucus that every Conservative MP would be at risk of losing their seats with Diefenbaker as leader.

Meanwhile, the *Globe and Mail* editor, Oakley Dagleish, had inserted himself into the mix after concluding Diefenbaker had to go. He had been in touch with various cabinet ministers, who together were plotting the timing of a *Globe* editorial and calculating its impact. If not Diefenbaker, who would lead the Progressive Conservative party in the campaign? There was no heir apparent, which unsettled caucus members. The editorial writers at the *Globe and Mail* did not seem to care much who took the helm provided there was a change: "If Mr. Diefenbaker continues in the leadership, he will do the party irreparable harm and perhaps destroy it as a national force."

Diefenbaker told his caucus that he needed unanimous support. He was feisty, and caucus members began to think the Chief had yet another good fight left in him. Caucus roared approval and gave the prime minister a standing ovation. The few ministers left seated were barely visible. Diefenbaker turned to Hees: "George, we've got this election, and you and I are going to fight it together. I've got to have you beside me. I'll change the defence policy to better suit your fellows' views." Hees was overcome by the moment and later said, "I was so excited I jumped up on my feet, and I was crying; there were tears in my eyes. I figured here we were at last, in with the defence policy that meant something."

Despite caucus support, Diefenbaker was savaged in the press, ridiculed over his unwillingness to step aside, his indecisiveness as prime minister, and for dividing his party. The *Globe and Mail* took to task those cabinet ministers who had threatened to resign but ultimately got cold feet.

> Today, the Prime Minister is still in office, and the rebels, having deserted their cause, are still in Cabinet. They purchased their jobs for a few weeks... these men lead a tattered party into the election with lies on their lips and a dual standard of morality in their hearts.... They have abandoned the one among them who had the courage to resign, defence minister Douglas Harkness.

Diefenbaker recalled in his memoirs that "the tears ran down (Hees) face like rain in an Asiatic monsoon." The demands for Diefenbaker's resignation were withdrawn. "We're going to knock the hell out of the Grits," Hees told the parliamentary press gallery, who were expecting a different outcome from what they believed was a civil war within Tory ranks.

Meanwhile, the Kennedy administration gloated and boasted about Diefenbaker's demise. Ambassador Butterworth sent a communiqué to Washington that read:

> Preponderance of evidence available—news media, editorial comment, private citizens expression of views—indicate shift of public attention from U.S. statement to clear recognition Diefenbaker indecisiveness, with frequent and widespread reaffirmation of identity of U.S. and Canadian interests and explicit acknowledgment that Canada has somehow gone astray.
>
> Department will recall this was basic aim of exercise, to bring Canadian thinking back to state of relevance to hard realities of world situation. For past four or five years we have—doubtless correctly—tolerated essentially neurotic Canadian view of world and of Canadian role. We have done so in hope Canadians themselves would make gradual natural adjustment to more realistic understanding. For long period there were good grounds for hope this shift would occur relatively painlessly and without our help. Inconclusive outcome last June's general elections, GOC fumbling and indecision during Cuban crisis, continued GOC evasiveness on vital defence matters suggested reappraisal necessary.
>
> However, we had been encouraged in recent weeks that liberal opposition was beginning to crystallize and were beginning, at long last, to press the government to focus on major questions. GOC performance in Commons January 24 and 25 nevertheless clearly showed Prime Minister Diefenbaker determined to carry on in dream world as long as possible and continue to postpone the acquisition of nuclear warheads for Canadian forces to carry their share of defence of continent, at the same time, refusing us permission stockpile for our own use, not to mention failure arm 104 G's of Canadian air division in NATO..... In effect, we have now forced the issue and the outcome depends on the common sense of the Canadian people....

> In short, we think the Canadian public is with us even though some Liberal politicians may have been afraid we have handed Diefenbaker an issue he can use against them and the United States. We think Canadians will no longer accept irresponsible nonsense which political leaders all parties, but particularly Progressive Conservatives under Diefenbaker, have got away with for several years.... Over the long run, this exercise will prove to have been highly beneficial and will substantially advance our interests.[17]

Kennedy's national security advisor, McGeorge Bundy, wrote to his president, "I might add that I myself have been sensitive to the need for being extra polite to Canadians ever since [United States Under Secretary of State] George Ball and I knocked over the Diefenbaker (government) by one innocuous press release."[18] In these messages, we see the smoking guns brandished in American hands to defeat the duly elected Canadian government by overt and covert means.

The polls looked bleak for Diefenbaker. He was 15 points behind Pearson. In the aftermath of the Cuban Missile Crisis, Canadians were inclined to believe that Canada should accept nuclear weapons. But Diefenbaker did not believe leaders should be influenced by polls, especially concerning matters of principle and sovereignty. He was ready to take his position to the Canadian people, even if his party was divided. He had been ridiculing Pearson, who Diefenbaker alleged was risibly pliable on important issues, noting that just three years earlier, he stood in the House of Commons and said Canada should pass on accepting BOMARC missiles.

Despite George Hees' position in caucus that the Tories would trounce the Liberals in the 1963 election, he soon had a change of heart. After Parliament was dissolved and the election set for April 8, Hees visited Diefenbaker very early on Saturday, February 9, along with the associate minister of national defence, Pierre Sévigny. "Here's my resignation," is how Hees began the conversation. "Your what?" replied a stunned Diefenbaker. Before Hees could reply, Sévigny said, "Mine too," a decision he said he later regretted. Diefenbaker immediately understood the gravity of the situation and asked for time for them to consider the matter. To Hees, it was a matter of personal honour, and there was nothing to discuss.[19] After sensing his ministers could not be persuaded, Diefenbaker became dismissive. "I don't have to listen to you. You represent Bay Street and I represent the common man."[20] In his letter of resignation, Hees stated he could not accept Diefenbaker's position on relations with the United States.

> Dear Mr. Prime Minister:
>
> As you know, I have been extremely concerned for some time about our defence policy and our relations with the United States. I have outlined to you, to my colleagues, and to the caucus of the Conservative party why I consider that our present defence policy does not either fulfil our international commitments or provide for the security of our country. I have also stated clearly that I consider the present attitude of the government cannot but lead to a deterioration of our relations with the United States.
>
> I had hoped that the views which I expressed would lead to changes in policy which would permit me to remain a member of the government. However, since that time there has been no indication of such change. I feel these matters to be of vital importance to the welfare and security of our country, and therefore I have no alternative but to tender my resignation as a member of your cabinet. I do not propose to be a candidate in the forthcoming election.
>
> Yours sincerely,
>
> George Hees

Diefenbaker contended in his memoirs that without these resignations, especially George Hees, he would have won the 1963 election. On the campaign trail, he had no good answer to the question, "What happened between the Wednesday, when [Hees] came out of the caucus and announced to the press, 'We're all together,' and Saturday morning, when he resigned?"[21] Oddly enough, Harkness, who had been Diefenbaker's most outspoken critic, chose to run in the 1963 election while Hees took a pass.

But it was more than Harkness, Sévigny, and Hees who jumped ship. Davie Fulton, who had held the justice and public works portfolios, and Donald Fleming, who had held the finance and then justice portfolios, also decided not to seek re-election. Diefenbaker offered a brave face to his team: "Elections are not won except in the last week. I am the underdog now, and that means the fight must be strongly waged," adding, "We can win a majority. Pearson isn't a campaigner. He's afraid of me and he should be."[22] Ever confident, he later said, "My golly, I'd hate to run against myself."[23]

Diefenbaker's attempts to shore up his cabinet team were uninspiring. Senator McCutcheon, who Diefenbaker appointed in 1962, a member of the eastern business establishment, was given a cabinet portfolio, an unusual posting for an unelected parliamentarian. Diefenbaker came to regret his choice, noting that McCutcheon had threatened to resign during the campaign. Diefenbaker later said McCutcheon was "the biggest political double-crosser I had ever known"—which was significant given the events in the party, caucus, and cabinet over the prior weeks.

Quebec Premier Jean Lesage supported Pearson's Liberals, criticizing the financial arrangements that Diefenbaker imposed on the Quebec government. Diefenbaker accused the Lesage administration of using the Quebec Provincial Police to harass Diefenbaker's candidates, conducting searches of Tory meetings for illegal alcohol.[24]

In another accusation that would become common in conservative circles in years and decades to come, Diefenbaker thought the CBC had become the voice of the Liberal party, quoting in his memoirs his assessment of the editor of the Fredericton Gleaner, "I would say, from my own observations, that the CBC commentators were one-sided Liberal propagandists, giving tongue to the most prejudiced, tendentious utterances on every phase of the campaign, invariably referring to Pearson with the tone of pride, Diefenbaker with disgust."[25]

Diefenbaker's primary concern was how he would get his message across amidst the noise and confusion. He began the campaign 15 points behind the Liberals in the polls. Defeat appeared a certainty. He wanted to be viewed as not in the back pockets of the Americans, not because he had anything against them but because he was pro-Canadian. However, had he known the extent of American interference in the election campaign, he might have made Kennedy's involvement more explicit.[26] In one of the more ironic twists of history, a future Liberal prime minister, Pierre Trudeau, then a university professor, came to

Diefenbaker's defence. Trudeau had little doubt that American hands were all over the election call, which he described in the April 1963 edition of the publication *Cité libre*.

While the Liberals had been actively recruiting Trudeau to run as a candidate in 1963, that was impossible after he called Pearson "the defrocked pope of peace" who had fallen under the spell of the Kennedy "hipsters." He noted that Pearson took a position on nuclear weapons contrary to a policy adopted at a party congress and that he had not consulted with Liberal MPs on his change in stance. "The Pope had spoken; it only remained for the believers to believe." Trudeau's provocative essay and a series of questions left no doubt about American influence on Canadian politics:

> You think I dramatize? But how do you think politics works? Do you think that General Norstad, the former supreme commander of allied forces in Europe, came to Ottawa as a tourist on January 3 to call publicly on the Canadian government to respect its commitments? Do you think it was by chance that Mr. Pearson, in his speech of January 12, was able to quote the authority of General Norstad? Do you think it was inadvertent that, on January 30, the State Department gave a statement to journalists reinforcing Mr. Pearson's claims and crudely accusing Mr. Diefenbaker of lying? You think it was by chance that this press release provided the leader of the Opposition with the arguments he used abundantly in his parliamentary speech on January 31? You believe that it was coincidence that this series of events ended with the fall of the government on February 5?
>
> But why do you think that the United States should treat Canada differently from Guatemala when reason of state requires it and circumstances permit?

Diefenbaker made Dalton Camp the national campaign chairman. Camp proved immediately effective, taking the offence when, in a February 18 *Newsweek* article titled "Canada's Diefenbaker: Decline and Fall," the magazine ridiculed Diefenbaker's facial features and gestures on its front cover: "The India rubber features twist and contorted in grotesque and gargoyle-like grimaces...

the eyebrows beat up and down like bats' wings; his agate blue eyes blaze forth cold fire... his enemies insist that it is sufficient grounds for barring Tory rallies to children under sixteen." The bureau chief for *Newsweek*, Ben Bradlee, later a *Washington Post* editor, was not so coincidentally a good friend of President Kennedy.

Newsweek was an American publication entirely outside the influence of the Opposition parties. Yet, Camp, who made his living in advertising, was able to use the article and its inflammatory cover photo to his advantage. Camp contended the magazine was friendly to the American administration, which wanted Diefenbaker out of office because he stood up for Canada. A bemused Diefenbaker remarked, "Satan saw my picture in *Newsweek* and said he never knew he had such opposition in Canada." Diefenbaker would indeed tremble, contort, and shake when he spoke as if he had Parkinson's disease. But he suffered no physical ailment. It was simply his style of speaking, developed in his youth and maintained throughout his life.[27]

Diefenbaker turned the personal attacks into an issue of discrimination in the same manner Jean Chrétien would do with a similar situation three decades later—and to his benefit in the 1993 election—when he responded to Conservative party ads that seemed to belittle his facial features.

Diefenbaker boiled the controversy over national defence down to a message Canadians could understand:

> Insofar as Canadian soil is concerned... we shall place ourselves in the position, by agreement with the United States, so that if war does come, or emergency takes place, we shall have available to us readily accessible nuclear weapons. But in the meantime, we shall not have Canada used as a storage dump for nuclear weapons. The Liberal high command seemed to mistake our country for the United States.

Diefenbaker's passion and evangelical zeal sharply contrasted with the mild-mannered and intellectual Lester Pearson. Diefenbaker was making headway, and his magic was not to be dismissed. His sense of destiny that he was meant to be prime minister and would ultimately win the hearts of ordinary Canadians was undiminished. When asked if he intended to appear on television with his competitors, he brusquely replied, "I have no competitors."[28]

Diefenbaker's message had not changed from his early days in Parliament as he undertook his tour by train, "I'm down on the ground with you. I'm not asking for the support of the powerful, the strong, and the mighty, but of the average Canadian, the group to which I belong."[29] He often remarked, "There are powerful interests working against us, national and international. Everyone is against me, but the people." Those "powerful interests" included the establishment, the press, and the American president. Critics scoffed that Diefenbaker was just being paranoid. But he backed up his charge with evidence. On boarding the Tory plane, reporter Val Sears of the *Toronto Star* was overheard saying to his fellow reporters: "To work, gentleman. We have a government to overthrow."[30]

He was not alone. Respected journalist Bruce Hutchison told the former U.S. secretary of state Dean Acheson in 1963 that he was "doing his best to make Mike Pearson prime minister."[31] When the *Globe and Mail* ran a front-page editorial that declared Diefenbaker unfit to lead, Diefenbaker responded, "The eastern magnates ran an editorial on the front page in Toronto Saturday, saying they wouldn't support us. The only reason they put it on the front page was because nobody would read it on the editorial page."

Towards the end of the campaign, American Defense Secretary Robert McNamara unwittingly lent proof to Diefenbaker's allegations that Canada would be in harm's way if it accepted, without conditions, American nuclear weapons on its soil. McNamara appeared before the House Appropriations Subcommittee and, in response to a question, said: "At the very least, [Bomarc missile sites] could cause the Soviets to target missiles against them and thereby increase their missile requirements or draw missiles onto these Bomarc targets that would otherwise be available for other targets."

Despite an attempt at clarification by the White House, Diefenbaker launched his own missile:

> The Liberal party would have us put nuclear warheads on something that's hardly worth scrapping. What's it for? To attract the fire of the intercontinental missiles. North Bay—knocked out. La Macaza—knocked out. Never, never, never, never has there been a revelation equal to this. The whole bottom fell out of the Liberal program today. The Liberal policy is to make Canada a decoy for intercontinental missiles.[32]

Diefenbaker had not lost his touch. The Americans called it a "low blow."

Kennedy was distressed by the turn of events and let McNamara know it:

> It might be worthwhile to bring to the attention of those who read your testimony on the Bomarc in Canada that their failure to catch the political significance has strengthened Diefenbaker's hand considerably and increased our difficulties. It would seem to me that every word in those sentences flashed a red light. They should be on the alert for our political, as well as military, security.[33]

Pearson feared that remarks from the Kennedy's administration would sink the Liberal campaign. The president's national security adviser took the unprecedented step of sending a memorandum to the secretary of defense and the secretary of state outlining the president's wishes to avoid any appearance of interference in the Canadian election. But had Kennedy not already interfered—on multiple occasions—such re-direction would not have been necessary.

During the campaign, Kennedy used the Washington correspondent of the *Winnipeg Free Press*, Max Freedman, as an intermediary to advise Pearson. Freedman had just met with Kennedy and called Pearson from the White House. And he delivered: "For God's sake," Pearson told Freedman, "Tell the president not to say anything. I don't want any help from him. This would be awful."[34]

Pearson was aware of the risk, partly because his American pollster, Lou Harris, told his team that Diefenbaker was gaining ground with his message that Canadians should make decisions about Canada And partly, as Pearson well knew, because such allegations of interference were true—whether from the U.S. State Department, the U.S. embassy, the Kennedy White House and via diplomats, journalists, and a pollster. In a last-minute mirage of neutrality, Kennedy's national security advisor sent a message to the Canadian embassy and all departments to avoid the appearance of interference, even if it meant not commenting on distortions or unethical commentary issued by Diefenbaker or at least clarifying anything that was said with the White House beforehand, regardless of the degree of non-attribution.

But the Americans and Pearson had already handed the prime minister a club, and he fully intended to use it. "We are a power, not a pauper," Diefenbaker bellowed on the campaign trail. "I want Canada to be in control of Canadian soil." And reaching back to his political hero, Sir John A. Macdonald, for grounding, he declared, "A Canadian I was born; as a Canadian, I will die."

Momentum was building for Diefenbaker. But he would need a big push in the campaign's final week. That's when news reports of a wayward presidential briefing memorandum, the one where Kennedy wrote he wanted to "push" the Canadian government, appeared in the *Ottawa Citizen*. While Diefenbaker denied it, he was the likely source. This flummoxed the Americans. "Pretty clear use of the 'push' document without using it," noted McGeorge Bundy, Kennedy's national security advisor.[35] Another official admitted to being outfoxed by Diefenbaker. The story was out, but Diefenbaker appeared to have clean hands.

Diefenbaker took his message to Canadians at train stops across the country. Ironically, he harkened back to the Truman presidential campaign in 1948 when facing a divided party, he ran a come-from-behind and stunning victory where he gave his opponents hell from a railway caboose. Years later, in his 1963 book *Renegade in Power*, Peter C. Newman conceded that Diefenbaker had achieved what appeared impossible. "He had taken his party, which had seemed demoralized beyond redemption at the start of the campaign, to a position of realistic hope for re-election. And he had achieved this entirely by himself."[36]

***

On election night, April 8, 1963, with the results showing a Progressive Conservative defeat, Diefenbaker was not inclined to concede the loss until the votes of the armed forces were counted. "I gave the best that was in me, and I followed the course that I believed right. That course was based on my conscience and my faith in the future of Canada."[37] The results were less damaging than feared at the start of the campaign: Diefenbaker's government lost just 21 seats, ending up with 95, compared with 128 for Pearson's Liberals. Diefenbaker could take some consolation. Under his fight-back strategy, he swept Saskatchewan, took 14 of 17 seats in Alberta, 10 of 14 in Manitoba, and seven of 12 in Nova Scotia. However, losses in Ontario and Quebec were sufficient to give the Liberals a minority government. Diefenbaker lost the most seats in the big cities and affluent neighbourhoods, winning only one of 39 seats in Montreal and Toronto. The Tories' popular vote declined by 4.5 percentage points to 32.8 percent, with the Liberals up by the same margin to arrive at 41.5 percent. With the Liberals only five seats short of a majority government, there was no realistic prospect of Diefenbaker testing his confidence in the House of Commons. Lester B. Pearson was sworn in as prime minister on April 22, 1963.

It was the second election in a row where voters put a minority government in place. The math for the other parties mattered. Had the Socreds not eaten away at the Tory vote, earning 11.9 percent nationally (compared with 2.6 percent in 1958), Diefenbaker might have held government. He was bitter when he heard that Socred members were offered a twenty-five-thousand-dollar bribe to align themselves with a Pearson Liberal government. Six Creditiste members were allegedly involved, although they swore in an affidavit that they only gave their assurance of support because they believed Lester Pearson would treat French Canadians and English Canadians as equal partners in Confederation and increase family allowances. The affidavit notes, "This offer is made voluntarily and freely. We do not expect any favour in return other than the satisfaction of duty accomplished."[38]

Diefenbaker thought that with 95 MPs he could mount a serious opposition, "provided the Conservative Party... could stop its lemming-like tendency, established over the years, of rushing into the seas of dissension and defeat."[39] The media thought that while Diefenbaker lost the government, he exceeded expectations and won the campaign. In a *La Presse* editorial, they remarked on Diefenbaker's raw political skill and stamina:

> The party was threatened by a complete rout and an unprecedented defeat. Only the spirit, the personality, and the magic of Mr. Diefenbaker explain that the catastrophe has been averted.... [A]bandoned by several of his most prestigious lieutenants and left by himself during the campaign, he accomplished the quasi-miracle of lifting himself off the floor of the arena where he was supposed to have been out cold and of ending the fight strongly.

The Kennedy administration was pleased that Diefenbaker was out and proud of its role in putting in place a leader that was more in tune with its views. Kennedy summoned his pollster, Lou Harris, to the White House to celebrate their win. "One of the highlights of my life," Mr. Harris told *The Canadian Press*, "was helping Pearson defeat Diefenbaker."[40] Harris said he had "made a lifelong friend in Mike." Richard Starnes, a columnist for the *Washington Daily News*, could well have been speaking for Kennedy when he wrote: "The victory occurred in Canada where adroit statecraft by the American State Department brought down the bumbling crypto anti-Yankee government of Prime Minister John

Diefenbaker and replaced it with a regime which promises to be faithful to the concept of Canadian-American interdependence. The Kennedy Administration must congratulate itself in private for its coup."[41]

Meanwhile, the American administration indeed rejoiced. "U.S. Hails Pearson's Win" was the headline of a story by the *Globe and Mail's* correspondent to Washington D.C.[42] Not to overstate how vital Diefenbaker's defeat was to the American president, Kennedy's principal speechwriter and biographer, Theodore C. Sorenson, in his epic 783-page biography of Kennedy, mentions Diefenbaker only twice. After the Liberal win, Pierre Trudeau remarked, "I am only concerned with the anti-democratic reflexes of the spineless Liberal herd. Power beckoned to Mr. Pearson; he had nothing to lose except his honour. He lost it. And his whole party lost it, too."[43] It was no accident that years later, upon becoming prime minister himself, no one would have cause to accuse Trudeau of being too close to the Americans.

Despite Diefenbaker's attachment to the monarchy, the British press was universal in its editorials, expressing satisfaction that he had fallen to defeat. They claimed Prime Minister Macmillan shared their views.[44] The only disappointment among Diefenbaker's critics was that Pearson was denied a majority government. The lead editorial in the *Globe and Mail* made the same point:

> The new government will not have the strong working majority that this paper would have wished. We believe, however, that the New Democratic Party will recognize that the future of Canada requires that partisan ambitions be put aside and that it recognize its duty to support a Liberal government in a program calculated to attack Canada's serious economic problems... to lead the country out of the problems that have beset it.[45]

Pearson had a different view of American influence despite the self-congratulations south of the border. After the campaign was over and Pearson was sworn in as prime minister, he candidly told Kennedy that the release of the State Department memo had cost him 50 seats and a majority government.

Seven months after the election, John F. Kennedy was assassinated in Dallas, Texas. Diefenbaker spoke diplomatically without bypassing the tension in their relationship: "Free men everywhere would bow their heads in sorrow. Whatever the disagreements may have been throughout the years, he stood as the embodiment of freedom, not only in his country but throughout the world."[46] A few days later, he commented that the world Kennedy left was "dangerous and untidy." While he expressed confidence that the United States would not falter, he also observed, "The assassination will add to the uncertainties of the world scene."[47]

***

Looking back to 1957, Diefenbaker won the leadership over the objections of the party establishment. By necessity, his cabinet included many MPs who doubted Diefenbaker from day one. They continued to question him as prime minister, especially during the Cuban Missile Crisis and on the question of the acceptance of nuclear weapons on Canadian soil. At a decisive moment, many abandoned Diefenbaker, dooming his government to defeat. He did little to win them over. Diefenbaker's personality was also partly to blame. He was a stubborn loner and possessed insecurities about his standing with the eastern-based power brokers in the Progressive Conservative party. Diefenbaker was a westerner with clear rural roots. Not all of his disputes with establishment figures were necessary. A more polished, engaged, and secure political operator could have managed the conflicts while still standing up for Canada and getting what was in the country's national interest.

John A. Macdonald famously said, "I don't need caucus when I succeed; I need them when I fail." Diefenbaker's stubbornness was a virtue when, as a lawyer, he fought for the poor, dispossessed and unjustly accused. However, this quality proved to be fatal to his government by 1963. Even after winning two minorities and a majority government, Diefenbaker failed to gain the loyalty he needed from his ministers to govern the country in periods of stress when a leader's standing to make difficult decisions needs to be assured.

\- 18 -

LIVE TO FIGHT ANOTHER DAY

No one since the days of Macdonald has gone through the like.... My friends, they believe they will succeed in this way. I will follow the will of the people. Will it be the will of the people or those that are all-powerful?

Political parties typically consider the question of leadership after an election defeat if the leader does not otherwise resign in the aftermath. Diefenbaker submitted his resignation to his cabinet after the 1963 election. It was not a sincere offer, designed instead to expose his detractors. He believed they had no viable alternative among them. But after the loss to Pearson in 1963, Diefenbaker was not prepared to make it easy on those who wanted a change at the top. He believed he could win again, and so long as Pearson was on the scene, he believed he was his party's best combatant.

There was precedent for Diefenbaker's hope: John A. Macdonald remained leader after losing the 1874 election. Conservative Sir John A. would go on to win four more contests (1878, 1882, 1887, and 1891); Liberal Mackenzie King lost power in 1930 before winning three more elections (1935, 1940, and 1945). Diefenbaker held the Liberals to a minority government, leaving his record at an impressive three wins and one loss. That gave him a more than respectable .750 "batting average." Only Macdonald had a better record than Diefenbaker among Conservative leaders who fought more than two elections. Brian Mulroney remains the only undefeated Conservative leader, winning two significant majorities.

To Diefenbaker's credit, the 1963 result was less of a drubbing than expected. After ministerial resignations that precipitated the election and the mid-campaign devaluation of the Canadian dollar, it was stunning to political commentators that Pearson could muster only a minority government. Diefenbaker's political skills on the stump and his vision of an independent Canada enabled the Tories to hold on to 95 seats. But a loss is a loss, and the Chief, at 68, looked every bit of his age.

While many in the party thought his time was up, Diefenbaker would not leave gracefully. As he wrote in his memoirs, it was time to heal the wounds in the party and keep fighting for his vision of Canada.

> I did not declare war on any person or group within the Conservative Party. Although I beat back challenge after challenge, there was never a point when I was not prepared to agree to let bygones be bygones. For example, when I addressed the meeting of the National Executive of the Conservative Party at Ottawa's Chateau Laurier Hotel on 26 October 1963, I stated sincerely that I was not going to resurrect what took place within the party in February 1963. I summed up my views with these words: 'I want to see the spirit of this Party directed to fighting Grits, not fighting Tories from within.[1]

In what appeared to be a post-election political obituary for John Diefenbaker, 32-year-old journalist Peter C. Newman authored *Renegade in Power: The Diefenbaker Years*. Released in October 1963, it established a new genre of political analysis designed to expose and take down a party leader in real-time in a tell-all book. In Canada, a book that sells 5,000 copies is considered a bestseller. Newman's publishers sold over 100,000 copies.[2] Newman claimed to be non-partisan but admitted his effort was crafted as "the unmaking of the Prime Minister." Diefenbaker thought the book was muckraking and slander: "I am considering commencing an action for libel. It is full of falsehoods." At the Diefenbaker Museum at the University of Saskatchewan, there is a handwritten note that describes his feelings:

> Then there is Newman. He is the literary scavenger of trash. Manufactured and concocted. He is in close contact with the Liberal hierarchy and gets his briefings from them as to what he should publish. False propaganda. Vicious. Health of my wife. Cruel Stories, Caricatures.

The *New York Times* took a keen interest in the book, calling it "a clinical, almost psychiatric, analysis of the complex and devious character of the most controversial figure in Canadian politics."[3] The reviewer told Americans that Diefenbaker's indecisiveness "threatened the safety of the whole North American continent" and that "his pro-Canadianism was hard to distinguish from anti-Americanism."

Newman had access to cabinet ministers, MPs, and party officials who thought Diefenbaker was erratic, indecisive, and paranoid. Having cast themselves as opponents of Diefenbaker, any content that reflected poorly on Canada's 13th prime minister was, for them and Newman, fair game. There was no holding back. Stories of Diefenbaker's successes were omitted or minimized. "No other Canadian politician in this century," wrote Newman, "could claim the emotional conquest of a generation; yet no prime minister ever disillusioned his disciples more.... He gave people a leadership cult, without the leadership."[4]

Despite Diefenbaker coming to office with a national vision to develop Canada's resources and to pass a bill of rights to protect minorities, Newman wrote he had "not the least inkling of what he wanted to do when he achieved high office." While many Canadians admired Diefenbaker's persistence in sticking with politics after so many early defeats, Newman wrote, "No Canadian politician before him ever rose so steadily through a succession of personal humiliations."[5] While the Newman book remained a "go-to" source for those who sought insight into the Diefenbaker regime for many decades after he left office, a more favourable book to Diefenbaker's point of view of Canada was George Grant's 1965 tome, *Lament for a Nation*. Grant supported Diefenbaker's instinctual nationalism and noted, "It took the full weight of the North American establishment to bring him down."

With no provision in the constitution of the Progressive Conservative party requiring a leadership review—even after an election defeat—and with Diefenbaker showing no signs of retirement, those who wanted a change at the top had to bring out their knives. For those who wanted a change in leadership, matters came to a head at the February 4, 1964, Progressive Conservative Party meeting in Ottawa, where Diefenbaker stared down his detractors and reasserted his position at the top of the party:

> I am not leading the Conservative party into the wilderness. I intend to lead this party to another task ordered by Canada's destiny. I am

> reminded of the motto of Count Frontenac: 'I will answer the enemy from the mouths of my cannon.' Ferment inside a party is a sign of life. But ferment carried on when the time comes for political battle is something else. It is treachery. I have always given the leader under whom I have served my complete loyalty and support. I expect no less today as leader.

Diefenbaker did not want to be seen as fearing a secret ballot when the question of his leadership came before delegates on the afternoon of the 4th:

> I come before you knowing that you are about to decide a question of leadership, which I want decided. No leader, no man, whatever his dedication to his country and his party may be, can ever march forward facing the foe if he is afraid that there is somebody behind him who is interfering directly or indirectly.
>
> I now come to a question that is on the minds of many. I have never given my opinion on the question of a secret ballot on the motion of confidence except to say that the annual meeting would decide. The constitution of the party says that the regular course shall be followed. In the wisdom of the years, the vote has always been an open one. I know there are many as conscientious as I am, who feel there should be a secret vote. I will not say to you what that will mean in the years ahead.
>
> On the other hand, I do not want to leave here and say that if we had had a secret vote, the results might have been otherwise. I want you, the delegates, to decide, and if you decide on the secret vote, that is fine with me. I want you to know where I stand. I want to know where you stand, too.[6]

A motion on the floor to make the confidence vote a secret ballot was defeated by a three-to-one margin. With no opportunity for private dissent, Diefenbaker received nearly unanimous support from convention delegates. It wasn't quite a Soviet-style re-election reenactment for an aging Politburo General Secretary, but the lack of a secret ballot and the potential for intimidation meant it wasn't exactly a no-holds-barred democratic wrestling match either. Diefenbaker had his way for the time being.

The front page of the *Toronto Star* carried the news of Diefenbaker's entrenchment with the headline, "Diefenbaker Beats Rebels: Party Hails him as Leader." However, the editorial page at the *Globe and Mail* offered this damning assessment:

> Mr. Diefenbaker offered himself yesterday not as the leader of the Conservative Party but as leader of the Diefenbaker Party. And the delegates accepted him on that basis, not as a Conservative leading a great party devoted to conservative principles, but as one man running a political machine from which he demands obedience.... The Conservatives are going away from this meeting with disunity smoldering in their ranks, with a leader who has demonstrated his inability to command a government, and having made no real attempt to re-examine their principles and re-define their policies. This is a very sad story.[7]

Newspaper elites aside, Diefenbaker mistakenly believed that the question of his leadership had been put to rest at the convention. While he won an open vote, the convention also chose Dalton Camp as party president. Under Camp's direction, the party's executive asserted its authority and set the party on a course to jettison Diefenbaker. Camp believed party members should engage in free expression and fresh thought, somewhat divorced from the edicts of the leader or the parliamentary caucus. Signaling his intentions, Camp said, "In the process of making a god of our Leader, we made sheep of ourselves.... I am not prepared to listen to those who would speak to us on Friday and leave us on Saturday unless we do as we are told."

Diefenbaker believed he had overwhelming caucus support. Indeed, many thought they owed their seats to Diefenbaker's defiant performance in 1963. While Diefenbaker infrequently attended caucus meetings, his respectful view was his MPs "carry the load and bear the ultimate democratic responsibility." Consequently, Diefenbaker thought the party's national executive held an advisory and consultative role but were more trouble than they were worth. "It cannot be denied that whenever the effective management of the party fell into the hands of non-parliamentary pashas, electoral disaster had followed."

In a plea for unity to party members, he said, "There must be more inviting targets on which to fix our aim than on one another. I would rather fight Grits than Tories... it is only self-inflicted wounds that are slow to heal, and that can be mortal."[8]

Beyond ambition and his sense that he remained the Tories' best shot at regaining power, Diefenbaker returned to his vision of One Canada. That meant no special status for any province and treating all Canadians equally regardless of ethnicity. This vision faced stiff opposition among Quebecers, who believed that Confederation was an evolving partnership that united French and English within a framework that enabled especially the French—a minority in Canada and a sliver of a population in North America—to protect and advance their language and culture. Diefenbaker thought the only groups that deserved special treatment were the poor and the disadvantaged.

Brian Mulroney, then a practicing lawyer, party activist, and dealmaker concluded that Diefenbaker had become tone-deaf to the aspirations of Quebecers and that a new vision and leader was required. At a meeting of Quebec Tories, he proposed a resolution with a preamble that acknowledged obstacles that prevented the full development of the French "nation" and that statements made by the party leadership were harming English-French relations.[9]

Mulroney was in the camp of Sir John A. Macdonald. Canada came into being in 1867 under Macdonald's design to address the dysfunction of the predecessor government that operated in a single parliament with divisions between Upper and Lower Canada—Canada East and Canada West. Diefenbaker believed in the rights of French-speaking Canadians as they were constitutionally guaranteed in the British North America Act. He reinforced those rights by introducing simultaneous translation into the proceedings of the House of Commons, a change that Liberals initially opposed on reasons of cost and the ridiculous fear that it would prevent MPs from becoming bilingual. "For the first time in our history," noted Diefenbaker, "Members could take their full part in debate. In the past, important debates had been in English."[10]

He broke ground with civil service reform, including actively recruiting French-speaking talent. He insisted that government documents, including cheques to citizens for pension and family allowance, be produced in a bilingual format. Prior governments had resisted the change due to the cost. With his only opportunity to appoint a Governor General, Diefenbaker chose General George Vanier in June 1959. Vanier, a decorated military officer and former Canadian ambassador to France, was a hero in Quebec. He was the first Francophone and the first Quebecer to hold the post. Vanier deserved the role. The added benefit of the appointment was the Tories rose by 10 percent in Quebec polls.[11]

Diefenbaker was responsible for establishing the National Capital Commission, which covered a vast territory in Quebec and Ontario, and building the Macdonald-Cartier Bridge to better link Ottawa and Hull. Other capital building initiatives including establishing Dominion Day on Parliament Hill and launching of the Changing of the Guard ceremony. In preparation for Canada's Centennial celebration, the Diefenbaker government championed the idea of a world exposition in Montreal to honour the 100th anniversary of Confederation: Expo 67. "We vigorously pursued this objective internationally," noted Diefenbaker, "to compensate for the lateness of our application, and we succeeded."[12]

Pierre Trudeau, then a Quebec-based intellectual and provocateur, was unimpressed by Diefenbaker's measures. In his memoirs, he referred to the translation of House of Commons proceedings as "table scraps" and that Diefenbaker was "tempestuous." However, he agreed with Diefenbaker on no special recognition of Quebec within Canada's constitutional framework.[13] It was why, when Brian Mulroney was prime minister, Pierre Trudeau vehemently opposed the Meech Lake and Charlottetown constitutional accords that at various times had the endorsement of the federal parliament and all provincial parliaments, largely because they included a recognition that Quebec constituted a distinct society within Canada. Diefenbaker believed a hyphenated Canadian was a diminished Canadian. He wanted all Canadians and all provinces to be equal. To him, there were no French Canadians or English Canadians, just Canadians. He rejected the view that Canada's founding was a coming together of two races with embedded constitutional protections vital to Quebec.

Conservative MPs from Quebec did not agree with Diefenbaker's view that Quebec had the powers it required to protect the French language. They saw his continued leadership as fatal to the party's electoral prospects. They remembered feeling snubbed by Diefenbaker when he became leader because he did not have a proposer or seconder from Quebec. Following the debate over a national flag, described in the following chapter, Léon Balcer, the MP from Trois-Rivières, issued a demand on January 14, 1965, to the party's national president. In the name of the Quebec caucus, he called "for a meeting of the national executive of the party to fix a date for a national convention to decide upon the leadership of the party."[14]

Balcer charged Diefenbaker with nourishing an anti-Quebec backlash and stated, "Our firm conviction, reached after the most careful consideration, that the Conservative Party can no longer carry on as a great national party under its present leadership and the policies which that leadership have engendered." Going further, Balcer claimed that Diefenbaker's policies were "the direct antithesis of the great work of union wrought by Macdonald and Cartier—the first Canadian to master the art of governing this difficult country of ours." Diefenbaker's main campaign organizer in Saskatchewan, Dick Spencer, concluded that his leader valued French Canadians but only in the abstract. "In person, he was uneasy with them, and kept his distance. He found few individuals to respect among them and no real friends."[15]

Party President Dalton Camp, called a national executive meeting for Saturday, February 6, 1965, a decision he made without consulting Diefenbaker. The national executive—an odd term, considering it comprised 116 people—met to discuss the party's future and its leadership. They debated four questions: First, should there be a leadership convention? Second, should the leader resign? Third, should there be a policy advisory committee? And fourth, should the party fully accept the new Canadian flag?

Diefenbaker claimed the executive had neither the authority nor the mandate regarding question number two. The delegates removed it from the agenda by a narrow vote of 55 to 52. Most leaders would have interpreted this result as a loss of confidence, but not Diefenbaker. Diefenbaker would not submit to the will of the party's executive. He believed his mandate came from the Canadian people. In a television interview, Diefenbaker remarked: "I have been maligned. I have been condemned. No one since the days of Macdonald has gone through the like.... My friends, they believe they will succeed in this way. I will follow the will of the people. Will it be the will of the people or those that are all powerful?"

Diefenbaker survived the executive meeting with what he called "unanimous support." However, the stories reported from the meeting revealed dissension and hard feelings, with one member saying Diefenbaker wins battles and loses wars."[16] While fighting off rancour in his party, Diefenbaker also had his sights on Lester Pearson, whom he saw leading a schizophrenic government that, at times, cozied up to the Americans and, at others, pursued knee-jerk nationalist policies. Liberals claimed to be strengthening national unity but, as Diefenbaker noted, were doing so by caving into provincial demands for power that would weaken the national government.

***

As expected, the Pearson government followed through on the promise to accept American nuclear weapons on Canadian soil in September 1963. This followed what Diefenbaker dubbed Pearson's "honeymoon" visit to Hyannis Port, the summer home of the Kennedy clan, where the two leaders walked the beach. On leaving the compound, Kennedy gave Pearson an American flag as a token of appreciation. It was a gift of subservience and not something Pearson could easily discuss or display.

Pearson came to power with a platform that called for "Sixty Days of Decision." Diefenbaker called it "Sixty Days of Derision." What Diefenbaker saw was not "cooperative federalism" but a surrender to the demands of the Quebec government. He feared one demand would lead to another and that Quebec would never be satisfied until it was a separate country.

Pearson struggled to form his cabinet. When Ontario MP Pauline Jewett made her pitch for a cabinet post, Pearson told her, "But we already have a woman in the cabinet, Judy LaMarsh." Jewett had a PhD from Harvard and was the Director of the Institute of Canadian Studies at Carleton University.[17] But his biggest blunder, perhaps of his entire government, was appointing Walter Gordon as finance minister. The first Liberal budget was tabled more than two months after the General Election, on June 13, 1963. It was as bold as it was fundamentally flawed. Gordon blamed economic drift on Diefenbaker: "The year 1962 was a remarkable one in Canada's economic history. It was marked by an exchange crisis, which followed upon five years of economic stagnation. It was also marked by the adoption of a fixed rate of exchange for the Canadian dollar, an action which was taken three weeks after the government of the day had indicated that it was not its policy to do so." Despite criticizing Diefenbaker, Gordon declared, "I do want to make it clear, however, that this government intends to maintain the fixed exchange rate at its present level." The Liberal promise to bring the dollar back to par with the U.S. buck was abandoned.

The budget's overall theme was nationalism, including a 30 percent tax on the sale of Canadian firms to foreign interests. The stock market tanked in disapproval, falling over six percent in the month the budget was released. Kennedy was equally shocked that American investors would be subject to a punitive, discriminatory, and financially devastating tax.

One media report called the budget a "Canadian financial declaration of independence," and an American journalist was quoted as saying, "This will rock people back home. Diefenbaker talked a lot about Candianizing industries but didn't do anything about it. Now some Americans will be crying about bringing Diefenbaker back again because the Pearson program is going to pinch our toes."[18]

There was a rush to prepare the budget, and it showed. Sloppiness abounded. Diefenbaker called it "the largest monstrosity ever brought before Parliament." This included Gordon relying on "budget whiz-kids" who remained on the payroll of Toronto-based investment houses while they sat at the decision-making tables in the Finance Department. These were the same young guns that helped the Liberal election team craft the platform.[19] Gordon revealed but did not apologize to the House of Commons for the conflict of interest for having Bay Street insiders operating inside the Liberal government.

On the substance of the budget, the president of the Montreal and Canadian stock exchanges said he would tell investors to short Canadian stocks. The takeover tax, its prime feature, was rescinded less than a week after its announcement. Gordon offered his resignation, which Pearson refused to accept. Diefenbaker railed that the government had bypassed the trained public servants and relied on "three novices" to set public policy.

Despite the Liberal inclination to nationalism, it agreed to tariff-free automobile trade with the U.S. in 1964 through the Canada-U.S. Automotive Products Agreement, known as the Auto Pact. The ultimate result was a dramatic rise in employment in the Canadian sector and a decrease in the prices of new cars for consumers. It proved that "Free Trade" with the United States, something both Diefenbaker and Pearson opposed, made economic sense. It was not until the 1988 federal election under Prime Minister Mulroney that Canadians fully endorsed the concept.

When the Liberals introduced a national contributory pension plan—the Canada Pension Plan (CPP)—it was a program that Diefenbaker had previously proposed. His only objection was that it would operate in all provinces but one, with Quebec establishing its plan and fund with investment leanings that bolstered the Quebec economy. Diefenbaker recoiled that one province was not like the other and could opt out of what was otherwise a national program. The Canadian Constitution gave the provinces this power, which Quebec used to its advantage.

***

In June 1964, Tom Kent, a key Pearson advisor, wrote to his boss in unflattering terms: "Your government is weak and disorganized because it depends on you, and you are making it impossible for yourself to be a good Prime Minister."[20] Monitoring the fumbling of the Pearson government kept Diefenbaker engaged and relevant. In his book, *The Duel*, John Ibbitson contends that Diefenbaker was happier in opposition than in government so he could "concentrate on attacking them for their missteps, rather than having to explain his own."

One scandal involved a mob-connected union leader from the United States who was welcomed into Canada by the Liberal government despite an extensive rap sheet that included writing bad cheques, burglary, and murder. Hal Banks had been sentenced to a maximum of 14 years in San Quentin Penitentiary. He came to Canada in 1940 to bust up the Canadian Seamans Union and install the Seafarers International Union as its replacement. Canadian government officials denied Banks' standing in Canada and issued a deportation order. Despite his sordid past, Banks persuaded the Liberal minister in charge to overturn the order. On July 6, 1954, through an order-in-council granted under the powers of the Immigration Act, Banks became a landed immigrant. Then-Citizenship Minister Walter Edward Harris spoke of Banks's "successful rehabilitation."

Bank's ruthless ways had paid off in addressing Canadian union unrest, which pleased the Liberal government. However, a commission of inquiry found that Banks was a "hoodlum" and a "bully." While in Canada, Banks was charged with physical assault. However, he escaped to the United States in 1964 rather than face the Canadian criminal justice system. Efforts to extradite him to Canada were perfunctory and ignored by the American government. What Diefenbaker saw in Banks was "a valued source of Liberal campaign funds and election muscle," someone he called "the pampered pet of the Liberal Party." He alleged that the Canadian government had enabled Bank's exit from Canada to hide how they had been complicit in his dubious undertakings.[21]

While the Bank's affair rocked the Liberal government, it was small potatoes compared with a story that was much easier for the public to follow. Lucien Rivard, a well-known mobster from Montreal, was arrested on June 19, 1964, under a United States warrant for smuggling heroin. Rivard was incarcerated in Montreal's Bordeaux Jail while awaiting an extradition hearing. Efforts were made on Rivard's behalf to prevent the hearing from taking place, including the offer of a $20,000 bribe to the attorney for the United States government if he stated that he did not oppose bail for Rivard.

As it turned out, the bribe was not offered by a fellow mobster but by Raymond Denis, the executive assistant to the Honourable René Tremblay, Canada's minister of immigration. When the bribe was rejected, it was offered to other Liberal political staffers to apply pressure on the American attorney. They were the assistant to the justice minister and Prime Minister Pearson's parliamentary secretary. All of this was reported to the RCMP for investigation.

Erik Nielsen, the Conservative MP for the Yukon, had learned of the brewing scandal and challenged the Liberal front bench in the House of Commons to come clean. As Diefenbaker described it, Nielsen carefully told the story of alleged incompetence and bribery in a narcotics case with the alleged involvement of those closely associated with cabinet ministers and the prime minister. Also, the government was warned that charges would be levelled in the House of Commons, so they should have been ready with the facts. Their first response was that it was a pack of lies, muckraking, and casual smears against senior government officials. The following day, however, Pearson fired his parliamentary secretary. The justice minister agreed with the Opposition's demands to a call for a judicial inquiry, which was headed by Chief Justice Frédéric Dorion of the Quebec Superior Court. While Pearson was initially thought to have responded quickly to the allegations, in the days that followed, he admitted he had known of the scandal months earlier. Diefenbaker said Pearson was trying to "explain the unexplainable, unscrew the inscrutable, and resolve the unresolvable."[22]

The report from Justice Dorion was tabled in the House of Commons on June 29, 1965, with this conclusion:

> Mr. Guy Rouleau tried to use his influence as parliamentary assistant to the Prime Minister to secure the release of Lucien Rivard on bail... an intervention of this sort, particularly coming from a person in authority, certainly constitutes a reprehensible act, because it comes into conflict with the normal course of justice; but it does not constitute an act within which are to be found the elements essential in the perpetration of a criminal act.... There is no doubt that Mr. Letendre's (assistant to Liberal ministers) intervention was reprehensible... this step was taken without malicious intent, the sole purpose of being agreeable to his friend... for whom he wanted to do a favour.

Diefenbaker was perplexed that the only visible response to the damning revelations and an inquiry was a letter that Pearson sent to all his ministers outlining a "code of political conduct." With the attention given to Rivard, it would seem advisable that the government would do all in its power to ensure Rivard was prosecuted to the full extent of the law. That was not to be. While in jail, Rivard was given VIP treatment. Guards reported that Rivard enjoyed a "palace" life where he could roam freely around the prison, watch hockey games on television when he wanted, play high-stakes dice games, listen to the radio, and had a stove to make meals.[23]

On a warm evening in early March, Rivard and another prisoner sought permission to flood the skating rink at the Bordeaux Jail. The rink had already melted. There was six inches of standing water for all to see. Rivard and his accomplice used the hose to scale the prison walls. About three months later, Rivard was recaptured and faced Canadian charges and an extradition order.

The Rivard affair became a Diefenbaker favourite, the gift that kept on giving, As Diefenbaker put it in the House of Commons:

> After all this came the findings of the Dorion Commission, which have left Canadians shocked, whatever their political party may be, that there could be such carryings-on in high places; that international crime and the Mafia had been able to work itself into the higher echelons of government. Now that he has been recaptured, there is a great desire to get him out of the country. They do not want him here before an election. They do not want him to give evidence.[24]

Diefenbaker wanted Chief Justice Dorion's mandate extended and broadened to examine the circumstances of Rivard's escape, hinting at the possibility of further government involvement. An independent investigation was undoubtedly something Diefenbaker would promise in the next election, which, as it turned out, took place later that year. Diefenbaker clarified, "We will get to the bottom of the mess. There will be no pussyfooting... the time has come to outlaw the outlaws in Ottawa."

Diefenbaker did not wait until the election to remind voters of Liberal incompetence or worse. He would say in many hot and steamy community centres that summer, "It was on the night such as this that Rivard went to water the rink." The line, always anticipated, never failed to bring the crowd to its feet.

- 19 -

THE FLAG DEBATE

Neither the Union Jack nor the fleur-de-lis
was a sign of subservience to a colonial past.
There was no colonialism in honouring our history.

No attention was given to the Canadian flag at the time of Confederation. Canada was a colony of Great Britain with no authority over foreign policy. The country's top court was not in Ottawa but in London. Canada's flag was Great Britain's flag. In 1891, Sir John A. Macdonald ran under the banner of "The Old Flag. The Old Policy. The Old Leader." The flag that Sir John carried in the campaign poster was the British Union Jack placed on a simple red background.

It was not until 1945 that Canada could even claim to have an official flag. This was not done by a resolution of the House of Commons but from a cabinet decree, an order-in-council. It came with the caveat that the decree would be valid "until such time as Parliament takes action for the adoption of a national flag." The cabinet-endorsed flag was known as the Canadian Red Ensign, a variation of the same flag that Canadian soldiers had carried during two world wars. It featured the Royal Union flag and a shield divided into four quarters comprising the coats of arms of England, Scotland, Ireland and the Kingdom of France. There was also the Canadian Blue Ensign that continued to be flown by the Royal Canadian Navy. The British admiralty had approved its usage in 1868, as all ships in international waters needed to be flagged to designate the country of registration.

Much has been written about Diefenbaker's opposition to adopting a new flag that ultimately was raised on February 15, 1965. He did not like Pearson's process of legislating a flag without consulting Canadians. And he was not a fan of the ultimate design that lacked a connection with Canadian history.

However, three years earlier, Diefenbaker brought the matter of the flag before his cabinet on April 23, 1962, when he asked his colleagues to support a Dominion-provincial meeting on the matter. In June, while on a three-day election tour of Quebec, Diefenbaker proposed a national conference on a distinctive Canadian flag and national anthem. The matter appeared more officially in the September 27 Speech from the Throne that called for "a significant step in rounding out the concept of Confederation." What was proposed was the "repatriation" of the Constitution of Canada and to "invite the concurrence of the provinces to this end." The throne speech added, "As another means of manifesting the Canadian identity, my government will invite the provinces to a conference for consultation regarding the choice of a national flag and other national symbols."

Globe and Mail editorialists dumped on the idea and thought it took Canada in the wrong direction: "We are not much for flags because we are possibly the least national nation in the world, and it is time we stopped deprecating this state of mind. If the world is to find permanent peace, national boundaries and national symbols must decline in importance; the citizens of nations must be replaced with citizens of the world."[1] This was a sentiment that a youthful Pierre Trudeau would have endorsed. In 1944, he posted a self-made sign on his Harvard University residence door that read, "Citizen of the World." When the flag issue was raised, Trudeau said, "Quebec does not give a tinker's dam about the new flag. It's a matter of complete indifference."

Pearson also spoke of the need for a new flag. In the 1962 and 1963 elections, he proposed that a Liberal government would address the matter early in a mandate. It distressed Diefenbaker that Pearson wanted a flag that had no relationship with Canada's past, with "nothing to indicate our heritage: the greatness of the French régime or the contribution of Great Britain."[2] To Diefenbaker, the Red Ensign honoured Canada's historical ties to the British Empire and the sacrifices made by its soldiers in times of war. He believed the Canadian flag should include a nod to the Union Jack of Great Britain and the fleur-de-lis of France:

> I realized that such a flag would be objected to by some on the grounds that it had the Union Jack thereon and by others who would object to it because it had the fleur-de-lis thereon, but I believed the Canadian people would realize that such a flag would be most acceptable in the interests of Canadian unity. Neither the Union Jack nor the fleur-de-lis was a sign of subservience to a colonial past. There was no colonialism in honouring our history.

While Diefenbaker wanted the Union Jack represented on the flag, his Conservative MPs from Quebec were adamantly opposed. These MPs also told Diefenbaker that the fleur-de-lis was unimportant in Quebec. Diefenbaker could not persuade his caucus, let alone the country, of his views. To charges that he was obstructing Liberal intentions, Diefenbaker responded that Pearson had not even consulted him before the formal process to adopt a new flag was launched. On May 17, 1964, Pearson announced at a Royal Canadian Legion Convention of 2,000 delegates in Winnipeg that Canada would have a new flag. Most of those in attendance were wearing Canadian Red Ensign pins. Pearson asked delegates to rally around a symbol that indicated pride in the nation that would inspire all Canadians, and not just those of British descent:

> It's quite clear tonight that there are others who disagree strongly, honestly and deeply with me... I believe most sincerely that it is time now for Canadians, in the course of our national evolution, to unfurl a flag that is truly distinctive and truly national in character, as Canadian as the Maple Leaf on your badge; a flag identified as Canada's; a flag which cannot be mistaken for the emblem of any other country; a flag of the future which honours also the past; Canada's own and only Canada's.[3]

Accompanying Pearson on the trip was John Matheson, the Liberal MP for Leeds in eastern Ontario. Matheson, who was wounded in the Second World War and was a member of the Heraldry Society of England, would play a critical role in the flag's design.

Diefenbaker was alarmed at the development and charged that Pearson's action on the flag had "caused to this nation cleavages and fissures and separations that more than a generation of people will come to recall."[4] In August 1964, Diefenbaker said he was open to a compromise on the flag and that a committee of the House of Commons should consider the matter. Diefenbaker also expected committee members to return to their ridings and consult with constituents. While Diefenbaker wanted to give the committee months to do its work, Pearson preferred to provide it with a few weeks.

On August 21, Pearson said that it would not be a partisan issue and that MPs would be "free" to vote their conscience on the matter. Diefenbaker preferred to settle the matter in a national referendum rather than a vote of parliamentarians.

Pearson's preferred design featured two horizontal blue bands, top and bottom, with three maple leaves on a white background in the middle. That design was modified to make the blue bars vertical to signify that Canada was situated between the Atlantic and Pacific oceans. This became known as the "Pearson pennant." He had quietly indicated his preferred design to selected journalists, which Diefenbaker charged was evidence that the work of parliamentarians was a sham and the outcome had been pre-determined.

While Pearson saw adopting a new flag as a unifying force for all Canadians, with a particular emphasis on French Canadians who were disinclined to rally around the Union Jack or new Canadians with no British or French ancestry, the debate on the flag itself was highly divisive. "To tamper with our traditional flag—the Canadian Ensign," wrote the editors of the *Toronto Telegram*, "was at this time mischievous and dangerous,"

The debate in the House of Commons on a new Canadian flag was launched on June 15, 1964, asking Parliament to:

> Establish officially as the flag of Canada a flag embodying the emblem proclaimed by His Majesty King George V on November 21—three maple leaves conjoined on one stem—in the colours red and white then designated for Canada, the red leaves occupying a field of white between sections of blue on the edges of the flag and also provide that the royal union flag, generally known as the Union Jack, may continue to be flown as a symbol of Canadian membership in the Commonwealth of Nations and our Allegiance to the Crown.

Permitting the flying of the old Red Ensign flag on designated occasions may have been a nod to history and tradition, but it was more likely done to mollify the traditionalists as an exercise in change management.

As a minority government with a free vote on offer, the Liberals needed support from the other parties in the House of Commons. When the debate began, no other party was onside with Pearson. Ultimately, by September, the question was referred to a committee of 15 MPs. The committee comprised seven Liberals, including its chair, John Matheson. While Matheson supported Pearson's design, an independent historian from the Royal Military College, George Stanley, persuaded him of the virtue of simplicity and that a single maple leaf was better than three. It also had the benefit of being stylized after the Royal Military College flag.

While almost 6,000 designs were submitted by Canadians for Parliament to consider, the committee had three designs before them by October. First was a Union Jack and Fleur-de-lys combination that Diefenbaker preferred, a three-maple-leaf design that was Pearson's choice, and a simple white and red flag featuring a single maple leaf. One professional artist, A.J. Casson, from the Group of Seven, was unimpressed with the single leaf design, remarking that it looked like some 6-year-old's kindergarten project.[5]

The Conservative committee members were not simply tasked with choosing a preferred design. Instead, they wanted a divided committee to undermine the prime minister's desire for a speedy resolution. Believing the Liberals would select Pearson's three-leaf preference, Conservatives voted for the single maple leaf design. Unknown to them, this was Matheson's preference as well. At that point, Pearson was more concerned about unity than design choice and was prepared to compromise. When the votes were tallied, the single-leaf design was the unanimous choice. That was before four Conservatives changed their mind to avoid a unanimous recommendation. Diefenbaker was unhappy with the turn of events and dismissed the proposed flag as one that Peruvians would salute, given its similarity.

Parliamentary debate ensued. After about two weeks, with no end in sight, a Conservative MP from Quebec, Léon Balcer, Diefenbaker's seatmate in the House of Commons who was the party's deputy leader and Quebec lieutenant, urged the government to invoke closure, to force the end of debate, a measure supported by the Social Credit leader from Quebec. The Conservative House Leader rose to say that Balcer was not speaking on behalf of the Conservative caucus.[6] Any notion that Balcer was Diefenbaker's "Quebec lieutenant" had vanished.

On principle, Diefenbaker would have preferred a Parliament where closure did not exist.[a] Balcer and seven other Conservative MPs from Quebec voted

a It was particularly offensive when it was proposed from his front bench. He liked to tell the story of a Liberal MP from Quebec, David Arthur Lafortune, when at 14 hours and ten minutes of his remarks, said, "I now have laid the basis for the argument I intend to advance." Not wanting to compliment a Liberal, he noted that it took Grits more time to explain their point of view, but they should not be restricted from speaking because of time limitations.

against Diefenbaker's wishes and endorsed the new flag.[7] Whether this was a vote on policy or a matter of conscience remained an open question. "I always made it clear in caucus that on matters of principle, we had to stand together," Diefenbaker wrote in his memoirs. "But when a member felt he could not conscientiously support a measure, he was entitled to do as he pleased, providing he gave the Whip advance warning." But Balcer never tested Diefenbaker on the question. He chose to leave the Conservative caucus to sit as an independent MP. The closure motion passed by a vote of 152 to 85. The flag we know today was adopted by a vote of 163 to 78 on December 17, 1964, at 2:15 A.M.

Tempers flared on Parliament Hill the next day when Progressive Conservative MP Bob Coates and Liberal MP George McIlraith got into a shouting match in a crowded elevator over the flag debate. Future prime minister Jean Chrétien jumped into the fray, grabbed Coates by the lapels of his suit jacket and pushed him up against a wall.[8]

Diefenbaker undermined the credibility of the debate and the outcome, calling it a "flag of closure." In a comment that has not aged well and was even then a clear exaggeration, Diefenbaker thundered to Pearson, "You have done more to divide the country than any other prime minister." What was not in doubt was that the flag debate and Diefenbaker's adherence to the British tradition had divided his caucus. In addition to Balcer, several Quebec MPs from the Progressive Conservative caucus left the party. Diefenbaker said he was not impressed by a "clique" or a "claque." Balcer was never again a candidate for the Progressive Conservative party.

On February 15, 1965, the flag was raised for the first time on the grounds of Parliament Hill. Diefenbaker was present to observe the event, and a photo of him in newspapers the day following showed a tear flowing down his cheek.[9] Never one to forget a battle, when Diefenbaker died in 1979, his coffin was draped with two flags: the Maple Leaf and the Red Ensign. It was Diefenbaker's message to Canadians of the importance of preserving the past while accepting what Parliament had determined.[b]

---

b February 15 is celebrated each year as Flag Day in Canada. No anniversary was more memorable than in 1996 when Prime Minister Chrétien marked the occasion with a group of schoolchildren before being obstructed by belligerent protestors. Chrétien grabbed one of the agitators by the throat and threw him to the ground in a maneuver now known as the "Shawinigan Handshake."

Canadians quickly forgot the heated debate, and the new flag was widely embraced. The enduring response was not what Diefenbaker had predicted; that Pearson's decision "would leave cleavages and fissures and separations that more than a generation of people will come to recall." The flag became what Diefenbaker aspired it to be: a source of unity, inspiration and Canadian independence. Canadians of all ethnicities and regions accepted it. The flag debate is thus noteworthy and forever tied to Diefenbaker, but mainly for the wrong reasons and negatively: the debate left Diefenbaker and the Progressive Conservative party damaged and divided.

THE FINAL ACT

- 20 -

ONE LAST SHOT

Regularly, the pundits and prophets have predicted my demise. I allow the pundits and prophets to enjoy themselves while I continue to serve the Canadian people. There were times when the prognosticators said there was no hope. I knew differently.

The flag debate and defection of Quebec MPs depleted Diefenbaker's standing and the strength of the Progressive Conservative party across Canada. While MPs like Dr. Lawrence E. Kindt of Macleod, Alberta, urged Diefenbaker to continue the fight, the Chief understood that the efforts of Léon Balcer and other former ministers to oust him as leader had been damaging.

> In all, the experience left me depressed. I brooded on the situation and came finally to the conclusion that I would resign as leader. I decided that I simply had had enough. Over several days, I drafted the letter announcing my decision. This I would give to caucus, to the National Executive, and to the press on 22 March 1965. On Sunday, 14 March, I invited a few close friends and trusted colleagues to Stornoway to inform them of my decision.[1]

An uninvited MP arrived at Stornoway and assured Diefenbaker that everything he heard would be kept in strict confidence. Instead, the interloper seized on the news that Diefenbaker was stepping down and began an immediate campaign to secure the position of the party's interim leader. The betrayal and the shadow campaign that began before Diefenbaker was allowed to resign incensed him. "I was so aroused by the necessity of denying to the press my decision to retire," Diefenbaker wrote in his memoirs, "that I decided not to retire." It was an impetuous decision by Diefenbaker in response to an untimely leak of no national consequence. But it was not just the personal slight that motivated Diefenbaker to continue to fight on:

> That year, I celebrated my seventieth birthday. At an age when most men had turned their thoughts to the quiet joys of retirement, why didn't I? The answer is simply that I had fought a lifetime to bring substance to my *One Canada* dream. Everything that my government had achieved in equalizing the opportunities for all Canadians in every section of this nation was being imperilled by the policies of the Pearson government and by the hostility of powerful interests within the Conservative Party, who did not want these changes entrenched. I was portrayed as a dangerous man for staying on to fight for all our rights.[2]

Diefenbaker thought the country was going in the wrong direction and was reckless in responding to emerging nationalist and even separatist threats emanating from the province of Quebec. He was a firm detractor of the "Deux Nations" theory of Canada and Confederation. He opposed any notion of "special status" for one province over another or that any Canadian province was a state within a state. He thought back to the battles that Macdonald waged in placing as much power as possible in the hands of the federal government to avoid the strife that had brought America into a bloody and catastrophic Civil War that was fought not just over the matter of slavery, but state rights.

However, Macdonald and Diefenbaker held different views regarding Quebec's place in Canada. Macdonald thought of Confederation as a partnership—even a marriage—that joined together British North American colonies. He saw the coming together of British colonies as necessary to withstand American manifest destiny and a claim to Canadian territory. Macdonald understood that the precursor to Confederation was the divorce of Upper and Lower Canada, which struggled to govern English and French in the same legislature. When Lord Durham was asked to explore the Rebellions in Upper and Lower Canada in 1837 and 1838, he expected to find a conflict between the government and the people. But instead, he discovered two warring nations within a single state, a struggle not of principles but of races.

In 1841, Canada East (mostly Quebec) and Canada West (mostly Ontario) became the Province of Canada in a single legislature where Macdonald served.

While the populations differed, both sides of the legislature held the same number of seats. Legislation required a "double majority," which meant a plurality of votes from each of Canada East and Canada West. It made for a dysfunctional marriage.

Macdonald lambasted the anglophone attitude towards the French in Canada East: "The truth is that you British Lower Canadians never can forget that you were once supreme—that Jean Baptiste was your hewer of wood and drawer of water." Macdonald believed any attempt to assimilate or dominate the French was pointless and ignored reality: "No man in his senses can suppose that this country can, for a century to come, be governed by a totally unfrenchified government. If a Lower Canadian Britisher desires to conquer, he must 'stoop to conquer.'"

Macdonald's moderate and respectful views enabled him to build bridges with French Canadians. Ahead of his time, he was perhaps the first English politician to recognize the French people of Quebec as a nation: "(We) must make friends with the French, without sacrificing the status of his race or religion or language (we) must respect their nationality. Treat them as a nation and they will act as a free people generally do—generously. Call them a faction and they become factious." Presciently, Macdonald foretold how French Canadians would react when threatened:

> Supposing the numerical preponderance of British in Canada becomes much greater than it is, I think the French would give more trouble than they are said now to do. At present, they divide as we do, they are split up into several sections, and they are governed by more or less defined principles of action. As they become smaller and feebler, so they will be more united; from a sense of self-preservation, they will act as one man and hold the balance of power.

Macdonald and his nemesis in Parliament, George Brown, agreed on Confederation for different reasons. To Brown, Confederation was a way to segregate Canada West and Canada East and achieve representation by population, with a diminished influence by the French over Canada West. Macdonald disagreed with Brown's intent to isolate the French but agreed with the design.

In Canada West, George Brown triumphantly declared, "constitution adopted—a most credible document—a complete reform of all the abuses and injustices we have complained of. Is it not wonderful?" In Canada East, Quebecers viewed Confederation as a framework allowing them to control their destiny. Editors at *La Minerve,* a newspaper closely aligned with the Tories, proclaimed, "As a distinct and separate nationality, we form a state within a state. We enjoy the full exercise of our rights and the formal recognition of our national independence. In giving ourselves a complete government, we affirm our existence as a separate nationality."

These two views embody the question of Canada as an equal partnership of individual and equal provinces or a compact that kept French Quebec in Canada. The British North America Act did not create Canada in isolation or as an abstract idea. It begins with the pedestrian phrase, "Whereas the Provinces...", unlike the poetry of the American Constitution that begins with, "We the People, in Order to form a more perfect Union."

***

Diefenbaker understood that he was "portrayed as the instrument of an English-Canadian backlash, an anachronistic bigot who had missed the wave of the future." None of this bothered him. He sympathized with the concern of French Canadians, who feared the loss of their identity through assimilation and absorption into the English-Canadian and American cultures, and felt that their fears were justified in their belief because they were denied a fair share of the economic gains enjoyed in other regions. Diefenbaker contended that:

> Quebec could gain within the Confederation what it was impossible to achieve outside it. The separation of Quebec would not change the fact of Quebec's cultural bombardment by the industrial society of North America, of which Quebec was and would remain a part. My idea was that without Confederation, there would be neither Canada nor French Canada.[3]

Taken to its natural conclusion, Diefenbaker believed that the "two nations" theory would isolate Quebec and ultimately lead to its separation from Canada. When the Pearson government, according to Diefenbaker, abdicated federal leadership, the Lesage government in Quebec filled the resultant vacuum.[4] Diefenbaker opposed the creation of the Royal Commission on Bilingualism and Biculturalism, which Pearson established on July 19, 1963:

> I was convinced that its appointment and composition would encourage alienation and separatism. To begin with, the problems of biculturalism and bilingualism were both federal and provincial. This Royal Commission could only make recommendations to the federal government. As I could not conceive of any party attempting to solve the problems of national unity through unilateral federal action.... I thought the Commission, at best, a dodge.
>
> At worst, I saw it giving rise to a popular false hope that solutions to the problems of Confederation would be achieved through a Commission of socialists and outspoken protagonists of particular constitutional changes. The only legitimate forum was a Dominion-Provincial Conference.[5]

Pearson created the commission in response to rising Quebec nationalism. Under the rubric of "equal partnership," the commission had three primary missions: bilingualism in the federal government, the role of public and private organizations in promoting better cultural relations, and opportunities for Canadians to become bilingual. In a preliminary 1965 report, the commissioners concluded that Canada was experiencing a national unity crisis and that the "two founding Peoples" justified establishing English and French as Canada's official languages.

While in Quebec, Diefenbaker refuted the charge by Liberals that he was anti-French because he believed in the equality of provinces rather than the two-nations view of the country:

> I was pictured in Quebec as your enemy, but I was always your greatest friend. Nothing matters more to me than the unity of this nation. Nothing means more to any Canadian than that. I don't come to you in 1965 and say, 'Today I have certain views.' I have always held these views....

> When I read these attacks upon me, I wonder whether we are living in a democracy or not.... [T]he Honourable Bona Arsenault (Quebec Liberal MNA) described me as 'worse than the atomic bomb, cholera and rats.' Let us have a constitution made in Canada for Canadians and by Canadians. Canadians in every province want to have you; they want you to be in this nation. They want you to have equal partnership. We must join hands in equality.[6]

One of the most shocking aspects of Diefenbaker's 30-minute speech was that it was delivered entirely in French. Most Canadians had not heard Diefenbaker speak French and assumed he could not speak the language. The media called the remarks "le miracle de Ste. Perpétue."

Diefenbaker wanted to make Liberal wrongdoing and Pearson's weak leadership the defining issues in the next election. "The Prime Minister talks of a majority, and I believe in majorities, but if the present government had a majority, would the truth ever come out? Instead of condemning wrongdoing, they will not talk about it.... [T]he Prime Minister's attitude is that of the three monkeys: see no evil, speak no evil, and if you hear any evil, forget it."

Pearson was not initially inclined to call an election in 1965. His parliamentary secretary, Jean Chrétien, advised against it. But the logic of going to the polls was compelling. The economy was strong, unemployment was low, the budget was essentially in balance, and Diefenbaker was yesterday's man, even within his party—which made a snap election more tempting. Pearson's inner circle pressed hard to go after a majority while the polls were favourable. Had they waited much longer, the odds of facing a different Tory leader would have increased, and they wanted one last kick at the 70-year-old Diefenbaker before his party would be good and done with him.

With the blessing of his cabinet, Pearson had Parliament dissolved on September 8 for an election on November 8. However, the Liberals had no clear issue to take to the people other than their desire to win a majority government. Diefenbaker was older but had not lost form. When the Liberals could not define the campaign, he did it for them with sarcasm: "Throw the bums in—scandals included," Diefenbaker cautioned voters. He said the Liberal code of conduct was, "Be good. And if you can't be good, be careful."[7] With a Liberal majority, he alleged the malfeasance would be well-hidden. Diefenbaker campaigned less to win than to hold the Liberals in check. "We shall get to the bottom of this and assure Canadians that the cobwebs of the Mafia, the wrongdoings of the narcotics peddlers and the corruption of public officials does not make a way of life."[8]

Diefenbaker went into the 1965 campaign with little, if any, organizational support. Communication between headquarters and the leader was nonexistent, and tension within the party ran high. In an account by Peter C. Newman, there was a prediction that if Diefenbaker won, "there'll be the biggest political bloodbath this country has ever seen... (and) the entire Tory headquarters crew would join hands and leap off the roof of the Chateau Laurier."[9]

Diefenbaker sought to quell internal dissent by welcoming back those who had questioned his leadership. This included the candidacies of those who had served with him in Parliament, such as George Hees, Davie Fulton, Richard Bell, Frank McGee, Douglas Harkness, and Paul Martineau. He encouraged Dalton Camp and George Hogan to run in Toronto area ridings. He accepted the support of Pierre Sévigny and Egan Chambers in Montreal. He appointed Eddie Goodman as national campaign director, who had been part of a cabal seeking Diefenbaker's resignation in 1963.

The campaign was run under the Diefenbaker name, but the slogan was a generic "Policies for People—Policies for Progress." At its core, it was a continuation of the policies and programs that Diefenbaker had pursued as prime minister. This included a commitment to medicare, which gained ground following the Royal Commission on Health Service launched by Diefenbaker on June 20, 1961, under Supreme Court Justice Emmett M. Hall. While Diefenbaker's government had delivered hospital insurance to Canadians, Hall's report, completed in 1964, called for a broad, universal health-care system. He called human health a societal obligation and a sound economic investment in human capital. Diefenbaker's proposal in 1965 was a national health insurance plan to cover all sicknesses, including mental illness.

Diefenbaker proposed the doubling of university grants to help lower tuition fees. An unconventional measure would allow a tax deduction for the payment of municipal taxes of up to five hundred dollars. Building on his record as prime minister, Diefenbaker proposed increasing old age pensions to one hundred dollars a month without a means test. Another attempt at vote buying was a pledge to enact consumer loan legislation to reduce interest paid on instalment buying, which studies showed had risen to usurious interest rates of up to 30 percent.

But this was not a policy-driven or ideas campaign. As in most contests, it came down to leadership and the connection that either Diefenbaker or Pearson could make with ordinary Canadians. Despite his age, his struggles in Quebec, and the battles over his leadership from within the ranks of the Conservative party, Diefenbaker remained a great campaigner. He was a draw at rallies, often requiring overflow space to accommodate the thousands of Canadians who wanted to hear him speak.

Even Quebecers turned out in numbers, with over 4,000 people attending a rally in the Maurice Richard Arena in Montreal on November 3. This compared with just over a thousand people who had attended a Pearson rally the night before. Diefenbaker ignored a death threat to greet supporters at a packed Edmonton Jubilee Auditorium. At Toronto's Varsity Arena, it was standing-room only, leaving thousands in an overflow area outside the stadium.

Despite being his fifth election as party leader, Diefenbaker was energized and enjoyed poking fun at Pearson. On October 28, Pearson made the pitch for a majority government and said that if he were returned with a minority, there would be another election in a year to 18 months. When the media asked Pearson to elaborate on the statement, he denied he had ever said such a thing. When confronted with a recording of his remarks, he stumbled and said he didn't mean what he had appeared to say. Diefenbaker offered his translation to the amusement of the media and his audiences by mimicking Pearson: "I didn't say what I said when I said it. What I meant to say, when I didn't say it, was that I wouldn't have said what I said, when I did say it."[10]

While Diefenbaker's tour was a roaring success, not all was well at campaign headquarters. Diefenbaker complained that his instructions were ignored and blamed Eddie Goodman, who had reluctantly been appointed campaign director, and Flora MacDonald, a confidante of Dalton Camp, another Diefenbaker detractor. On election night, when it became clear that the 1965 Parliament had not changed much, Diefenbaker chastised the media:

> Regularly, the pundits and prophets have predicted my demise. I allow the pundits and prophets to enjoy themselves while I continue to serve the Canadian people. There were times when the prognosticators said there was no hope. I knew differently. I approached the future in the same spirit I had followed: my country always first, my Canada, your Canada.[11]

The Liberals picked up three seats to stand at 131, lost 1.3 percentage points of the popular vote, and returned with a minority government. The Tories gained four seats to arrive at Parliament with 97 in total. Diefenbaker believed his party was stronger after the election and that no other party represented all parts of Canada so widely. The Liberal party had one MP from Manitoba and none in Saskatchewan, Alberta, or Prince Edward Island. Outside of Quebec, Diefenbaker held 14 more seats than the Liberals. If there was a loser beyond Pearson in the 1965 election, it was the Social Credit party that had split into two factions, English and French, and surrendered ten seats.

Pearson held government but was dispirited: "I had never been so depressed in my political life," Pearson wrote in his memoirs. "We had gone through it all for nothing." He offered to resign as leader, which his caucus rejected. The campaign director, Keith Davey, took the fall only temporarily. Pearson soon appointed him to the Senate at the age of 39.

Diefenbaker and Pearson were damaged by their inability to move their parties forward. But in defying expectations, Diefenbaker looked and felt like he had won the 1965 election. It would make the Chief even more reluctant to let a new generation and a new leader take charge so long as Pearson was sitting in the prime minister's chair.

- 21 -

A VERY TORY SEX SCANDAL

A diplomat is a person who lies away from home.
You are no diplomat.

After losing the 1963 and 1965 elections, most observers thought Diefenbaker's days as Tory leader were numbered. While looking over his shoulder for fire from within his ranks, he did not take his eyes off Pearson and the missteps of the Liberal government.

On March 4, 1966, Liberal Justice Minister Lucien Cardin announced that a postal worker, George Victor Spencer, had been accused of spying for the Russians and had been dismissed. Although charges were not laid, the government rescinded Spencer's pension. Diefenbaker demanded an inquiry. When Diefenbaker asserted Cardin mishandled a national security file, the Liberal minister pointed his finger at the leader of the Opposition. "He is the very last person in the House who can afford to give advice on the handling of security cases in Canada... and I'm not kidding... I want the right honourable gentleman to tell the house about his participation in the Monseignor (sic) case when he was prime minister of this country."

Whether Cardin's revelation was planned, spontaneous, or an error of judgment, the hint of a sex scandal rocked the House of Commons and the parliamentary press gallery. It became a much more exciting scandal when it emerged Diefenbaker's onetime associate minister of defence, Pierre Sévigny, was involved with a German woman in 1960. But it was not a woman named Monseignor, as Cardin noted in the House of Commons, but Gerda Munsinger.

In 1952, Gerda Heseler married Michael Munsinger, a U.S. serviceman stationed in Germany. She told reporters that she had been a European refugee. After being denied immigrant status by the United States, she landed in Montreal, where she cleaned homes for a living. But before being accepted as a refugee, she had to overcome a past that included being a convicted prostitute and thief. What dramatized the affair was that Munsinger had been connected to a minor Russian intelligence officer. After settling in Canada, she acknowledged encountering Sévigny and a second Canadian cabinet minister, George Hees.

The affair between Sévigny and Munsinger began in 1959. Sévigny, a war hero, denied the affair when it was first raised in the House of Commons, but he later acknowledged his love interest. Sévigny's side of the story was simple: "What happened between us is what happens between a beautiful woman who likes a man and a man who likes a beautiful woman, and that's all." While state secrets were not revealed, a Sévigny staffer made calls to support Munsinger's citizenship application. Believing the matter should never have been raised publicly, Sévigny called Cardin a "despicable, rotten, little politician."

Diefenbaker had been informed of Sévigny's affair with Munsinger by his justice minister, Davie Fulton in December 1960 based on files held by the RCMP. Diefenbaker summoned his associate minister of national defence and demanded answers. Without moralizing, he asked his minister, "What in the hell did you do?" Diefenbaker secured a commitment that the liaison be terminated. Satisfied that his minister had not revealed state secrets, Diefenbaker kept Sévigny in his cabinet. The prime minister was not judgmental towards his minister's sexual conduct except to the extent it represented a potential risk to Canada's national security interests. He was sensitive to the personal upheaval that a revelation of the affair would have on Sévigny and his government.

Pearson, tired of being on the defensive, wrote a chilling letter to Diefenbaker on December 4, 1964, inquiring about the former prime minister's steps to protect Canada's national security when he was made aware that one of his cabinet ministers was associated with Munsinger:

> I have been greatly disturbed by the lack of attention which, insofar as the file indicates, this matter received. This minister was left in a position of trust. In order to assess the need for corrective action, I have asked for a full report of instances in the last ten years or so in which political intervention was involved in investigations. This information will enable me to see how such matters could and should be dealt with. I have decided that I cannot, in the public interest, let the matter lie where it was left and that I must ask the R.C.M. Police to pursue further enquiries.

> I recognize that the file before me may not disclose all the steps that were taken. In view of this, it is my duty to write to you about the matter in case you might be in a position to let me know that the enquiries that were pursued and the safeguards that were taken reached further than the material before me would indicate. That material now indicates that the Minister of Justice brought the matter to your attention and that no action was taken. Because national security is involved, this is the most serious and disturbing of the matters that have been brought to my attention.

Pearson went on to indicate that he would use the incident as the rationale for conducting a sweeping review of the entire Diefenbaker administration's conduct, an unprecedented and chilling political intrusion into the conduct of a predecessor government. Pearson had, in effect, politicized the RCMP:

> But I assure you [Diefenbaker] that all incidents during the last ten years are being thoroughly examined and will be followed up without fear or favour if and when the evidence requires it. If there is further information you can provide about the Munsinger case, I will be grateful if you will let me know.

The letter was a not-so-thinly veiled threat: keep up the attacks on Liberal ministers, and the Munsinger affair would be brought out into the open. It was political blackmail designed to silence the government's official Opposition. Pearson's judgement was clouded by Diefenbaker, a man he not only held in contempt but considered evil.

On December 11, Diefenbaker met Pearson at the prime minister's East Block office. Diefenbaker told Pearson that he would agree that "a full examination should be made regarding political intervention in the operation of the law and that any investigation that he chose to have made by the RCMP would, of course, be welcomed." Diefenbaker assured Pearson that he was unaware of any incident that compromised Canada's national security interests, and he did not take kindly to any "attempt to blackmail Her Majesty's Loyal Opposition into silence on the scandals rocking his government." Pearson rose from his chair, approached Diefenbaker, and said, "We should not talk to each other like this, John." Diefenbaker responded, "I didn't write the letter that you sent me, Mike.

And neither did you." Clearly, in the uncomfortable position of being directly challenged, Pearson added, "You know I am not a politician, I am a diplomat," to which Diefenbaker replied, "A diplomat is a person who lies away from home. You are no diplomat."[1]

Cardin held a press conference and went public with specific accusations about Diefenbaker's handling of the Munsinger affair. He claimed that Munsinger had died, although it took intrepid reporter Robert Reguly of the *Toronto Star* only a few days to find her alive and well, living in Munich, Germany, running a coffee shop.

Diefenbaker had chastised but did not fire his minister. The RCMP officers who listened to Munsinger's wiretaps found humour in the noise that was made when Cardin's wooden leg hit the floor at some inevitable point during his encounters with Munsinger. There was also press coverage that Munsinger had an affair with another Diefenbaker cabinet minister, George Hees. Munsinger told reporters that she had only had lunches with Hees.

The *Globe and Mail* labelled the ensuing public inquiry headed by Supreme Court Justice Wishart Spence as an unprecedented, "vague, vengeful... witch-hunt." Spence confirmed the breadth of his work when he wrote, "Not only did I study the details of this case... but I examined other security cases in the last ten years, certain cases which were of very direct and immediate concern to the government of the day, which was the government preceding this government."

Diefenbaker, who refused to testify before the two-month inquiry, noted that Justice Spence had a solid Liberal background before his appointment and was a friend of the Honourable Paul Martin, Pearson's secretary of state for external affairs. Diefenbaker added that other Supreme Court judges had refused to lead the commission as they considered the inquiry politically inspired.

In the end, the inquiry headed by Justice Spence drew damning conclusions about the conduct of Diefenbaker and his ministers in the Munsinger affair. Spence concluded that there was not a "scintilla of evidence or any indication that there was any disloyalty involved." However, he determined Sévigny was nonetheless unsuitable "to hold any portfolio in the Cabinet, let alone the most sensitive one of Associate Minister of National Defence."[2] Spence concluded that George Hees's conduct related to Gerda Munsinger was "slight but regrettable."

As to Diefenbaker, Spence ruled that as prime minister, he had taken the matter too lightly and should have fired Sévigny and pursued the matter more diligently as soon as he was aware of the indiscretion. Spence did not comment that Pearson knew of the Munsinger affair two years before Cardin revealed the matter in the heat of a parliamentary debate and only asked for an inquiry when the issue was inadvertently exposed and became a potent political weapon to use against the charging Leader of the Opposition.

The affair was not sufficiently objectionable to preclude Sévigny from being appointed to the Order of Canada in 1994. Cardin ultimately regretted raising the matter in the House of Commons: "All that came of it was sorrow and pain to many people." As far as Diefenbaker was concerned, he concluded the commission report gave Dalton Camp "the edge he needed in his new campaign to force me out as leader of the Conservative Party."[3]

- 22 -

1966: THE LEADERSHIP REVIEW

It's time that French Canada started opting in rather than opting out. I was criticized for being too much concerned with the average Canadian. I can't help that; I'm one of them.

On May 19, 1966, Dalton Camp, after failing to win a seat in the 1965 election, returned to his duties as national president of the Progressive Conservative party. He had one goal: to ditch John Diefenbaker as leader. The "dump Dief" movement sought to weaken him by neglect and disrespect. At a fall meeting of the Ontario wing of the party, a group of young Tory activists took prime seating at a speaking venue and were told to sit on their hands during Diefenbaker's speech.[1]

On September 20, 1966, Camp spoke at a private meeting at Toronto's Albany Club, an elite backroom of the Tory Party, if there ever was one, and called for a leadership review. He delivered a similar speech soon after at the Toronto Board of Trade. Camp was laying the groundwork leading up to the Conservative party convention scheduled for November of that year.

Gordon Churchill, who had served Diefenbaker in several portfolios, called for Camp to resign for having failed to honour his duty as party president:

> Your immediate resignation as national president should be submitted to the national executive. You have flagrantly abused the privilege of your position in making a public attack on our Leader. You have no authority from the membership at large for your action. For a national president to attempt to undermine and disrupt his party under the specious guise of attacking the leadership of the Liberal party as well is too obvious a subterfuge. As a private member of the Party, you may

> speak your mind as you see fit. As national president, you have a duty to strengthen the Party, not weaken it. You have taken advantage of your temporary position in a manner that admits no excuse or explanation. Your resignation should be made effective today.[2]

When Diefenbaker addressed the November convention, he was uncharacteristically unaware of the scheme that was in place to take him down. Instructions had been widely circulated to the "dump Dief" delegates not to stand when he entered the room, not to applaud his speech, to heckle and boo him frequently, and to offer no ovation after his remarks. Conversely, when Dalton Camp was at the podium, the instructions read that he should receive a rousing ovation and shouts of "Go, Camp, Go." And at the stage, though Camp's resolution offered "full-hearted appreciation of his universally recognized services to the party," the preamble in his remarks made it clear that Diefenbaker had no future as party leader:

> Leaders are fond of reminding followers of their responsibilities and duties to leadership.... What is seldom heard, however, is a statement on the responsibilities of the leader to those he leads... The leader should give at least as much loyalty to his followers as he demands from them. This is not personal loyalty but rather loyalty to the party, to its continuing strength, best interests, and well-being. Where the leader does not know the limits of his power, he must be taught, and when he is indifferent to the interest of his party, he must be reminded.

Diefenbaker experienced in real time how the convention deck had been stacked against him when he appeared on the rostrum, and there was no podium for him to place his notes. As Diefenbaker gave an account of the party's standing, he could barely be heard over the jeers that urged him to shut up and sit down. In anger, he said he would not turn the Conservative party over to the forces of reaction and inaction. Perhaps tone deaf, but wanting to highlight the hypocrisy on display, he quoted all the great things that Camp had said about him the year before. This only intensified the booing. "Is this a Conservative meeting?" Diefenbaker asked the crowd. "I've had years in the service of this party and this country." The heckle in response was, "Too many."

Diefenbaker had support in caucus, but he lost the rank and file in the party, at least of those elected as delegates to national meetings. Those delegates included Brian Mulroney, who got a bloody nose after a Conservative MP from the Gaspé in Quebec took a swing at him in the jostling on the convention floor.[3] Mulroney's view was the party needed a change at the top.

Diefenbaker saw the uprising as an attempt at his ouster and the middle innings of a campaign that would have him replaced by Dalton Camp. But Camp's tactics had been too bold and brazen, even for those who had little sympathy for Diefenbaker. The President of the Winnipeg North Conservative Association addressed the convention and said the Conservative party had nothing without loyalty.

Arthur Maloney, a Tory MP from 1957 to 1962, told delegates that when the leader of his party enters the room, "Arthur Maloney stands up." Camp would achieve his first objective of undermining Diefenbaker's leadership, but his blatant disloyalty killed any leadership ambitions he may have held. Camp retained his presidency by a vote of 564 to 502. Flora MacDonald, whom Diefenbaker had fired from national party headquarters because of her allegiance to Camp, was elected national secretary.

The Annual Meeting passed a resolution on November 16 by a vote of 563 to 186, calling for a leadership convention before January 1968, which, as it turned out, took place in September 1967. Diefenbaker had wanted the matter settled earlier to remove uncertainty and to focus the party's energies on the Liberals in the House of Commons. Diefenbaker offered no clues on his intentions but wrote in his memoirs that he had "absolutely no plan of running to succeed myself." He wanted to see if those who put their name forward to lead the party shared the fundamentals of his vision of a strong federal government. "Had any one of them done so to him, I might have been able to give my blessing. But in every case, while protesting care and concern about national unity, there was nothing but promises to give more and more to the provinces."[4]

Thus, Diefenbaker had a renewed purpose and a cause to take to the September 1967 convention, where his fate would be settled once and for all. In what was a suicide mission, Diefenbaker let his name stand for leadership. He wanted his views to be heard after the party, at a "thinkers' conference," had adopted a resolution supporting the two nations theory of Canada. Diefenbaker, somewhat detached from historical accuracy, said, "This was the absolute reverse of everything I had stood for in life, and the reverse of everything the Conservative party had stood for, from Macdonald to me." For Diefenbaker, the two nations theory excluded people like him. "When you talk about special status and two nations, that proposition will place all Canadians who are of other racial origins than English and French in a secondary position. All through my life, one of the things I've tried to do is to bring about in this nation citizenship not dependent on race or colour, blood counts or origin."

In a keynote address, convention co-chair and Member of Parliament Roger Regimbal paid tribute to Diefenbaker in what would typically be said of a retiring leader:

> Our country has been blessed with some great Canadians, and some great leaders, The man who gave us the Bill of Rights is one of these. The man who united this far-flung disparate land 10 years ago is a great Canadian. To the establishment, he is a radical. To the radicals, he is a maverick. To the mavericks he is a hoosier [frontier rough]. To the hoosier, he is an idealist. To the idealists, he is the establishment. To all, he is a fighter, an innovator, a friend to men who are alone, to the men who suffer, to the man who needs a friend. To friend and foe alike, he is a great Canadian.[5]

Senator Wallace McCutcheon refused to speculate on Diefenbaker's next move. "I learned a long time ago never to guess what Mr. Diefenbaker will or won't do." Diefenbaker submitted his nomination papers 15 minutes before the deadline. "I realized that I would be clobbered in the voting, as I told my friends and supporters, but as no other candidate was prepared to pit himself against this monstrous course, it was up to me."[6]

Fearing that a resolution on two nations would divide the convention and cause enduring acrimony and media attention, it was pulled from its agenda. Diefenbaker could say he was victorious at the convention because of this outcome alone. When delegates asked Diefenbaker how long it took him to prepare the speech that galvanized the convention on such a divisive topic, he responded, "My entire life." But it was not just party resolutions that bothered him. More important were the actions of the federal and provincial governments. In his convention remarks, he spoke of the federal government "frittering around" in their relations with the provinces. Cooperative federalism, he said, was neither cooperative nor federalism but capitulation. To Quebec, he lamented, the Liberals promised everything under the sun:

> They have opted this out and opted that out. It's time that French Canada started opting in rather than opting out. I was criticized for being too much concerned with the average Canadian. I can't help that; I'm one of them.
>
> The adoption of the two-nations concept would segregate French Canada. I am not going to agree, whether it's popular or not, to take the stand to erect a Berlin Wall around the province of Quebec.... We don't want any checkpoint Charlies in our nation... That is what this proposition will do.
>
> I feel privileged to have had the opportunity to continue serving Canada in the House of Commons. The Canadian people, without regard to political affiliation, have given me their affection. I bear no ill feeling to those who, in the past, opposed me. But I stand today, as I have always stood, for principle: freedom and equality for all Canadians, however humble their lot in life and whatever their racial origin. One Canada, One Nation.

Primarily to avoid embarrassing the former prime minister, 271 delegates supported Diefenbaker on the first ballot. That placed him fifth out of eleven candidates, with less than half the total votes of frontrunner Robert Stanfield. Diefenbaker stubbornly remained on two more ballots, falling to 114 votes, before he finally bowed out. "I am still making history," he boasted to the media.

After Stanfield was declared the winner, Diefenbaker appeared onstage, calling for unity. "My course has come to an end. I fought your battles, and you have given that loyalty that led us to victory more often than the party has ever had since the days of Sir John A. Macdonald. In my retiring, I have nothing to withdraw in my desire to see Canada, my country in your country, one nation."

In Stanfield's concluding remarks, he quipped, "Personally, I'm determined to get along with that fellow Camp." Diefenbaker was incensed. Stanfield later apologized and ensured that Camp was invisible when Diefenbaker was around. Camp neglected the lessons of Brutus, one of the assassins of Caesar; those who wield the sword against the leader rarely replace them.

- 23 -

A TROUBLESOME BACKBENCHER

The Conservative Party has suffered a calamitous disaster.

Despite his pledge of loyalty to the new Conservative Party leader, Robert Stanfield, Diefenbaker took private and public pleasure at the demise of those who followed him as leader.

Given his many attempts to get into Parliament, he would not leave it willingly. He remained a member of Parliament until his death on August 16, 1979, serving from 1940 for 39 years, four months, and 21 days in the House of Commons. Only three other members of Parliament have served longer than Diefenbaker. That meant winning four more elections in his Prince Albert riding after he lost the leadership. And he never gave up hope that the party would again turn to him to lead. He humorously quipped in his speeches, "You know, Gladstone was British prime minister at the age of 84." To the cheers in response, Diefenbaker would pause: "Ah. You see, it's everywhere." He often arrived or left the podium to the stirring theme song "The Impossible Dream."

In the 1968 election, Diefenbaker refused to campaign with Stanfield. He had threatened not to run in the election if the leader did not put forward basic policies acceptable to him.[1] Stanfield posters were barred from Diefenbaker's local campaign offices.

Pierre Trudeau, the onetime lawyer, associate professor of law at the University of Montreal and justice minister under Pearson, surprisingly won the leadership of the Liberal party in April 1968, ascending to the prime minister's office. The bilingual and charismatic Montrealer quickly called an election for June 25. It was the right political decision: Trudeau's Liberals won 155 seats, a comfortable majority out of 264 seats, and reduced the Tories to 72 seats, 25 seats lower than Diefenbaker won in 1965.

Trudeau's win gave the Chief a reason to gloat on CBC about his own party's failure: "The Conservative party has suffered a calamitous disaster." While Diefenbaker was not on speaking terms with Stanfield, he nonetheless enjoyed mutual respect with Pierre Trudeau as they were aligned in opposition to "deux nations." It was in that 1968 campaign when Stanfield had referenced "two founding peoples with historic rights to maintain their language and culture." But Diefenbaker was not upset that his party went down to defeat. For his part, referencing Diefenbaker, Trudeau said to his colleagues "I really love that old guy."[2]

In the House of Commons, Diefenbaker split with his party and leader over the Liberal bill on official bilingualism in 1969. He and sixteen other Tories insisted on a recorded vote (as opposed to a voice vote where MPs are not identified) causing Stanfield to remark, "Their stupidity was exceeded only by their malice. There are some things in a political party one simply does not do to one's colleagues." Given that Diefenbaker had established simultaneous translation in the House of Commons and had government documents issued in English and French, it is surprising that Diefenbaker opposed official bilingualism. Diefenbaker justified his opposition by saying he was distressed by the provision that created a commissioner of official languages who had the power to investigate complaints. In his view, this politicized the position as, at the time, it would be under the influence of a federal politician (Gerard Pelletier), who Diefenbaker said was "known to be the sworn enemy of anything in (this) country that is in the British tradition. This official will become the grand inquisitor of the realm."[3]

In the 1974 election, where Trudeau regained a majority government by winning 60 of Quebec's 74 seats and losing the rest of the country, Diefenbaker railed on a Liberal blind spot: "In Western Canada, the situation is such that everybody realizes that Mr. Trudeau doesn't give a tinker's damn for Western Canada... and his whole attitude throughout has been one of contemptuous disregard of the equality rights of our Western provinces."

Because of Diefenbaker's stature in the House of Commons, he would invariably be recognized by the Speaker during Question Period whenever he arose. To Stanfield's dismay, this could occur at heated moments when a Liberal minister was on the ropes. Diefenbaker would alter the rhythm of questioning by asking a question about something obscure, such as the loss of the coat of arms from government letterhead. On some occasions, the leader's office would ask Diefenbaker's staff to arrange an extended lunch for him to ensure there would not be a distraction during question period.

The feud with Dalton Camp never ended. Asked how he felt seeing Camp in a position of power, Diefenbaker proved he had not lost his touch for a pithy quote and was near-Churchillian in that skill: "Psychologists have long since determined that nothing is more disturbing for the human mind than for a person to have his victim still around after an assassination." He was quick with other quotes that got the media's attention. When chided from government benches, Diefenbaker remarked, "The Honourable Member for Halifax [Gerald Regan] does nothing but engage in occasional desk-tapping. It shows his intelligence that he makes that his major contribution."

When Liberal MP Paul Martin Sr. suggested Diefenbaker was "putting a gun to the opposition's head," he replied, "I do not know what it would do to put a gun to the honourable Gentleman's head. There would be no damage in any event."[4] During one debate, a Liberal MP interrupted Diefenbaker's remarks to the House of Commons by asking if he would take a question. After the second such interruption, Diefenbaker turned to his inquisitor and said, "A big game hunter is never diverted by rabbit tracks." Similarly, his wit showed when 51-year-old Pierre Trudeau married 21-year-old Margaret Sinclair in March 1971. Diefenbaker quipped that Trudeau had two choices: marry or adopt her.[5]

Diefenbaker had previously referred to Trudeau's penchant for kissing women—young ones mostly, on the campaign trail in 1968, and posed the question, "Have you ever seen him kissing a farmer?" He said the young women Trudeau kissed were children and it was a shameless act for the prime minister to engage in.[6] He said Trudeau was intent on turning Parliament into an "institutional eunuch."[7]

With yet another "zinger," Diefenbaker condemned Nixon for calling Trudeau an asshole but added that he had "demonstrated an excellent knowledge of human anatomy."[8] When his party proposed wage and price controls in the 1972 election, he quipped, "Every man believes his wages should increase and his prices should fall. We can't sell this."[9] He could make jokes at his own expense, remarking in 1976 that accolades that came his way embarrassed him, adding, "I have not often been embarrassed." In 1979, the year of his death, he said of those who thought he was too old to serve that he would take them on for a three-mile race, "providing they agree to a (medical) exam from the neck up." He said at age 83 he felt like a (tough) twenty-minute egg, "but the doctors scared the hell out of me. They said I was as sound as a dollar."[10]

He used his wit and sharp tongue, even when dealing with ordinary citizens who took undue exception to his political positions. He kept close tabs on his mail and spent much of his day reading letters and dictating replies to Canadians from all walks of life and all regions. However, he often sent the same short reply to writers who took an exceptionally harsh moral tone against himself and his party:

> Dear Sir,
>
> I have just received from some crackpot who is using your stationary, even forging your name, a letter. I know how shocked you will be to know that your name is being used in this way. If you would like to have the letter in question returned to you so that you can use it and take such action against the wrongdoer as counsel may advise, I will be glad to send it by the next post.
>
> John Diefenbaker

He took most letters he received, especially as prime minister, seriously. In response to a letter-writing campaign of citizens in 1959, concerned about federal government officials declaring that two hundred and fifty ponies on Nova Scotia's Sable Island were surplus and were to be destroyed, Diefenbaker reversed a departmental administrative decision.

Diefenbaker remained sensitive to slights. Lavishly praised in a *Globe and Mail* editorial for his support of the Gardiner Dam in Saskatchewan, adjacent to Lake Diefenbaker, the Chief, who was getting his hair cut while reading the editorial, turned to his barber and said, "They're trying to destroy me." A few days later, his office photocopied and distributed the editorial.

The one place he felt totally secure was at home with his wife. Diefenbaker had once remarked during the 1963 campaign, "Where's Olive? If I lose her, I'll lose everything." In the video documentary "The Chief," Diefenbaker said of his wife, "Without my wife, it would be impossible to carry on, or to have carried on.... she has the infinite capacity of being able, when I enter the home to close the door on problems and give me that undivided attitude of, not appreciation, but of encouragement.... know(ing) that criticism comes from the heart." She had been alive to see her husband recognized by the Queen as a Companion of Honour on January 1, 1976, one of only 65 who could hold the distinction at any time.[a] His beloved wife died on December 22, 1976. He was devastated by Olive's death and became a lost and lonely soul.

***

After the leadership battle, Diefenbaker spent time embellishing his reputation and settling old scores. That could, on occasion, include pettiness. After days of planning to get Diefenbaker to a campaign event in 1972, his executive assistant Lee Richardson recalled that seconds before arrival, the Chief inquired who had previously held the riding in the prior election. Upon hearing it was Douglas Harkness, the Chief curtly commanded his driver to turn around in full view of those waiting hours for his arrival. Before Lester Pearson's funeral, a reporter asked Diefenbaker for his reflections. He paused briefly and said, "He shouldn't have won the Nobel Prize."

In 1974, RCA Victor produced a record album, "I Am a Canadian," featuring Diefenbaker's remarks about individual freedom and the Bill of Rights. The album also included Diefenbaker telling witty stories about his heroes—Winston Churchill, John A. Macdonald, R.B. Bennett, and others. As an indication of the enduring affection the public held for Diefenbaker, it had the highest advance order in the company's history.[11]

At the 1976 leadership convention, Diefenbaker was given a prime-time speaking role, which he used to settle a score with Brian Mulroney, one of many who had called for a leadership vote of the party when the Chief was battling to remain at the helm. That year, the contest was expected to produce the first Quebecer to lead the party: Claude Wagner or Brian Mulroney. Diefenbaker warned the delegates not to consider a contestant without parliamentary experience. It was a not-so-oblique reference to Mulroney. As Mulroney noted in his memoirs, when John Diefenbaker swung, he rarely missed his target. Mulroney looked at his wife, Mila and said, "Honey, we're dead in the water." Diefenbaker responded to media questions by saying he did not know who Mulroney was, what he stood for, or who stood with him.[12]

---

a In more exclusive company, Pearson was recognized by the Queen under the Order of Merit, which is restricted to only 24 individuals at a time.

The reality was that Mulroney had organized "Youth for Diefenbaker" in 1956, regularly spoke with Diefenbaker when he was prime minister, and offered advice on the rising separatist sentiment in Quebec. Diefenbaker wrote a letter to Mulroney's father extolling the virtues and potential of his young protégé. It defied credibility that Diefenbaker would claim not to know the person who came in a strong second on the first ballot at the leadership convention, 80 votes ahead of the ultimate winner, Joe Clark. The outcome was such a shock that the *Toronto Star* headline the next day was "Joe Who?" (Clark and Wagner battled it out on the fourth ballot after Mulroney was dropped after the third.) Diefenbaker knew Mulroney well and pretended they were unacquainted to diminish the status of his one-time protégé, who defied Diefenbaker when the party wanted a change at the top in 1967 and when the Chief dug in yet again. Before the convention, Diefenbaker also knocked Mulroney down in the press about Mulroney's claim to being the party's chief organizer in Quebec for the 1972 election. "And how many members did we get?" Diefenbaker posed rhetorically. "Two. I'd mention that."[13]

Diefenbaker was also no fan of Joe Clark, whom he remembered as one of the "Campers" who sought to remove him from the leadership. When Clark wanted his MPs to vote to abolish capital punishment in Canada in a 1976 vote, Diefenbaker shockingly went against his leader's request. His rationale was that the Queen was set to open the Olympic Games in Montreal, and doing away with the death penalty might be an "invitation to regicide." In 1979, in another withering witticism, Diefenbaker said Canada celebrated the International Year of the Child by electing Joe Clark as prime minister. Clark was sworn in as Canada's 16th prime minister on June 4, 1979, one day short of his 40th birthday. Diefenbaker predicted Clark would be a "disaster."[14]

With the Progressive Conservatives back in power under Clark, Diefenbaker found himself seated next to External Affairs Minister Flora MacDonald in the House of Commons. She reached out to Diefenbaker to shake his hand, but the man who had ceremoniously fired her from party headquarters some fifteen years earlier was having none of it. "You! You! He should never have made you foreign minister!" he bellowed. "Minister of health, perhaps, or postmaster general, but never foreign minister!" So much for reconciliation. Another Clark minister, Ray Hnatyshyn, often referred to Diefenbaker as the "independent member for Prince Albert."[15]

Just before a long-planned trip to China, on August 15, 1979, Diefenbaker was on hand to inaugurate a new snooker table at the National Press Club. The following day, he died alone in the study at his home. He had planned his state funeral under the title "Operation Hope Not," the same title Winston Churchill chose for his funeral. One of his honorary pallbearers was Brian Mulroney, a man Diefenbaker had sabotaged a few years earlier at the 1976 leadership convention, who he claimed not to know. Perhaps Diefenbaker knew Mulroney had a bright political future ahead and was hedging his bets.

Historians weighed in on the Diefenbaker legacy in the days after his death. "Vindictive visionary Dief's best epitaph" was the headline under Richard Gwyn's *Toronto Star* column. Under the title, "Greatness eluded him, historians say," the *Star* offered perspectives from leading Canadian academics:[16] They all agreed that Diefenbaker's six years as prime minister "will not stand out in glory."

Macdonald biographer Donald Creighton wrote of how Diefenbaker "had certain talents and certain lacks, but the actual business of government suffered rather than prospered.... He didn't surmount his problems well... of a party whose leadership was not fond of him." Creighton also thought Diefenbaker's stance not to welcome South Africa back into the Commonwealth was a mistake. York University history professor William Kilbourn wrote that "(Diefenbaker) was an egomaniac, but you could not help loving him as long as he was out of power." The University of Toronto professor Paul Rutherford offered that Diefenbaker "[w]asn't all that intelligent. You can't be a tragic figure if you have no substance."

Canadians thought otherwise. Lying in the state on Parliament Hill, ten thousand people silently paid tribute to the Chief as they passed the casket. He was taken by train from Ottawa to Prince Albert, accompanied by 84 passengers, with frequent stops at small towns where huge crowds gathered to salute a great leader—they recognized the man, the lawyer, the fighter—who had always recognized them. In a petty move—all too often repeated in Canada at the expense of preserving and promoting the history of prime ministers and premiers alike—the Liberals rejected Diefenbaker's offer to donate his Ottawa home in the posh area of Rockcliffe Park as a museum. The Chief was buried at the University of Saskatchewan; Olive's remains were transferred from Beechwood Cemetery in Ottawa, and she was reinterred beside her husband.

- 24 -

TRUE NORTH, STRONG AND FREE

All my defeats were fortunate for me in the light of subsequent events. I never lost hope that ultimately, I was going where I intended to go from the time I was nine years of age.

Diefenbaker was a charismatic leader with a deep connection to ordinary Canadians. He said he never campaigned; rather, he continuously visited the people.[1] He was a visionary prime minister who advanced the rights and freedoms of individual Canadians, where all citizens were treated equally. He fought for an independent Canada with allies, but with the conviction and courage to chart its own course. In pursuit of his vision, he could not be intimidated or thrown off course by the wealthy, the media, and world leaders, including the president of the United States. He was not a transactional or incremental leader. Diefenbaker enthralled the country and gave it hope. He became prime minister to fulfill a destiny ingrained in him in his youth of a Canada free from discrimination. This purpose enabled him to withstand a succession of defeats before earning the trust of the Canadian people in three elections, including the largest electoral landslide in Canadian history. For 39 years, he served in Parliament, winning thirteen consecutive elections between 1940 and 1979. After his passing, his seat of Prince Albert, Saskatchewan, became an NDP stronghold.

Before Diefenbaker, the Progressive Conservative party had a penchant for losing, eking out just one victory in the previous nine contests. Six months after being elected leader, Diefenbaker won a minority government, followed by a majority, and then another minority government. Even in the two elections he lost as party leader, Diefenbaker performed valiantly, exceeding all expectations while denying Liberal majority governments. In his time, he was the most formidable opponent for Liberals to handle since Sir John A. Macdonald.

He held the highest office in the land, yet he instinctively mistrusted authority, the rich, the powerful, and even some members of his cabinet. As a populist, he hoarded his political capital, avoiding bold moves that Canadians instinctively opposed. Diefenbaker held to a maxim that a successor Liberal prime minister, Jean Chrétien, would embrace—*trust the people*. His mandate was less about policy and tactics than vision and helping struggling Canadians. Unlike his predecessors, Diefenbaker built a new coalition of voters and remade the Conservative party in his image.

While Diefenbaker warned of the dangers of communism and socialism, he was not burdened by an ideology that came with a consistent policy framework. He led with a grand vision and was not mired in detail. Rather than following inherently predictable policy prescriptions, he was open-minded. During his time in government, he launched or concluded 18 Royal Commissions to inform himself and the nation how the government could solve long-festering problems. To contemporize, Canada has not launched a Royal Commission since 1991, although it has struck inquiries of national importance, such as the Truth and Reconciliation Commission.

Some of Diefenbaker's biographers accentuated Diefenbaker's erratic behaviour, leaving the impression he was something of a madman. But what was so irrational about asserting Canadian sovereignty over American intrusions into domestic policymaking? Why does the reluctance to keep nuclear weapons off Canadian soil unless necessary for national security seem irrational? And why should the governor of the Bank of Canada go unchallenged when many experts and the duly elected government thought his monetary policies and other actions were damaging the economy? And who could call Diefenbaker paranoid over interference in Canadian elections by an American president when the evidence is overwhelming that Kennedy did all he could—overtly and covertly—to engineer Diefenbaker's defeat?

Those who thought Diefenbaker was paranoid and a blowhard were from a different class than ordinary Canadians. They were the elites who engaged in groupthink and who looked down on rural Canada and those without graduate degrees. They thought standing up to an American president was unwise. Giving Bay Street bankers a hard time, as Diefenbaker did, was considered to be economically dangerous—and sometimes could be. However, these were qualities Canadian voters appreciated in Diefenbaker.

Canadian prime ministers are often evaluated in four broad categories.[2] First, there is economic prosperity and the nation's general welfare. Without a strong economy, economic opportunity, and what is perceived as a "fair" sharing of wealth, a nation suffers. Second, a great prime minister maintains and enhances national unity. This challenge has vexed many political leaders in a country as diverse as Canada. Third, national security and Canada's standing in the world matters. The country loses influence and becomes vulnerable when it is not respected in the capitals of the world that matter. Finally, there is political leadership. Holding a party together and winning elections is essential to success in politics.

***

During Diefenbaker's six years in power, Canada suffered two economic recessions. Neither was prolonged, steep, or caused by the direct actions of his government. The first began in March 1957, before Diefenbaker came to power and continued until January 1958. The evidence is clear that the prior Liberal government hid the coming economic downturn from voters in 1957. It did not hurt Diefenbaker politically, as he would go on to win the largest majority in Canadian history in March 1958. The second recession endured from March 1960 to March 1961 and largely mirrored the economic circumstances in the United States. It was a cyclical downturn, not caused by reckless fiscal policy but by reduced consumer demand for manufactured goods, growing competition from imports, and an unwarranted tight money supply that had spiked interest rates.

Diefenbaker's response to both recessions was to stimulate economic activity with tax relief and spending on public infrastructure on borrowed money, strategies that have enjoyed a broad following to this day, despite legitimate critiques that can be made.[a] During the second recession, the Diefenbaker government pressured the governor of the Bank of Canada to lower interest rates.

---

a Too much debt is a tax on the next generation; tax relief without grasping not all tax cuts pay for themselves in the short-term will increase deficits that are normally not preferred by conservatives. Jean Chrétien cut spending, balanced the books and then reduced taxes.

Due to the governor's intransigence on the issue, where Canada was slower to lower interest rates than the United States, the economy rebounded sluggishly.

When Diefenbaker came into office, there was no glaring need or call for a shift in economic policy. Diefenbaker was critical of the St. Laurent government to the extent it was arrogant in specific national projects, such as constructing a natural gas pipeline from Alberta to central Canada without sufficient parliamentary debate. However, Diefenbaker's vision and imagination took us in a different geographic direction by investing in infrastructure to support the development of natural resources in the Far North.

The construction of "roads to resources" provided immediate jobs, but the more meaningful benefits were realized over the long term. It is remarkable by today's standards that from a standing start, over 6,000 kilometres of highways were completed under his government by the spring of 1963. This infrastructure was a made-in-Canada building block of economic independence and interdependence. It included the Mackenzie Highway, paving portions of the Canada-Alaska Highway, the Whitehorse-Dawson Road, the Dempster Highway from Dawson City to Inuvik, and the Pine Point Railway.

Each of these projects led to the opening of mines, the building of gas pipelines, and the development of new communities. Diefenbaker's vision was drawn from the past and reached far ahead: "I can see this northland of ours with developments envisaged by D'Arcy McGee in his magnificent speech at the time of Confederation as he saw that great Canada." From this seat in the House of Commons, he said, "I can see cities in northern Canada north of the Arctic Circle. There are vast power potentialities in that area. I can see cities developing as they are developing today in Norway if only the government would catch the vision of possibilities." He wanted Canadians to own and develop their resources, adding incentives to that end: "I believe that the entire tax structure in Canada needs to be overhauled to provide encouragement to the promotion of primary and secondary industries in our country."

While monetary policy was in the realm of the Bank of Canada, led by its obstinate governor, James Coyne, Diefenbaker chose to invest in the Canadian economy even though this increased the deficit in the short term. This put him on a collision course with Coyne, who had no tolerance for modest inflation and was determined to exploit his public perch to berate the Diefenbaker government over its fiscal policies. The nationalist Coyne took center stage to proclaim the Diefenbaker government did not go far enough to diminish foreign investment in Canada. If there was a renegade, it was Coyne and not Diefenbaker. During his time in office, Diefenbaker's spending increases and deficits were modest. While he governed during two recessions, he added less relative per capita national debt than most other prime ministers.[3]

There is little doubt that James Coyne's actions to increase interest rates dramatically, his zeal to save Canada from foreign influence, and his inclination to scold the government for not "living within its means" were well outside his mandate and damaging to the country. However, the method by which Diefenbaker legislated Coyne out of his post reflected poorly on the prime minister's competence as the head of government. Politically, it would have been wiser to let Coyne complete the remainder of his term or not use the shocking rise in the governor's pension arrangement as a partial justification for his dismissal. In Diefenbaker's defense, after Coyne veered into the political theatre, it was reasonable for him to conclude that the Bank of Canada governor would not leave office voluntarily. The prime minister was left with a Hobson's choice where there was no clear win; Diefenbaker took a political hit to restore sound monetary policy.

Sound finances were a priority for Diefenbaker, and he abhorred waste in government. It was most evident in his cancellation of the Avro Arrow fighter jet program. That decision was politically damaging, but continuing the development of the program would have been reckless and irresponsible. He took seriously the duty of parliamentarians to scrutinize the government's expenditures, a task that he remarked had steadily deteriorated over his time in the House of Commons. That's why he instituted a permanent reform where the public accounts committee chair comes from the official Opposition and not the government benches, even though it gave more power to his opponents while he was prime minister.

Of the notable shifts in economic policy, Diefenbaker launched the Carter Commission, which led to a fundamental change in Canada's tax system with the introduction of a tax on capital gains. This did not make him popular on Bay Street, where he sought no friends. When the issue of collusion or price fixing was raised, Diefenbaker said those who pursued anti-competitive practices and were found guilty should be imprisoned rather than subjected to fines.

He did nothing that damaged the economy. An attempt to divert trade away from the United States and replace it with greater activity with Great Britain and Commonwealth countries was more political posturing than a concerted effort to alter established trade patterns. Exports to Britain over Diefenbaker's tenure rose by $190 million, and a much larger $762 million with the U.S.[4]

While Canada had an export surplus with Britain, it carried a deficit with the Americans. Both countries remained number one and two in trade, with Japan ranking at a distant third. His attempts to bolster Canadian ownership in the economy by penalizing foreign investors were modest and dwarfed in scope and scale by the Liberal administrations that followed. This included Pearson's failed foreign takeover tax and Pierre Trudeau's establishment of the Foreign Investment Review Agency (FIRA). As noted in a summary of prime ministerial performance in *Policy Options*, with Diefenbaker, "there was continued rhetoric but little serious effort to reduce Canadian dependence on the U.S. market or to reduce U.S. investment in Canada."[5]

With his sour relations with President John F. Kennedy, Diefenbaker risked Canada being economically punished by its largest investor and trading partner. Kennedy's efforts contributed to the devaluation of the Canadian dollar in 1963, which politically harmed his Canadian counterpart. Nonetheless, Diefenbaker's resolve to sell wheat to China and maintain economic ties with Cuba over the objections of American administrations was economically advantageous to Canada. Diefenbaker put Canadian farmers above the wrath that the popular John F. Kennedy consistently invoked.

Despite the alarm bells pulled at the Bank of Canada, inflation remained low during Diefenbaker's time in office, peaking at 4.2 percent in his early days and sitting at 1.3 percent when he was defeated. A decade later, Canadian inflation was much higher—nearly ten times the rate when Diefenbaker was in power. Diefenbaker understood that inflation hurts poor people more than any other group in society. That's why he increased social payments at rates above inflation. He also understood that discrimination of any sort was not just damaging to the individual, but limited opportunities and was thus a drag on the economy. For Canada to achieve its national potential, he believed every Canadian must be enabled to reach their personal potential. Whether respecting women or minorities, for Diefenbaker, good social policy was sound economic policy. More broadly, he said, "We must restrain the undermining of our Canadian Confederation through encouraging or developing a dislike of Canadians of other racial origins, for Canada's destiny and Canada's future can and never will be achieved on the basis of racial prejudice."[6]

The major change in economic variables during Diefenbaker's tenure was the value of the Canadian dollar. It had traded at or above par to the U.S. buck over the 1950s and was fixed at 92.5 cents in Diefenbaker's final month in power. That devaluation was abrupt and belied Canada's economic fundamentals. Currency speculators smelled an opportunity, fueled in part by the determination of an American administration to weaken Diefenbaker. Yet, after Diefenbaker lost government, and with the less fiscally responsible governments that followed him, the dollar slid in value for much of the following generation.

In the final analysis, Diefenbaker neither transformed the economy nor left issues for his successor to repair. He made life easier for those who were struggling, especially seniors and farmers. He believed in regional economic development and initiated capital projects in areas of Canada facing duress. There was modest variability in unemployment, but the rate was never far removed from five percent during Diefenbaker's time in office, which was below the average rate over the following generation. Opening the North to resource development was his legacy economic accomplishment.

John Diefenbaker was a prudent manager of the tax dollars of Canadians. Economists may, quite correctly, not have liked his nationalist rhetoric and saber-rattling, but these were of little consequence to the functioning of the economy. Compared with his successors, notably Pierre Trudeau—who inflicted massive operating deficits, rampant and sustained inflation, out-of-control spending, and structural unemployment that brought misery to the nation—Diefenbaker was an economic superstar.

****

Canada's unity, even its existence as a nation-state, has been challenged throughout Canadian history. The ultimate test in Diefenbaker's time and the period thereafter was whether Confederation allowed Quebecers to achieve their linguistic and cultural aspirations, or whether greater flexibility in the constitutional arrangement was required. John Diefenbaker approached Canadian unity through a different lens. He was not preoccupied with the intersection of English and French but with the equality and social welfare of all citizens regardless of language, race, origin or religious belief.

He rejected the idea of hyphenated Canadians—including the terms French-Canadians and English-Canadians. He vigorously opposed any form of discrimination, both in Canada and around the world. Diefenbaker dismantled preferential immigration policies that favoured white applicants, substituting them with an objective points-based system that disregarded race. This replaced policies of prior Liberal governments, including that of Sir Wilfrid Laurier, that banned immigrant applications from the "negro race" as they were deemed to be "unsuitable to the climate and requirement of Canada." When he spoke to service clubs and the like, Diefenbaker reminded their members that so long as they were Canadian, they should be colour-blind. He consistently respected Indigenous Canadians and established crucial national institutions. He was a proponent of the fair treatment and liberty of all Canadians to pursue and fulfill their dreams.

His policy reforms laid the groundwork for Canada's enduring social safety net, including increases in old age security, programs for disabled individuals, and support for family farmers. He introduced hospital insurance and commissioned Justice Emmett Hall to lead the Royal Commission on the National Health System, a pivotal step toward modern medicare in Canada. He was compassionate and ahead of his time in providing support for those suffering from mental illness, some of whom he encountered when he acted as defence counsel in the justice system. He sought to redeem those incarcerated by establishing the Parole Board of Canada to ensure imprisonment decisions were based on rehabilitation rather than political considerations "without undue risk to society."[7]

Central to Diefenbaker's vision of national unity was maintaining Canada's political and cultural independence from the United States. His government sought to reduce the influx of American cultural content into Canada through initiatives recommended by the Royal Commission on Publications, which aimed to safeguard Canadian cultural sovereignty, including prohibiting the importation of periodicals containing advertising primarily directed to the Canadian market and to limit the deductibility of advertising costs by Canadian companies in foreign magazines that were imported into Canada. He was determined that Canada would be an ally, not an appendage of the United States.

Diefenbaker was critical of the CBC, Canada's "national broadcaster," for what he perceived as its Liberal bias that "indiscriminately embraced North American continentalism." He saw the CBC as "extravagant, in its spending, disappointing, even blasphemous in its programming and downright inimical to party interests."[8] He reduced the power of the CBC and stripped its authority to grant licenses to new stations by establishing a Board of Broadcast Governors (later the CRTC).[9]

Regarding Quebec's place within Confederation, Diefenbaker believed the British North America Act adequately empowered provinces. He thought that the provisions contained in Sections 92 and 93 of the BNA Act were sufficient to allow the distinctiveness of Quebec and every other province to flourish. This included provincial jurisdiction over health, education, municipalities, property and civil rights, marriage, administration of justice and the power to tax their citizens directly. His efforts to support the French language, such as introducing simultaneous translation in Parliament and appointing the first French-speaking Governor General, were consequential and respectful. However, as someone who grew up in Saskatchewan and fought for the social and economic underdog over his lifetime, he had a blind spot regarding the vulnerabilities Quebecers collectively felt over preserving the French language. Many Quebecers, including most Progressive Conservatives in that province, disagreed with Diefenbaker's approach to national unity.

Diefenbaker's obstinance in the flag debate was a breaking point, which caused leading Conservative Quebec MPs to call for his resignation. Some of his key Quebec MPs left the party in protest. Outside of the 1958 election, Diefenbaker won only 13 percent of Quebec seats. The party would remain irrelevant in the province until 1984 when Mulroney became the first Conservative leader from Quebec. He swept that province—and the country—with policies that Diefenbaker would have abhorred.

George Grant, the author of *Lament for a Nation* and a fervent admirer of Diefenbaker, noted, "The keystone of a Canadian nation is the French fact. English-speaking Canadians who desire the survival of their nation have to cooperate with those who seek the continuance of Franco-American civilization. The failure of Diefenbaker to act on this maxim was his most tragic mistake."[10] That must be balanced with the fact that what gave Diefenbaker pride was how he helped Canadians of neither French nor British origins feel welcomed and gave them a sense that every opportunity in Canada was open to them. He believed that while diversity is a Canadian characteristic, it is unity that is its strength. That was his reflection after winning the leadership of the Conservative party: "The opportunity that I had looked forward to was now given me, the opportunity to bring about, not a Canada of principalities, but a Canada in unity."[11]

***

In a 2023 book on the foreign policy legacies of Canadian prime ministers edited by Patrice Dutil, Michael D. Stevenson challenges the prevailing historical view of John Diefenbaker as a rogue and unstable prime minister. Stevenson contends that Diefenbaker ensured Canada's significant role in the western alliance, initiated crucial development projects and maintained principled stances on human rights.[12]

Diefenbaker enacted the NORAD agreement while staunchly defending Canadian foreign policy independence. He was a vocal anti-communist who directly confronted Soviet leadership. At the United Nations, he boldly exposed their hypocrisy and military oppression when the Cold War was nearing its peak in a speech as relevant today as it was when delivered in 1960. This is especially true for the people of Ukraine.

A devoted monarchist with a deep admiration for British traditions, Diefenbaker opposed Britain's entry into the European Economic Community out of concern that it would weaken its ties with Canada and lead Canada to further economic integration with the United States. He believed the Commonwealth of Nations—those with a connection to the British Empire—furthered the cause of peace by bringing together countries from around the world with different races, beliefs, and religions. One of his most notable international stands was his opposition to South Africa's readmission to the Commonwealth after becoming a republic unless apartheid was dismantled—a stance that garnered support from Nelson Mandela during his imprisonment and his marked appreciation when he was liberated.

While often criticized for his conduct during the Cuban Missile Crisis, Professor Asa McKercher at the Royal Military College of Canada praised Diefenbaker for his "deft handling of Latin America, with his actions reflecting a shrewd calculation of Canadian interests and abilities." McKercher added, "Diefenbaker's approach to Latin America should force some revisions to the typical characterization of him as a foreign policy ingénue for, with the western hemisphere emerging as a Cold War battleground, he charted a prudent course.[13]

Diefenbaker's relationship with President Kennedy was marked by personal and strategic tensions. Kennedy expected Canada to align with American policies, which often clashed with Diefenbaker's insistence on maintaining Canadian sovereignty. As noted by Stephen Azzi, Carleton University professor of political management, Kennedy's team dismissed disagreements with Diefenbaker as the "product of irrationality rather than of often-legitimate policy differences." They viewed Diefenbaker as "neurotic and emasculated." Azzi argues that Kennedy was overconfident and unwisely portrayed Diefenbaker as "a child or as a neurotic."[14]

Despite strained relations, there is little evidence that Canada, as a nation, suffered. Politically, it was a different story. Diefenbaker faced not only the Liberals under Lester B. Pearson in the 1962 and 1963 federal elections but also the Kennedy administration, determined to orchestrate his defeat. Even Lester Pearson believed Kennedy had acted inappropriately by intervening in Canadian affairs. Had Eisenhower been president during Diefenbaker's full term, tensions between the nations would unlikely have caused much of a ripple. Diefenbaker could have avoided much of the foreign election interference if he bowed before Kennedy and not flaunted diplomatic protocol to gain stature as someone who could not be "pushed around" by the most powerful nation in the world—his country's most important economic and military ally.

There is only one government in Canadian history that has allowed nuclear weapons on Canadian soil. Lester B. Pearson took that policy position to the Canadian people in the 1963 election when he said he had converted from diplomat to politician. Despite internal divisions within his cabinet and party, Diefenbaker staunchly opposed nuclear proliferation. As he said to delegates to a party convention, "Do not tie my hands in a quest for peace."

Nuclear weapons on Canadian soil were phased out when Pierre Trudeau became prime minister. This followed Canada's ratification of the Nuclear Non-Proliferation Treaty in January 1969. Trudeau boasted that Canada was the first country in the world to choose to divest itself of nuclear weapons, saying he would invest the money saved in developing nations. In 1969, Trudeau unwisely opined, "I am not interested in protecting a few Canadian cities if this means we will be consenting to a kind of policy which we think is dangerous to the world."

Trudeau's policy was based on moral rather than strategic interests. Diefenbaker wanted fewer nuclear weapons in the world. Still, his objection to Canada accepting atomic weapons in 1963 was largely motivated by a desire to keep Canada independent of the United States. The policy that Diefenbaker fought for, which severely ruptured his cabinet and was adopted by Pierre Trudeau, has been the policy of every Canadian government for the past 55 years and is unlikely to change. Diefenbaker told his campaign team in 1963 "It would have been easy for me to have agreed to the acquisition of nuclear weapons. But so long as I am prime minister, I am going to insist that a thing is right... because sooner or later, you are proven right."[15]

Diefenbaker's belief that Canada could exist beside the Americans without being subservient to them is similar to the doctrine that Jean Chrétien adopted when he refused to be intimidated by an American president, George W. Bush, who wanted Canada to go to war in Iraq in 2003. Chrétien was pilloried in the press, the business community and many members of his caucus for his decision at the time. His small-town wisdom and courage not to succumb to powerful forces helped to make him a great prime minister. Diefenbaker is in his company on many levels.

***

John George Diefenbaker was a man destined for greatness. He wrote in his memoirs: "All my defeats were fortunate for me in the light of subsequent events. I never lost hope that ultimately, I was going where I intended to go from the time I was nine years of age."

Though it took three attempts to secure the leadership of the Conservative party, Diefenbaker's victory did not guarantee a clear path to 24 Sussex Drive. Since the end of the First World War, electoral victories had heavily favoured the Liberals, with the Tories only securing one win compared to eight for their opponents. Few within his party or the media believed Diefenbaker stood a chance in the 1957 election. Yet, he defied expectations by winning that election and the two subsequent elections.

These victories were indisputably due to Diefenbaker's charismatic leadership, vision, and ability to connect with ordinary Canadians. He transformed the Conservative party almost overnight, replacing the traditional image of Bay Street bankers calling the shots with that of a populist folk hero who fought for the people. With Diefenbaker, the Tories became a winning party, something it had not experienced since the 19th century under Macdonald.

Despite his electoral success, Diefenbaker faced suspicion from the elites within his party throughout his tenure as leader. He eschewed long-held policy dogma that was suspicious of social engineering to lead a more active government that implemented or enhanced programs that helped the disadvantaged.

Diefenbaker's refusal to resign after losing the 1963 election led to internal party strife and distracted his party from preparations for subsequent elections. While he single-handedly held Lester B. Pearson to a minority government in 1963 and thwarted Liberal ambitions again in the 1965 election, his continued leadership ultimately became a hindrance rather than a benefit. Breaking his promise to party delegates when he was elected leader in 1956, he did not hand the reins of power "to whomever my successor may be, unimpaired and enhanced to the limits of my capacity and ability."[16] His reluctance to cede control and allow his successors to shape the party's message ultimately weakened the Conservatives in the 1968 election, where the Liberals under Pierre Trudeau won a majority government.

He held on until a bitter ending because of his zeal to oppose what he saw as the movement in the party to endorse the "two nations" theory of Canada. He said at the convention that chose his successor in 1967 that policies divorced from principle are dangerous and that all he stood for would be undermined if there were "two classes of citizenship." This, he warned, would result should there be a "nation within a nation."

Diefenbaker believed "two nations" was a popular thing that maligned Canada's heritage. "Some say the past is dead. Much has been done by the present government to depreciate the monarchy.... I say to my friends in French Canada, your freedom in our country came because there was a British monarchy, and that has to be underlined," he said. It was a message that few Quebec delegates thought would resonate in their home province.

Diefenbaker hung on because he said the future of Canada as an independent nation was at stake. He said the two-nation policy jeopardized those of non-French or British origin and that the theory could only lead to de-confederation. He reminded delegates that "two nations" had been tried in 1841 and failed. He threatened to leave the party and reject any leader that advanced elements of a theory he opposed. The vote at the 1967 convention demonstrated that the party had decisively and wisely moved on from Diefenbaker. But he did not leave the party. He ungraciously took delight in its defeats, as if each loss by his successors validated his leadership and stature.

Diefenbaker won four elections in the riding of Prince Albert under the leadership of Bob Stanfield and Joe Clark. He did not make their political lives easy. He carried grudges against ministers who were not loyal to him in 1963 and anyone who advocated for a change in leadership after that. If he had not intervened in the 1976 leadership contest, Brian Mulroney might have been the victor instead of Joe Clark. It would have been better for Diefenbaker's legacy and his party if he had kept his ego in check rather than settle old scores. As Mulroney said, Diefenbaker never missed when aiming at a target.

He could be petty, but his personality also had a kind, thoughtful and generous side. His foreign policy advisor, Basil Robinson, experienced Diefenbaker's moods and suspicions. But in his book, *Diefenbaker's World: A Populist in Foreign Affairs*, Robinson wrote that Diefenbaker was always accessible and was someone with whom he could speak frankly "without getting thrown out of the room." When they crossed swords, "Diefenbaker would nearly always find an early way of signaling that he did not want relations to be strained." Robinson marvelled at Diefenbaker's sense of humour and how considerate he was with someone coping with a family crisis. "One of my children still speaks gratefully of being taught to fish by the prime minister at Harrington Lake."

Diefenbaker maintained a clean record throughout his time in office, with no scandals tarnishing his name. His dedication to Canada and its people, especially its Indigenous people, was unwavering. He prioritized national interests over personal gain. He didn't care for the wealthy or worry about his financial security. He did not go on corporate boards or seek wealth after he ceased as party leader. Throughout his life, Diefenbaker remained steadfast in his convictions and goals, a testament to his unwavering commitment to the freedom and liberty of the people of Canada. His legacy as a man of the people endures as his greatest virtue. Diefenbaker worked for the people until the day he died.

- 25 -

THE CHIEF'S LEADERSHIP: VISION, COURAGE, CONTRARIAN

Strong men have strong opinions.

Diefenbaker has a record of accomplishment. Save for the introduction of nuclear weapons on Canadian soil for a brief period, none of the major reforms and policies he implemented as prime minister were reversed by his successors. Indeed, all subsequent prime ministers expanded upon his progress in social policy and protecting individual liberties. There is no doubt on the facts that he was a successful politician and prime minister. But what can be learned from his qualities of leadership?

The caricature of Diefenbaker as being erratic and egotistical is sensational, unfair and incomplete. His positive attributes and faults are instructive to any political leader as well as to those in business, community organizations and others who seek to realize a vision that betters the country.

Winston Churchill once wrote that courage is rightly esteemed the first of human qualities because "it is the quality which guarantees all others." Diefenbaker displayed courage in the face of many political defeats in elections and when contesting his party's leadership. He dared to cancel the Avro Arrow when he knew it would be unpopular. He stood up to the British when they were pursuing membership in the European Union. He took flak from President Kennedy and even some of his ministers who wanted Canada to accept U.S. nuclear weapons on Canadian soil. He condemned the apartheid regime in South Africa and the repression of the Soviet Union with notable public denunciations. We can question Diefenbaker's decision to remain leader after being defeated in 1963, but he did not fear the consequences of failure, even humiliation, in the 1967 leadership contest to stand up for the vision of Canada he had maintained over his political career. He was a courageous leader.

Inscribed on the wall of Centre Block on Parliament Hill are the words, "Without vision, the people perish." Taken from Proverbs 29:18, the message to politicians is they are elected to stand for something more than themselves. Peter C. Newman, in his seminal book *Renegade in Power*, wrote that Diefenbaker "had not the least inkling of what he wanted to do when he achieved high office." On the contrary, more than most Canadian prime ministers, Diefenbaker signalled his vision for Canada prior to becoming a member of Parliament in 1940, 17 years before he became the head of the cabinet. Even before entering the House of Commons, he stood for the common person and an end to prejudice and any form of hyphenated Canadianism. And he brought that vision to life with the Bill of Rights, open-minded reforms to the immigration system, and by extending the vote to Indigenous Canadians without conditions. He appointed the first woman to cabinet along with the first person of non-French or British origin. He relied on his vision when he rejected the call from the Newfoundland premier to have the RCMP intervene on the front lines of a worker's strike. He was optimistic about what Canada could become and thought on a grand scale. He was a visionary prime minister anchored in 19th-century liberalism, which thought the individual, not the group or collective, should be at the core of law and policy to protect citizens from government suppression. Diefenbaker was a man of destiny driven by a clear-headed vision for Canada.

Ronald Reagan was known as the Great Communicator. Pierre Trudeau once dismissively mused about how being an actor and a politician was possible. Reagan replied in reverse that it was impossible to be one and not the other. Whether in the courtroom, in Parliament, or on the campaign trail, Diefenbaker delivered his lines like thunderbolts. He used simple language with an economy of words that got directly to the point he wanted to make. He exceeded expectations in the six elections he fought as Conservative leader. His mastery on the campaign stump and his ability to draw crowds have few parallels in Canadian history. Connecting with people was a skill Diefenbaker honed over time, but he always had the intrinsic advantage of being his authentic self. His convictions were honestly and deeply held, which added to his powers of persuasion. He was a great communicator.

Voters hope that their elected leaders are bastions of integrity and honesty. In a competitive political environment, Diefenbaker was not immune to hyperbole, direct attacks on his opponents, or raising suspicions about his detractors. However, there was a reason one of his nicknames was *Honest John*. His personal conduct was beyond reproach; he sought no money for himself, and his government was remarkably free of malfeasance and scandal. Only one accusation is worth noting: allowing a minister to remain in place after being made aware he had an affair with a woman who was a possible security risk. There was little doubt in the minds of Canadians that Diefenbaker was in politics to serve the people and not himself. Diefenbaker was a man of honesty and integrity.

While a leader has a vision, it cannot be disconnected from the people they serve. Great politicians know their country and its history. Jean Chrétien's primary political maxim was "trust the people." Like Chrétien, Diefenbaker shunned groupthink. He was wary of intellects and academics who believed they had all the answers based on theories that may work in a classroom but didn't pass the basic political test of common sense.

A well-informed leader instinctively knows what is important to citizens and what will make a positive difference in their lives. Diefenbaker said he identified with ordinary Canadians because he was one of them. People responded to him with affection and admiration while the elites in his party thought Diefenbaker was over his head on national security and on the economy. Time has proven that he was on the right side of history on the big issues of his day and was rightly trusted by the Canadian people. That's because he trusted them and accepted he was their servant and not their master.

Diefenbaker was a cautious decision-maker, arguably to a fault. He held a record number of cabinet meetings and often sought consensus around the table when it was not within his grasp. Other prime ministers have forged ahead to set the path for others to follow. He was quick to join NORAD and was clear-headed in cancelling the Avro Arrow but was indecisive when it came to accepting nuclear weapons.

It is worth noting that Diefenbaker led under the shadow of Sir John A. Macdonald (nicknamed Old Tomorrow) and Mackenzie King (not necessarily conscription, but conscription if necessary), both of whom were slow to make decisions. Diefenbaker also led when power was not as tightly controlled in the hands of the prime minister as it has been in recent decades. Decision-making did not come easily to Diefenbaker, and he would have been a better prime minister if he had moved more quickly through the issues of the day.

Great leaders build strong teams. They know how to get the most out of the people around them and delegate responsibility for decisions within their sphere of responsibility. Diefenbaker was not a centralizer where all decisions needed to flow through him and his office. The cabinet table was the decision-making chamber, a committee he kept decidedly small for efficiency purposes, not control.

His cabinet included rivals and detractors, so it was anything but an echo chamber. However, for a cabinet to work effectively, there needs to be trust among its members, confidence that its deliberations would remain at the table, and the certainty that when disputes arose, the prime minister would bring matters to a resolution. The Diefenbaker team did not work well together. Time was wasted in meetings. There was confusion about where Diefenbaker stood on some issues. Eventually, his cabinet splintered in full public view, precipitating an election and the defeat of his government. Diefenbaker was not a team player when it came to his cabinet, his MPs or his party. What Diefenbaker did not appreciate was that he could better serve the people by getting the most and the best from the people around him.

A leader who is open to ideas and different perspectives, who does not come to every problem with a pre-determined and predictable solution, who looks at every issue on its merits and nuances, who is not determined to prove a theory or ideology, is more likely to produce results. As Winston Churchill once said, "My views are a harmonious process which keeps them in relation to the current movements of events." While Diefenbaker had a grand vision based on individual freedom, he did not oppose the imposition of the War Measures Act during the Second World War. He believed in an independent Canada but firmly supported NATO and concluded the NORAD agreement. He was a capitalist but supported farm income supports. He believed everyone needed to pull their weight but advanced social programs that supported those facing poverty. He believed in private enterprise but a government-sponsored health program.

He believed in balanced budgets and incurring deficits when the economy was weak. It didn't bother him if his solutions were theoretically contradictory or inconsistent. To the frustration of his opponents, he didn't hesitate to change past positions when dealing with new circumstances, new evidence, or unexpected events.

Like most Canadians, John Diefenbaker was a problem-solver with a deep appreciation of Canadian history and traditions, not an ideologue. Canadians are more interested in results than political theory and in this respect, Diefenbaker served the country well.

One of the most challenging aspects of being a leader is that there is little room for friendships and few opportunities for escape. Many leaders are overwhelmed by those who seek a favour or an appointment to a position they are not qualified for. As prime minister, those who serve at the cabinet table may have been by your side on the Opposition benches, may have contested the leadership and may think they would do a better job leading the country than the incumbent. Those who may think they are your friend or that you owe them something have expectations of a role or a status in an administration. In reality, old loyalties and friendships can undermine what a leader needs to do. This may include dismissing or demoting a minister, being scrupulously neutral on government contracts, and saying no to requests from major party donors. Stephen Harper boasted during the 2004 election, "I don't stand for patronage because I don't owe anybody anything." Jean Chrétien said he could only become friends with his staff or ministers after they no longer worked for him. Diefenbaker won the leadership with no personal or political debts. He owed no favours to his cabinet ministers or his MPs. Besides his wife and other family members, he had few, if any, deep friendships. He believed putting the country first meant a prime minister could have few close acquaintances, or a social life, despite the personal burden this added. It was a sacrifice he knowingly accepted for the greater good.

In a country as diverse as Canada—linguistically, culturally, geographically, and economically—any successful political leader must build broad coalitions representing all parts of Canada. Some call it making a "big tent" that welcomes diverse views and opinions sufficient to win elections. Coalition-building also helps keep the country united. A system built on the foundations of confidence and consensus also helps isolate extreme positions, making it difficult for toxic views to find a voice in decision-making. At its core, a system that requires consensus for success helps promote harmony, understanding, and tolerance. Successful leadership and political parties are not about letting one side of a political movement dominate but about fostering unity among a broad, multi-faceted coalition. A successful leader bridges the gaps, inspires unity, and draws the party together in a common cause. In any broadly based political party, internal battles are inevitable. Going back to 1940, Diefenbaker said, "Success of the Conservative Party today is not in turning to the left or to the right but in the establishment of policy in keeping with the changing times."[1]

Diefenbaker's initial coalition was broad. It included those who thought a "man of the people" was needed, someone who spoke to immigrants who faced discrimination, those who thought the disadvantaged needed a champion, and people who wanted a change from an arrogant Liberal administration. However, this was not a sustainable coalition after Diefenbaker lost ground in Quebec from those with a view different from his own of Confederation. Over time, the sentiment for change worked against him. Too much of his party's success was dependent on Diefenbaker's personal capacity to win the day. After winning three elections, Diefenbaker led a divided movement and party he could not hold together.

Great political leaders are also storytellers and humourists. They connect with people by taking the job more seriously than themselves. Mulroney rarely began a speech without telling a joke, often at his own expense. He learned from Macdonald, who had a line or a quip for every heckler and opposition politician who came his way. Chrétien rarely got to his feet without disarming his audience with a colourful yarn that revealed he understood what people were thinking, even if what he said was politically incorrect.

In the darkest days of the Second World War, Churchill could lighten the load on the people by making them laugh. When criticized for switching political parties twice, he replied, "Anyone can rat, but it takes a certain amount of ingenuity to re-rat." Diefenbaker was a quick-witted storyteller who enjoyed telling jokes as much as his audience enjoyed hearing him. He could ridicule his opponents, often harshly, and his rhetorical ammunition usually hit the bullseye. He did it spontaneously, without notes. It is what made Diefenbaker a great campaigner and drew tens of thousands to his public events. Diefenbaker had the ineffable leadership qualities of good humour, a razor-sharp mind, and the ability to tell stories that captured hearts and minds. It was said of Diefenbaker that the press was at a disadvantage as he usually interviewed himself, which often included a story that showed he understood what was on the minds of Canadians.[2] Diefenbaker was a campaigner like no other because he kept the people engaged and gave them hope. Storytelling, often at his own expense, was how he built his connection to ordinary Canadians.

Of all Diefenbaker's attributes that the Progressive Conservative party and its MPs should have embraced in Diefenbaker was his competitiveness. In short order and defying all expectations, he turned a party of losers into a party of winners. Yet his cabinet and his party turned on him, not just after he lost government but while he held office, and they precipitated not only Diefenbaker's downfall but the electoral fortunes of the Progressive Conservative party as well. Diefenbaker was a fighter who never backed down, even after a succession of defeats or when the odds were stacked against him, which they often were.

Few politicians succeed when they do not understand and appreciate all that has come before them. Diefenbaker was a voracious reader and a student of history, not just of Canada but the world. He knew well the foundations built over many centuries that had given us the liberties and freedoms that were the cornerstone of his beliefs and values. He saw his role as a leader that would build on the greatness of his predecessors. He saw his role as one to bend the arc of history towards a more just and fair society that lifted up those who needed not a handout but a hand up. He was not the traditional, pinstriped business-oriented Tory that was all business and no heart.

Diefenbaker was the antithesis of how Liberals like to portray Conservatives: that Tory times are hard times. He embraced his role as the folk hero to battle for the liberties that enabled every citizen to fulfill their potential and for an independent country to chart its own course. He was a man of destiny. Diefenbaker remained, until his dying day, a man of the people.

POSTSCRIPT:

CONTRASTING CONSERVATIVE PRIME MINISTERS

This book has demonstrated that John Diefenbaker was a Conservative leader who did not fit the mold. But how different was he?

When Brian Mulroney became prime minister in 1984, he offered a minor tribute by establishing the John Diefenbaker Award for a German scholar working in Canada. Stephen Harper, prime minister between 2006 and 2015, went further: "If ever there was a Conservative prime minister whose reputation needs to be reclaimed from Liberal slander," said Harper, it is the Chief, 'Honest John.'" The Harper government named a Canadian icebreaker in Diefenbaker's honour in 2008. In 2010, Harper's government also established a human rights award in Diefenbaker's name, although it has not been given since the Liberals came to power in 2015. In 2011, one of the two main offices of the Department of External Affairs was given the title The John G. Diefenbaker Building. Pierre Trudeau's government named the other after Diefenbaker's successor, Lester B. Pearson, in 1973.

It is one thing for a political party to honour its past leaders when it holds the levers of power. However, this does not settle how he compares relative to his peers. To move past the caricature of Diefenbaker as an erratic madman, we can compare his prime ministerial legacy with that of Conservative leaders who held office for a full term. This excludes Conservatives who served briefly in office, namely John Abbott, John Thompson, Mackenzie Bowell, Charles Tupper, Arthur Meighen, Joe Clark and Kim Campbell.

Diefenbaker most liked to fashion himself in the image of Sir John A. Macdonald. Both were lawyers who stood up for the underdog. Both were visionaries who were wary of American influence. They were electorally successful and sympathetic to the plight of ordinary citizens and Indigenous peoples. They were monarchists who cleaved to tradition. They were superb storytellers on and off the campaign trail with an engaging sense of humour and who enjoyed nothing more than beating Liberals and winning elections. Between 1867 and 1891, Macdonald won six majorities in seven elections; Diefenbaker won one majority in 1958 and two minorities, 1957 and 1963, in five contests. Macdonald faced challenges unlike any other prime minister.

Canada may not have existed without his guiding hand, and he managed to turn the gristle that was the nation at Confederation into bone that has endured. Macdonald and Diefenbaker respected the French language, but Canada's first prime minister understood and reconciled Quebec's aspirations in ways that Diefenbaker did not understand or embrace. Macdonald inspired loyalty within his party and admiration from his political opponents. Macdonald remains in a league of his own.

Borden held power between 1911 and 1920. Like Diefenbaker, he was a schoolteacher and a lawyer. It was his good fortune to gain office after Wilfrid Laurier unwisely went to the Canadian people in 1911, offering free trade with the Americans as his central platform plank when voters worried about political assimilation. Borden was consequential in that he navigated Canada through the First World War, including a conscription crisis. He proclaimed a uniquely Canadian voice on the world stage for what the country contributed and accomplished during the war. Borden's government extended the vote to women, although at first only to women in the armed forces and to female relatives of those serving in the military, a change that heavily favoured the Conservative vote. It was not, at first, done for reasons of equality in the same way Diefenbaker unilaterally extended the vote to Indigenous people in 1960 without preconditions. Borden's government interned 8,579 "enemy aliens," a program that Diefenbaker is likely to have opposed, and brought in the heavy hand of the RCMP to respond to the 1919 Winnipeg General Strike, where two men were killed. Diefenbaker refused a valid request of the Newfoundland government to deploy the RCMP to quell a strike.

Borden left the country more divided when he left office in 1920 than when he arrived, primarily because his decision to invoke conscription strained national unity. He also failed to defend French-language education rights in Manitoba. While Borden had to contend with the war, he left Quebecers wary of the Conservative Party. Borden went into the business world in retirement, while Diefenbaker, not motivated by money, remained a parliamentarian. An aggregate ranking of Canadian prime ministers lists Borden as the eighth best and Diefenbaker at twelfth out of 23.[1] Diefenbaker was more visionary than

Borden, and there is justification that he left a more enduring mark than the wartime prime minister.

After three losses following Borden, the Conservatives returned to power under R.B. Bennett, who governed during the worst of the Great Depression. Diefenbaker held Bennett in high esteem, primarily because Bennett fought the provinces to implement social programs that directly assisted the poor and the unemployed who were struggling for survival. However, it did not help Bennett's image that he was encamped at the luxurious Chateau Laurier hotel when in high office. While he was portrayed as priggish and aloof, he took his laissez-faire party against its grain to provide government relief for the oppressed, disadvantaged and hungry.

However, Bennett did not fully succeed in implementing the programs that he thought were necessary. The Conservatives split into two parties for the 1935 election, and Bennett became a one-time prime minister with a mixed record. While he implemented many institutional reforms that have endured to this day, Bennett does not have a record of accomplishment or political legacy that comes close to Diefenbaker.

Brian Mulroney is the only Conservative leader not to have lost a general election, winning two majority governments.[2] Mulroney and Diefenbaker won the largest majorities in Canadian history: Diefenbaker in 1958 with 208 seats and 53 percent of the vote and Mulroney in 1984 with 211 seats and 50 percent of the vote. Unlike Diefenbaker, Mulroney was popular in his caucus. Mulroney left a legacy of generational nation-building initiatives, such as free trade with the United States and Mexico, something Diefenbaker would have opposed. He replaced the Manufacturers Sales Tax with the widely despised Goods and Services Tax, scrapped the National Energy Program, and led massive privatizations of federal Crown Corporations. Similar to Diefenbaker, he took a bold stand against the apartheid regime of South Africa and imposed trade sanctions over the objections of American and British allies.

Mulroney was given significant credit for the release of Nelson Mandela and the end of the apartheid regime. For his part, Diefenbaker spoke out against apartheid and ensured that South Africa was not allowed to remain as part of the Commonwealth of Nations. Mulroney and Diefenbaker were hampered by obstinate governors of the Bank of Canada, although Mulroney was less inclined to a public feud. Mulroney admired Diefenbaker as a prime minister and regularly mentioned him when giving political speeches. Mulroney retold one story about Diefenbaker where, at a formal dinner, he insisted on a second pat of butter for his bread. Despite the waiter's insistence on adhering to the rule of one pat of butter per guest, Diefenbaker thundered, "Excuse me, but do you know who I am? I am the prime minister of Canada, and I would like another pat of butter, please." Mulroney delivered the waiter's response with impeccable timing: "Do you know who *I* am? I am the person who hands out the butter." Mulroney told this and other stories to make the point that the man who hands out the butter matters just as much as the prime minister.[3] On this point, the two prime ministers would agree.

Mulroney and Diefenbaker differed most in their views on Quebec's place in Canada. Diefenbaker advocated for "One Canada," where provinces and the citizens therein were equal in all respects. Mulroney believed that Quebec was a "distinct society" and that a failure to recognize that fact fanned the flames of separatism. Recognizing Quebec as a "distinct society" aligned with the views of Macdonald, who believed the French in Canada should be treated as a nation. Mulroney crafted the Meech Lake Accord with all provincial premiers to acknowledge that reality. The agreement was ratified in the Parliament of Canada with the support of all political parties. However, it failed re-ratification in Newfoundland and Labrador after its government had changed, and its new premier, Clyde Wells, was determined to defeat it. Wells was acting in line with the first principles enunciated not just by Diefenbaker and, more importantly at the time, by Pierre Trudeau, who also opposed special status for Quebec. With the failure of Meech, the Quebec wing of the Progressive Conservative party went its separate way, and western alienation deepened, exemplified best by the rise of the Reform party.

After Mulroney resigned in early 1993, an exceptionally weak performance by his successor, Kim Campbell, led to the near-death of the Progressive Conservative party. Such a fate never fell upon the party under Diefenbaker. Both Mulroney and Diefenbaker were given grand state funerals. Diefenbaker was remembered for his attachment to ordinary Canadians and Mulroney for having the courage to implement bold nation-building initiatives.

Stephen Harper is an unabashed admirer of Diefenbaker, and they have many similarities. Both men won one majority and two minority governments and lost two elections. Both identified with ordinary Canadians and were mistrustful of the public service. Neither much cared for the elite, academics or the wealthy. They were proud Canadian nationalists, though Harper, as an economist, worked to expand free trade deals with multiple countries while Diefenbaker retained a Macdonald-like suspicion of free trade, at least vis-à-vis the United States. Neither implemented many unpopular reforms, but when they did, there were solid reasons for doing so.

Diefenbaker cancelled the Avro Arrow because the airplane project had become wasteful. Harper cancelled income trusts, an innovative scheme that saved corporations and their shareholders billions of dollars in taxes. CEOs and seniors loved income trusts because companies with such structures could pay much less tax and much higher dividends. Harper's government pulled the plug on the scheme to protect federal finances from systemic erosion. Diefenbaker wanted to lower taxes, as did Harper, who notably reduced the federal GST rate from seven percent to five percent. As Mulroney said, it was good politics and bad economics since most who studied the cut advocated that income tax reductions would have produced better overall results.

Harper and Diefenbaker were guided by their sense of Canadian values but did not hesitate to treat their political opponents with disdain. Harper was more cunning, proroguing Parliament after opposition forces ganged up against him after he tried to strip away their public financing. Harper led a government of incremental change, always sensitive to public opinion. Harper controlled his party, caucus and cabinet more tightly and effectively than did Diefenbaker. They both governed during recessions, although the global financial crisis of 2007-08 was more consequential and potentially more catastrophic. In responding to the crisis, Harper took advantage of the exceptionally strong financial position that he inherited from Jean Chrétien's government. Harper believed the Québécois—the people and not the province—were a nation "within a united Canada." Harper placed a motion to that end before Parliament that passed by a vote of 265 to 16. Diefenbaker would likely have been one of the sixteen. Harper wisely resigned as leader after his government was defeated in 2015, while Diefenbaker dug in after losing in 1963 and ran again in the 1965 election.

Harper's legacy is more political, notable for partnering with Progressive Conservative leader Peter MacKay to create the Conservative Party of Canada and reclaiming power from the Liberals that had won four consecutive contests. While Harper had more of a libertarian orientation, Diefenbaker transformed social programs that paved the way for deeper and enduring reform of health care and pensions. Harper does not have an equivalent to Diefenbaker's Bill of Rights or extending the vote to Indigenous people, although his government issued a historic apology for residential school abuse. Diefenbaker's legacy is progressive. Harper is more as an incremental conservative.

Macdonald, Borden, Bennett, Diefenbaker, Mulroney and Harper are giants of the Conservative party and of Canada. The historians and political commentators who contend that Diefenbaker does not belong among the great prime ministers have misunderstood his meaning and legacy. He was a freedom fighter and he did battle for Canadian liberties and independence. In this respect, he was a great prime minister and a great Canadian.

BIBLIOGRAPHY

Berger, Thomas R. *Fragile Freedoms: Human Rights and Dissent in Canada*. Rev. ed. Toronto: Clarke, Irwin, 1982.

Black, Conrad. ***Duplessis***. Toronto: McClelland & Stewart, 1977.

- *Rise to Greatness: The History of Canada from the Vikings to the Present:* Toronto: McClelland & Stewart, 2014.

Blake, Raymond B., *Canada's Prime Ministers and the Shaping of a National Identity*, UBC Press, Vancouver-Toronto, 20124

Bliss, Michael. *Right Honourable Men: The Descent of Canadian Politics from Macdonald to Mulroney*. Harper Collins. Toronto, Canada, 1994.

Bothwell, Robert, Ian Drummond, and John English. *Canada Since 1945: Power, Politics, and Provincialism*. Rev. ed. Toronto: University of Toronto Press, 1989.

Bothwell, Robert, and William Kilbourn. *C.D. Howe: A Biography*. Toronto: McClelland & Stewart, 1979.

Bowering, George. *Egotists and Autocrats: The Prime Ministers of Canada*. Viking, Toronto, 1999.

Boyko, John. *Cold Fire: Kennedy's Northern Front*. Knopf Canada, 2016.

Brimelow, Peter. *The Patriot Game: National Dreams and Political Realities*, Key Porter Books, Toronto, Ontario, 1986.

Camp, Dalton. *Gentlemen, Players & Politicians*. Toronto: McClelland & Stewart, 1970.

— *Points of Departure*. Toronto: Deneau and Greenberg, 1979.

Campagna, Palmiro. *Storms of Controversy: The Secret Arrow Files Revealed*. Toronto: Stoddart, 1992.

— *The Avro Arrow: For the Record Paperback*, Dundurn Press; 2 edition, 2024.

Carrigan, D. Owen. *Canadian Party Platforms, 1867–1968*. Toronto: Copp, Clark, 1968.

Chrétien, Jean. *Straight From the Heart*. Key Porter Books, Toronto, Canada. 1985.

Cavell, Janice (Editor), Ryan M. Touhey (Editor): *Reassessing the Rogue Tory: Canadian Foreign Relations in the Diefenbaker Era*. UBC Press. Vancouver, Canada. 2019.

Coates, Robert C. *The Night of the Knives*. Fredericton: Brunswick Press, 1969.

Courtney, John. *Revival and Change: The 1957 and 1958 Diefenbaker Elections*, UBC Press, Vancouver, Canada, 2022.

Donaldson, Gordon, *Fifteen Men: Canada's Prime Ministers from Macdonald to Trudeau*, Doubleday Canada, Toronto, 1969.

Dow, James. *The Arrow*. Toronto: James Lorimer, 1992.

Diefenbaker, John G.

— *One Canada: The Crusading Years*

— *One Canada: The Years of Achievement*

– *One Canada: The Tumultuous Years*

– *The Wit & Wisdom of John Diefenbaker*. Hurtig, 1982.

– *Personal letters of a public man: The family letters of John G. Diefenbaker*, Editor Thad McIlroy. Doubleday Canada. 1985.

Dutil, Patrice. Ed. *Statesmen, Strategists, and Diplomats: Canada's Prime Ministers and the Making of Foreign Policy*. UBC Press, Vancouver, B.C. 2023.

Dutil, Patrice. *Sir John A. Macdonald & the Apocalyptic Year 1885*, Sutherland House, Toronto, 2024.

English, John. *Shadow of Heaven: The Life of Lester Pearson, vol. 1: 1897–1948*. Toronto: Lester & Orpen Dennys, 1989

– *The Worldly Years: The Life of Lester Pearson, vol. 2: 1949–1972*. Toronto: Knopf Canada, 1992

Fleming, Donald M. *So Very Near: The Political Memoirs of Honourable Donald M. Fleming, vol. 1:*

– *The Rising Years, vol. 2:* The Summit Years. Toronto: McClelland & Stewart, 1985

Gilbert, Martin. *Never Despair: Winston S. Churchill, 1945–1965*. Toronto: Stoddart, 1988

Glassford, Larry A. *Reaction and Reform: The Politics of the Conservative Party under R.B. Bennett, 1927–1938*. Toronto: University of Toronto Press, 1992

Goodman, Eddie. *Life of the Party: The Memoirs of Eddie Goodman*. Toronto: Canada, Key Porter, 1988

Grafftey, Heward. *Lessons from the Past: From Dief to Mulroney*. Montreal, Canada: Eden Press, 1987

Grant, George. *Lament for a Nation: The Defeat of Canadian Nationalism*. Toronto, Canada: McClelland & Stewart, 1965

Granatstein, J.L. *The Politics of Survival: The Conservative Party of Canada, 1939–1945*. Toronto: University of Toronto Press, 1967

Gwyn, Richard. *The Shape of Scandal: A Study of a Government in Crisis*. Toronto: Clarke, Irwin, 1965

– *John A: The Man Who Made Us*, Random House of Canada 2007.

– *Nation Maker: Sir John A. Macdonald: His Life, Our Times*, Random House of Canada, 2012

Haydon, Peter T. *The 1962 Cuban Missile Crisis: Canadian Involvement Reconsidered*. Toronto: Canadian Institute of Strategic Studies, 1993.

Holt, Simma. *The Other Mrs. Diefenbaker*. Toronto, Canada: Doubleday Canada, 1982

Horne, Alistair. *Macmillan 1957–1986*, volume 2 of the official biography. London: Macmillan, 1989

Hutchison, Bruce. *The Unfinished Country: To Canada with Love and Some Misgivings*. Vancouver: Douglas & McIntyre, 1985

Ibbitson, John. *The Duel: Diefenbaker, Pearson and the Making of Modern Canada*. Signal. 2023.

Ignatieff, George. *The Making of a Peacemonger: The Memoirs of George Ignatieff*, University of Toronto Press, Dec 15 1985, Toronto, 1985.

Jockel, Joseph T. *No Boundaries Upstairs: Canada, The United States, and the Origins of North American Air Defence, 1945–1958*. Vancouver: University of British Columbia Press, 1987.

Kilbourn, William. *Pipeline: TransCanada and the Great Debate, A History of Business and Politics*. Toronto: Clarke, Irwin, 1970.

Kyba, Patrick. *Alvin: A Biography of the Honourable Alvin Hamilton, P.C. Regina:* Canadian Plains Research Center, 1989.

LaMarsh, Judy. *Memoirs of a Bird in a Gilded Cage*. Toronto: McClelland & Stewart, 1968.

Legault, Albert, and Michel Fortmann. *A Diplomacy of Hope: Canada and Disarmament, 1945–1988*. Montreal: McGill-Queen's University Press, 1992.

Levine, Allan. *Scrum Wars: The Prime Ministers and the Media*. Toronto: Dundurn Press, 1993.

Lynch, Charles. *You Can't Print That: Memoirs of a Political Voyeur*. Hurtig Publishers, Edmonton, 1983.

Martin, Lawrence. *The Presidents and the Prime Ministers: Washington and Ottawa face to face: the myth of bilateral bliss, 1867-1982*. Doubleday Canada. 1982.

Martin, Paul. *A Very Public Life, Vol. 1. Ottawa:* Deneau, 1983.

– *A Very Public Life, Vol. 2*. Ottawa: Deneau, 1985.

Meisel, John. *The Canadian General Election of 1957*. Toronto: University of Toronto Press, 1964.

– Ed., *Papers on the 1962 Election*. Toronto: University of Toronto Press, 1964.

McMahon, Patricia. *Essence of Indecision: Diefenbaker's Nuclear Policy, 1957-1963*. McGill-Queens University Press. Montreal, Canada. 2009

Mulroney, Brian. *Memoirs*. Toronto, Canada: McClelland & Stewart, 2007.

Nash, Knowlton. *Kennedy and Diefenbaker: Fear and Loathing Across the Undefended Border*, McClelland & Stewart. Toronto, Canada. 1990.

Newman, Peter C. *Renegade in Power: The Diefenbaker Years*. McClelland & Stewart. Toronto, Canada. 1963.

Nielsen, Erik. *The House is not a Home: An Autobiography*, Toronto, Macmillan, 1989.

O'Sullivan, Sean (with Rod McQueen). *Both My Houses: From Politics to Priesthood*. Toronto: Key Porter, 1986

Pearson, Lester B. Mike: *The Memoirs of the Right Honourable Lester B. Pearson, vol. 1: 1897–1948;*

– Mike: *The Memoirs of the Right Honourable Lester B. Pearson: vol. 2: 1948-1957*

– Mike: *The Memoirs of the Right Honourable Lester B. Pearson: vol. 3: 1957-1968*.

Toronto: University of Toronto Press, 1974

Perlin, George C. *The Tory Syndrome: Leadership Politics in the Progressive Conservative Party*. Montreal: McGill-Queen's University Press, 1980

Pickersgill, J.W. *The Road Back*. Toronto: University of Toronto Press, 1986

– *Seeing Canada Whole: A Memoir*. Markham: Fitzhenry & Whiteside, 1994

Plamondon, Bob. *Full Circle: Death and Resurrection: Canadian Conservative Politics*. Key Porter, Toronto, Canada, 2006

– *Blue Thunder: The Truth about Conservatives from Macdonald to Harper*, Key Porter, Toronto, Canada, 2009

– *The Truth About Trudeau,* Great River Media. Ottawa, Canada. 2013

– *The Shawinigan Fox: How Jean Chrétien Defied the Elites and Reshaped Canada,* Great River Media, 2017

Powell, James, *The Bank of Canada of James Elliot Coyne: Challenges, Confrontation and Change.* McGill-Queen's University Press, 2009.

Reeves, Richard. *President Kennedy: Profile of Power.* New York: Simon & Schuster, 1993

Ritchie, Charles. *Diplomatic Passport: More Undiplomatic Diaries, 1946–1962.* Toronto: Macmillan, 1981.

Robertson, Heather. *More than a Rose: Prime Ministers, Wives and Other Women.* Toronto: Seal Books, 1991

Robinson, Basil. *Diefenbaker's World: A Populist in Foreign Affairs,* University of Toronto Press. Toronto, Canada. 1989.

Schmitz, Gerald. *Canadian Nationalism in the 1960s: The Voices of Walter Gordon.* Edmonton: Hurtig Publishers, 1980

Sevigny, Pierre, *This Game of Politics.* McLelland & Stewart, Toronto, 1965.

Simpson, Jeffrey. *Faultlines: Struggling for a Canadian Vision.* Harper Collins, Toronto, Canada. 1993

Skelton, H. Basil. *Diefenbaker's World: A Populist in Foreign Affairs.* Toronto: University of Toronto Press, 1989

Smith, Denis. *Rogue Tory: The Life and Legend of John G. Diefenbaker.* Macfarlane Walter & Ross. 1995.

Sorenson, Ted. *Kennedy.* Harper & Row. 1965

Spencer, Dick. *Trumpets and Dreams: John Diefenbaker on the Campaign Trail,* Douglas & McIntyre, Vancouver, 1994.

Stevens, Geoffrey. *The Player: The Life and Times of Dalton Camp.* Key Porter Books. Toronto, Canada. 2003.

Story, Donald C. (Editor), R. Bruce Shepard (Editor) at al. *The Diefenbaker Legacy: Canadian Politics Law and Society Since 1957.* Canadian Plains Research Center, Regina, Canada. 1998.

Stewart, Greig. *Shutting Down the National Dream: A.V. Roe and the Tragedy of the Avro Arrow.* Toronto: McGraw-Hill Ryerson, 1988

Stewart, Walter. *Stanfield: A Political Biography.* Toronto: McClelland & Stewart, 1976

Stursberg, Peter. *Diefenbaker: Leadership Gained, 1956–62.* Toronto: University of Toronto Press, 1975

– *Diefenbaker: Leadership Lost, 1962–67.* Toronto: University of Toronto Press, 1976

Tarnopolsky, Walter Surma. *The Canadian Bill of Rights.* 2nd rev. ed. Toronto: McClelland & Stewart, 1975

Van Dusen, Thomas. *The Chief.* Toronto: McGraw-Hill, 1968

Whitaker, Reginald, and Gary Marcuse. *Cold War Canada: The Making of a National Insecurity State, 1945–1957.* Toronto: University of Toronto Press, 1994

Williams, John R. *The Conservative Party of Canada, 1920–1949.* Durham: Duke University Press, 1956

Wilson, Garrett, and Kevin Wilson. *Diefenbaker for the Defence.* Toronto: James Lorimer, 1988

ENDNOTES

Preface

1. Right Honorable Men, Bliss. P. 186.
2. "Baird's Diefenbaker hero worship is unfounded," Andrew Cohen, Ottawa Citizen, March 31, 2014.
3. Years of Achievement, p. 265. The oral version of these remarks is widely available on the internet, such as <https://www.youtube.com/watch?v=gnlYr4wML2M&ab_channel=TributetoCanada>, accessed December 10, 2024.

Chapter 1: A Many of Destiny

1. Crusading Years, p. 1.
2. Crusading Years, p. 66.
3. Crusading Years, p. 66.
4. Crusading Years, p. 78.
5. Crusading Years, p. 55.
6. Crusading Years, p. 75.
7. Crusading Years, p. 83.
8. Crusading Years, p.53.
9. Renegade in Power, p. 26.
10. Crusading Years, p. 79.
11. "Dief," National Film Board Documentary, <https://youtu.be/-gWwVpkpsvM>, accessed July 17, 2024
12. Crusading Years, p. 87.
13. Rogue Tory, p. 30.

Chapter 2: An Early Calling: The Practice of Law

1. Crusading Years, p. 93.
2. Crusading Years, p. 70.
3. Crusading Years, p. 94.
4. Crusading Years, p. 95
5. Persons Sentenced to Death in Canada, 1867-1976: An Inventory of Case Files in the Fonds of the Department of Justice, <https://publications.gc.ca/collections/collection_2017/bac-lac/SB4-46-1994-eng.pdf>, accessed November 13, 2024.
6. Ken Whiteway, The Legal Career of John G. Diefenbaker <https://harvest.usask.ca/server/api/core/bitstreams/dccb1147-b55e-40d4-8d9d-dc87738f090c/content>, p. 13, accessed November 7, 2024.
7. J.A. Munro, ed., The Wit and Wisdom of John Diefenbaker (Edmonton: Hurtig, 1982), p. 71. See also, Spencer, p. 3.
8. Whiteway, 2024.
9. R. v. Harms, [1936] 3 D.L.R. 497, [1936] 2 W.W.R. 114, 66 C.C.C. 134 (Sask. C.A.).
10. "Court Gives Doomed Man Life Chance," Star Weekly, May 09, 1936, P. 1.
11. "L'affaire de l'école Éthier" (1992), Revue historique 3, 1 <http://musee.historiesk.ca/l-146-affaire-de-l-146-ecole-ethier-n155-t952.html>, accessed November 7, 2024.
12. Crusading Years, p. 115.
13. Diefenbaker for the Defence, Garrett Wilson, Lorimer, January 1, 1988, p. 274.

14. Whiteway, 2024.
15. Crusading Years, p. 124

Chapter 3: Unfulfilled Ambitions

1. Crusading Years, p. 64.
2. "Census debate is nothing new," Bill Curry, *Globe and Mail*, August 16, 2010
3. Crusading Years, p. 141.
4. Right Honourable Men, Bliss, p. 187.
5. Crusading Years, p. 166.
6. Rogue Tory, p. 81.
7. Crusading Years, p. 173.
8. Crusading Years, p. 175.
9. "States Albertans are Disillusioned," *Toronto Star*, May 26, 1938, P. 2.
10. "Hepurn Sows Disruption Conservatives are Told," *Toronto Star*, July 6, 1938, P. 35.
11. Crusading Years, p. 177.

Chapter 4: Ottawa-bound: Dief the Chief

1. Rogue Tory, p. 38.
2. "The Chief's unknown and vivacious first love: The other Mrs. Diefenbaker," Geoffrey Stevens, *Globe and Mail*; Toronto, ON, 25 Sep 1982: p. E.16.
3. Spencer, p. 4.
4. Crusading Years, p. 165.
5. "Mrs. J. Diefenbaker dies – Was popular in Ottawa," Douglas How, The Evening Citizen, February 8, 1951, P. 19.
6. Crusading Years, p. 222.
7. Hansard, April 23, 1947, p. 2331.
8. "Would life ban on communists and Jehovah's Witnesses," *Toronto Star*, February 27, 1943, P 21.
9. The Crusading Years, p. 233.
10. "Wants charter rewritten," The Toronto Star, November 27, 1945, P. 13.
11. "Ten thousand attend mass rally of Zionists," *Toronto Star*, October 9, 1945, P. 4.
12. Rogue Tory, p. 129.
13. Crusading Years, p. 251.
14. "Bracken Nearly Misses Out – Nomination Barely in Time," *Toronto Star*, December 11, 1942, P. 4.
15. Crusading Years, p. 252.
16. "Diefenbaker and Green will vote for allowances," *Toronto Star*, July 28, 1944, P. 6.
17. Rogue Tory, p. 169.
18. Rogue Tory, p. 170.
19. Rogue Tory, p. 171.
20. Rogue Tory, p. 156.
21. Spencer, p. 20.

22. Rogue Tory, p. 173.
23. Spencer, p. 10.
24. Crusading Years, p. 262.
25. Blue Thunder, p. 224.
26. Dalton Camp, Gentlemen, p. 145.
27. Blue Thunder, p. 221.
28. Rogue Tory, p. 567.
29. "Diefenbaker Pledges PC's To Be People's Party," *Globe and Mail*; Toronto, ON, 14 Dec 1956: 1.
30. "Baler Says Quebec Slighted by Favorite," Harvey Hickey, *Globe and Mail*; Toronto, Ont.. 14 Dec 1956: 1
31. Rogue Tory, p. 210.
32. CBC (1956), "Leadership at last for John Diefenbaker" <https://www.cbc.ca/player/play/video/1.3593853>, accessed July 17, 2024.
33. Brimelow, Peter, p. 59
34. The Crusading Years, p. 282.

Chapter 5: 1957: From Opposition to Minority

1. Years of Achievement, p. 4.
2. Rogue Tory, p. 214.
3. Years of Achievement, p. 6.
4. The Years of Achievement, p. 16.
5. The Player: The Life and Times of Dalton Camp, p. 101.
6. Rise to Greatness, Conrad Black, p. 795.
7. The Years of Achievement, p. 20.
8. Years of Achievement, p. 32.
9. Spencer, p. 32.
10. Lynch, p. 139.
11. The Duel, p. 166.
12. Years of Achievement, p. 34.
13. Bible, Matthew 20:27.
14. The Years of Achievement, p. 52.
15. Renegade in Power, p. 93.
16. The Years of Achievement, p. 51.
17. The Years of Achievement, p. 53.
18. "Canadian Medicare as a Policy Success," Gregory Marchildon, chapter in "Policy Success in Canada: Cases, Lessons, Challenges," July, 2022, Oxford University Press, p. 21
19. Government of Canada Canada Year Book, 1964, p. 262.
20. The Crusading Years, p. 75.
21. Years of Achievement, p. 191.
22. The Crusading Years, p. 79.
23. "John George Diefenbaker, 1895-1979 The Chief: a political survivor who knew his place in history," *Globe and Mail*; Toronto, Ont.. 17 Aug 1979: P.9.
24. https://www.cbc.ca/player/play/video/1.3593831, accessed July 17, 2024.

Chapter 6: 1958: Minority to Majority

1. House of Commons, Hansard, January 20, 1958.
2. Rise to Greatness, Conrad Black, p. 793.
3. Spencer, p. 49.
4. Spencer, p. 51
5. House of Commons Debates, January 21, 1958.
6. Lynch, p. 142.
7. Right Honourable Men, Bliss, p. 191.
8. Blue Thunder, p. 230.
9. Stevens, p. 113.
10. Cohen, Andrew, "Lester Pearsons lessons for today's defeated Liberals," Toronto Star, October 22, 2008.
11. "Dief," National Film Board Documentary, NFIB.ca/film/dief/ accessed July 17, 2024
12. One Canada, In Memoriam chapter, p. xx
13. One Canada, Years of Achievement, p. 299.
14. Crusading Years, P. 234.

Chapter 7: The 1960 Bill of Rights

1. Crusading Years, p. 16.
2. Hansard, March 21, 1946, p. 137-8.
3. *Globe and Mail* editorial, May 10, 1946.
4. The Crusading Years, p. 253.
5. Years of Achievement, P 253.
6. "Canada, Department of External Affairs, Statements and Speeches, No. 59/5, 12, January 1959.
7. The Crusading Years, p. 317.
8. Spencer, p. x.

Chapter 8: Our Home and Native Land

1. Crusading Years, p. 29.
2. Crusading Years, p. 29.
3. Crusading Years, p. 27.
4. "The Chief" video documentary, Part 2 of 4, 14:00.
5. The Crusading Years, p. 117.
6. Hansard, House of Commons Debates, April 8, 1942.
7. Aboriginal People: History of Discriminatory Laws, Wendy Moss, Elaine Gardner-O'Toole, Law and Government Division, November 1987, Revised November 1991
8. "To vilify Sir John A. Macdonald is to wrongly seek a single scapegoat for Canada's mistreatment of Indigenous people," Bob Plamondon, *Globe and Mail*, February 19, 2018
9. Dutil: 1885, p. 162.
10. Dutil: 1885, p. 173.
11. Diefenbaker Canada Centre, "The Enfranchisement of Aboriginal Peoples in Canada" <https://diefenbaker.usask.ca/exhibits/online-exhibits-content/the-enfranchisement-of-aboriginal-peoples-in-canada-en.php> accessed December 10, 2024.

12. House of Commons, Hansard, March 25, 1955

13. House of Commons, Hansard, October 29, 1957.

14. Crusading Years, p. 30.

15. Diefenbaker Canada Centre, <https://diefenbaker.usask.ca/exhibits/online-exhibits-content/the-enfranchisement-of-aboriginal-peoples-in-canada-en.php#RelatedDocuments>, accessed June 12, 2024

16. Hopper, Tristin, "Here is what Sir John A. Macdonald did to Indigenous people," National Post, Aug 28, 2018.

17. "Will the Indian vote turn any tides," James Gladstone, *Globe and Mail* Toronto, Ont.. 25 June 1960: A19

18. Statistics Canada, Canada Year Book. <https://www66.statcan.gc.ca/acyb_000-eng.htm>.

19. "In 1966, a sacred aboriginal rock was blown up to make way for a man-made lake. Now divers search for remnants," Published Aug 27, 2014

20. National Centre for Truth and Reconciliation, "Churchill" <https://nctr.ca/residential-schools/manitoba/churchill/>, accessed June 13, 2024.

21. Interview with the author, 2024.

22. Spencer, p. 94.

23. Spencer, p. 167.

24. National Centre for Truth and Reconciliation, University of Manitoba, https://nctr.ca/exhibits/residential-school-timeline/

25. Canada Year Book, 1964, p. 187.

26. Treble, Patricia and Jane O'Hara, "Residential Church School Scandal," Maclean's, March 17, 2003.

27. "Other Nations Envy Canada's Church Role," *Toronto Star*, May 30, 1958, P. 33.

28. "Indian Women on the Warpath," Ann Blanchard, Star Weekly, November 12, 1960, P. 42.

29. "The 'rational treatment' that made kids suffer. Residential schools were built for cultural assimilation,"Willow Fiddler, Globe and Mail, September 30, 2024

30. "Canada's Residential Schools: The History, Part 2: 1939 to 2000, Thee Final Report of the Truth and Reconciliation Commission of Canada (Volume 1), McGill-Queen's University Press, 2015, p. 399.

31. Canada's Residential Schools: The History, Part 2, 1939 to 2000, The Final Report of the Truth and Reconciliation Commission of Canada, published 2015, p. 20.

32. Canadian Geographic, "History of Residential Schools" <https://indigenouspeoplesatlasofcanada.ca/article/history-of-residential-schools/>, accessed December 10, 2024.

Chapter 9: The Avro Arrow

1. Library and Archives Canada, The Diefenbaker Papers, MG XIV/D/23.

2. Rogue Tory, p. 310.

3. Rogue Tory, p. 314.

4. Shattered Illusions: KGB Cold War Espionage in Canada, Donald G. Mahar, Rowman & Littlefield Publishers (Dec 31 2016)

5. *Globe and Mail*, September 25, 1958.

6. Fraser, Blair, "Backstage at Ottawa: What Led Canada to Junk the Arrow," Maclean's, October 25, 1958.

7. Saskatoon Star-Phoenix, September 25, 1968.

8. The Tumultuous Years, P. 42.

9. CBC (1964), "John Diefenbaker defends his Avro Arrow decision" <https://www.cbc.ca/player/play/video/1.3593864>, accessed July 17, 2024.

Chapter 10: A Declaration of Cold War Independence

1. Chrétien, My Years as Prime Minister, 265.
2. Knight, Amy. *How the Cold War Began: The Igor Gouzenko Affair and the Hunt for Soviet Spies.* (2005). Toronto, Ontario: McClelland & Stewart.
3. Edelgard Mahant and Graeme Mount, *Invisible and Inaudible in Washington*, UBC Press, April 15 1999, p. 31.
4. Renegade in Power, p.25.
5. The Crusading Years, p. 147.
6. "Under your Inspired Leadership – Dwight Eisenhower, Canadians, and the United States Consensus, 1945-1961" Asa McKercher and Michael Stevenson," International Journal, 2020 Vol 75(4), p. 473.
7. "Eisenhower Shoots 90 at Ottawa: Game Is Unimpeded by Extensive Hunt for 'Assassins'," Felix Belair Jr., New York Times, July 11, 1958, p. 3.
8. Cold Fire, p. 65.
9. Library and Archives Canada, Diefenbaker Papers. Reel M-9378.
10. Cold Fire, p. 71.
11. The Crusading Years, p. 165.
12. Memo from Secretary of State Dean Rusk to President Kennedy, JFK Library and Museum, Box 113.
13. Cold Fire, p. 86.
14. Rogue Tory, p. 382.
15. Right Honourable Men, Bliss, p. 210.
16. Interview with the author (2009).
17. Knowlton Nash, p. 113.
18. The American Presidency Project, "Radio and Television Report to the American People on the Berlin Crisis. July 25, 1961" <https://www.presidency.ucsb.edu/documents/radio-and-television-report-the-american-people-the-berlin-crisis>, accessed November 9, 2024.
19. The Guardian (Oct. 29, 2019), "Checkpoint Charlie by Iain MacGregor review – Berlin's secrets and spies" <https://www.theguardian.com/books/2019/oct/27/checkpoint-charlie-iain-macgregor-review-secrets-spies-cold-war-berlin>, accessed December 10, 2024.
20. "JFK's old pollster speaks on role in Canadian elections: 'Highlight of my life'", Alexander Panetta, The Canadian Press, Nov. 22, 2013.
21. "The Wordly Years: The Life of Lester B. Pearson," John English, Alred A. Knopf Canada, 1992, p. 247.
22. "Ultimate Destiny Delayed: The Liberals, the Organization of American States, and Canadian Foreign Policy, 1963-1968," Asa McKercher, Diplomacy and Statecraft, Taylor and Francis Group, 2014, p. 473.
23. May 17, 1961, John F. Kennedy, address Before the Canadian Parliament in Ottawa.
24. "In Bed with an Elephant," National Film Board, hosted by Kent Martin, 1986.
25. Years of Achievement, p. 181.

Chapter 11: The Commonwealth and South Africa

1. "Diefenbaker Carries Zealous Crusade for Unity to Heart of Commonwealth," The Ottawa Citizen, November 5, 1958.
2. The Crusading Years, p. 185.
3. Macmillan, Harold, *Pointing the Way*, p. 293.
4. CBC (1961) "John Diefenbaker stares down South Africa" <https://www.cbc.ca/player/play/video/1.3593846>, accessed July 18, 2024.
5. Janice Cavell and Ryan M. Touhey (eds), Reassessing the Rogue Tory: Canadian Foreign Relations in the Diefenbaker Era, p. 52, UBC Press: Vancouver; Toronto, 2018;

Chapter 12: Foreign Affairs and Taking on Nikita Khrushchev

1. Dean Acheson, transcript of interview with Lucius D. Battle, April 27, 1964. JFK Presidential Library and Museum
2. Rogue Tory, p. 303.
3. The Crusading Years, p. 107.
4. The Crusading Years, p. 121.
5. Nikita Khrushchev: Address to the UN General Assembly, Sept. 23 1960. <https://sourcebooks.fordham.edu/mod/1960khrushchev-un1.asp>.

Chapter 13: The James Coyne Affair

1. Crusading Years, p. 15.
2. Crusading Years, p. 42.
3. Crusading Years, p. 46.
4. "Notes for an address by the Prime Minister, the Rt. Hon. John G. Diefenbaker," on *The Nation's Business*, CBC Television, November 12, 1959.
5. "Fleming Sidesteps Question on Expenditure Cuts," Rickey Harvet, *Globe and Mail*, Toronto, Ont. 09 Dec 1957: 13
6. Government of Canada, Canada Year Book (1964), p. 989.
7. Government of Canada, Canada Year Book (1964), p. 293.
8. Government of Canada, Canada Year Book (1964), p. 295.
9. Government of Canada, Canada Year Book (1964), p. 298.
10. Government of Canada, Canada Year Book (1964), p. 310.
11. Budget Speech, House of Commons, April 9, 1959.
12. Government of Canada, Canada Year Book (1964), p. 902.
13. "Benidickson Says Fleming Somersaulted," *Globe and Mail*, 10 Apr 1959: 4.
14. "New Budget Said in Keeping With Fleming," *Globe and Mail*, 10 Apr 1959: 4
15. "Good May Come: Out of Budget: Manufacturer," *Globe and Mail*, 10 Apr 1959: 5.
16. "Washington Expects U.S. to Understand Budgetary Problem," George Bain, *Globe and Mail*, 21 Dec 1960: 25.
17. The Years of Achievement, p. 56.
18. Data on Canadian interest rates in this section were obtained from Statistics Canada, "Financial market statistics, last Wednesday unless otherwise stated, Bank of Canada."
19. Cabinet Conclusions, November 17, 1957.
20. Donald Fleming, So Vey Near, The Political Memoirs of the Honourable Donald M. Fleming Vol. 1, McClelland & Stewart, 1985, 456
21. House of Commons Standing Committee on Banking and Commerce, May 22, 1956, 373-5.
22. Renegade in Power, p. 298.
23. Statistics Canada, <https://www150.statcan.gc.ca/n1/pub/11-210-x/00000/t/4169418-eng.htm>, accessed August 26, 2024.
24. Memorandum to K.W. Taylor, "Mr. Coyne's Calgary Speech", October 14, 1960. National Archives of Canada, RG19, vol. 4099.
25. Hansard from the House of Commons, February 21, 1961.
26. Rogue Tory, p. 407.

27. The Crusading Years, p. 273.
28. Renegade in Power, p.304.
29. Powell, James, The Bank of Canada of James Elliot Coyne, p. 113.
30. Ibid, p. 125
31. "Coyne according to Coyne," National Post; Don Mills, Ont.. 20 Oct 2012: FP.7.
32. Renegade in Power, p. 313.
33. Renegade in Power, p. 316.
34. Years of Achievement, p. 56.
35. Bowering, p. 345.
36. Powell, James, p. 133.
37. Ibid, p. 125.
38. Years of Achievement, p. 277.

Chapter 14: The "Diefendollar"

1. "Fiscal Restraint: A Victory for Fleming," Bruce Macdonald, *Globe and Mail*, 11 Apr 1962: 7
2. Government of Canada, Canada Year Book (1964), p. 914.
3. "Bell Blasts Liberal Diefendollar Gimmick," *Toronto Star*, February 28, 1963, P. 19.
4. Tumultuous Years, p. 122.
5. Ibid, p. 137.

Chapter 15: 1962: Majority to Minority

1. Saturday Review, "The Terrain of Today's Statecraft," August 1, 1959.
2. Cold Fire, p. 151.
3. Cold Fire, p. 152.
4. George Ignatieff, p. 173.
5. Pierre Sevigny, p. 187.
6. Kennedy, Theodore C. Sorenson, p. 575.
7. Knowlton Nash, Kennedy and Diefenbaker Fear and Loathing Across the Undefended Border, p. 160.
8. "JFK's old pollster speaks on role in Canadian elections: 'Highlight of my life'", Alexander Panetta, The Canadian Press, Nov. 22, 2013.
9. Globe and Mail, Toronto, Ont. "In election collusion, JFK and Pearson showed the way," Lawrence Martin, 23 May 2018: A.15.
10. "JFK's old pollster speaks on role in Canadian elections: 'Highlight of my life'", Alexander Panetta, The Canadian Press, Nov. 22, 2013.
11. "'Renegade' Makes Liberals Blush too," Franck McGee, *Toronto Star*, Nov. 16, 1963, P. 8.
12. "JFK's old pollster speaks on role in Canadian elections: 'Highlight of my life'", Alexander Panetta, The Canadian Press, Nov. 22, 2013.
13. Renegade in Power, p. 323.
14. Renegade in Power, p 325.
15. CBC (1962) "Minority setback for Diefenbaker, Tories" <https://www.cbc.ca/player/play/video/1.3274830>, accessed July 17, 2024.

Chapter 16: The Cuban Missile Crisis

1. "Canada, the United States and the Cuban Missile Crisis," Jocelyn Maynard Ghent, Pacific Historical Review, 48:2, May, 1979, 163.
2. "Diefenbaker's World: A Populist in Foreign Affairs," H. Basil Robinson, University of Toronto Press, 1989, p. 166.
3. Tumultuous Years, p. 69.
4. "Canada, the United States and the Cuban Missile Crisis," Jocelyn Maynard Ghent, Pacific Historical Review, 48:2, May, 1979, 173.
5. Renegade in Power, p. 336.
6. Memorandum from Livingston Merchant to Dean Rusk, U.S. Department of State, FRUS, 1961-63, p. 1190
7. Cold Fire, p. 187.
8. Peter T. Haydon, The 1962 Cuban Missile Crisis: Canadian Involvement Reconsidered, Canadian Institute of Strategic Studies, September 1993, p. 124.
9. "A 'Half-hearted Response'?: Canada and the Cuban Missile Crisis, 1962,"Asa McKercher, Trinity Hall, Cambridge, The International History Review, Vol. 33, No. 2, June 2011, 335–352
10. "The Situation Room: The Inside Story of Presidents in Crisis," George Stephanopoulos and Lisa Dickey, Grand Central Publishing, May 14 2024.
11. Cohen, Lester B. Pearson, p. 145.
12. Janice Cavell and Ryan M. Touhey (eds), Reassessing the Rogue Tory: Canadian Foreign Relations in the Diefenbaker Era, p. 109, UBC Press: Vancouver; Toronto, 2018
13. Wit and Wisdom, John Munro, Hurtig Publishers, 1984, p. 103.
14. "Canada and the United States: Ambivalent Allies," John Herd Thompson and Stephen J. Randall, University of Georgia Press, 2002, p. 225.

Chapter 17: 1963: The Nuclear Election

1. Report of the Royal Commission on Taxation, 1966, <https://publications.gc.ca/collections/collection_2014/bcp-pco/Z1-1962-1-1-eng.pdf>, accessed June 6, 2024.
2. Rogue Tory, p. 463.
3. The Tumultuous Years, P. 1.
4. Knowlton Nash, Kennedy and Diefenbaker, p. 217.
5. "Resolution Comes Up Today: Don't Bind Our Hands on Nuclear Policy, Diefenbaker Pleads at PC Convention", Walter Gray, *Globe and Mail*, Toronto, Ont.. 19 Jan 1963: 4.
6. Renegade in Power, p. 342.
7. Toronto Telegram, editorial, January 5, 1963.
8. Renegade in Power, p. 354.
9. "The Wordly Years: The Life of Lester B. Pearson," John English, Alred A. Knopf Canada, 1992, p. 246.
10. Cold Fire, p. 219.
11. Lynch, p. 150.
12. Debates of the House of Commons, January 31, 1963.
13. Office of the Historian, "Telegram From the Embassy in Canada to the Department of State," Ottawa, February 3, 1963, 3 p.m. <https://history.state.gov/historicaldocuments/frus1961-63v13/d445>, accessed April 17, 2024.

14. Interview with the author, 2009.
15. Mulroney Memoirs, p. 79
16. Renegade in Power, p. 370.
17. 445. Telegram from the Embassy in Canada to the Department of State, Office of the Historian, accessed April 17, 2024.
18. The Presidents and the Prime Ministers, Lawrence Martin, Doubleday Canada; Jan. 1 1982, Page 7
19. Tumultuous Years, p. 175.
20. Renegade in Power, p. 378.
21. Tumultuous Years, p. 172.
22. Spencer, p. 85.
23. Spencer, p. 172.
24. Tumultuous Years, p. 180.
25. Tumultuous Years, p. 182.
26. Tumultuous Years, p. 185.
27. Right Honourable Men, Bliss, p. 206.
28. Renegade in Power, p. 384.
29. Renegade in Power, p. 385.
30. Fotheringham, Allan, "NDP hero finds party in shambles," *Globe and Mail*, March 2, 2002.
31. "The Wordly Years: The Life of Lester Pearson – Volume 2," John English, Alfred A. Knopf Canada, 1992, p. 204.
32. Rogue Tory, p. 504.
33. President Kennedy Memorandum to the Secretary of State, April 2, 1963, <https://www.aw-autographen.com/us-presidents/john-f-kennedy/>, accessed April 17, 2024.
34. Knowlton Nash, p. 279.
35. Rogue Tory, p.505
36. Renegade in Power, p. 398.
37. Tumultuous Years, p. 190.
38. The Tumultuous Years, p. 193.
39. The Tumultuous Years, p. 195.
40. Panetta, Alexander, "JFK's old pollster speaks on role in Canadian elections: 'Highlight of my life'"Winnipeg Free Press, Nov. 20, 2013.
41. Washington Daily News, April 23, 1963
42. "U.S. Hails Pearson Win," George Bain, *Globe and Mail*; Toronto, Ont.. 09 Apr 1963: 7.
43. Tumultuous Years, p. 266.
44. "British Happy About Election Outcome, but Disappointed by Lack of Majority," Robert Duffy, *Globe and Mail*; Toronto, Ont.. 10 Apr 1963: 10.
45. "The Next Government," editorial, *Globe and Mail*, Toronto, Ont.. 09 Apr 1963: 6.
46. Pearson Terms Loss of Kennedy A Tragedy for Canada, WorldStanley Westall, *Globe and Mail*; Toronto, Ont.. 23 Nov 1963: 4.
47. "JFK leaves 'untidy world' Dief," *Toronto Star*, November 26, 1963, P. 1.

Chapter 18: Live to Fight Another Day

1. Tumultuous Years, p. 214
2. "The defining Canadian political blockbuster, 50 years later," Allan Levine, National Post, October 2, 2013.

3. "Made—and Unmade—in Canada," Raymond Daniell, The New York Times, August 2, 1964.
4. Renegade in Power, xi.
5. Renegade in Power, p. 5.
6. "Diefenbaker Beats Rebels: Party Hails him as Leader," Norman Phillips," *Toronto Star*, February 5, 1964, P. 1
7. "The Diefenbaker Party", editorial, *Globe and Mail*, Toronto, On, 05 Feb 1964: p. 6.
8. Remarks to the Executive Officers of the Progressive Conservative Association of Canada, October 16, 1963.
9. Mulroney Memoirs, p. 112.
10. The Crusading Years, p. 299.
11. Renegade in Power, p. 166.
12. The Crusading Years, p. 303.
13. Trudeau, Pierre Elliot, Memoirs, p. 182.
14. Tumultuous Years, p. 235.
15. Spencer, p. 55.
16. "Dief's Hour of Trial," Norman Phillips, *Toronto Star*, February 6, 1965, P. 1.
17. "Pauline Jewett Blazes Trails for Women," Doris Anderson, *Toronto Star*, July 16, 1963, p. J1.
18. "The Bird View," John Bird, *Toronto Star*, June 14, 1963, P. 7.
19. "Budget Storm in Commons: Gordon Admits 2 Aides Paid by Private Firms Minister Defends His Action." Walter Gray, *Globe and Mail*. 15 June 1963: 1.
20. The Wordly Years: The Life of Lester B. Pearson, 1949-1972, Alfred A. Knopf Canada, P. 295.
21. Tumultuous Years, p. 217.
22. "PM's Words Unexplainable says Dief," *Toronto Star*, December 18, 1964, P. 27.
23. "Bordeau was 'Palace' for Crime Big Shots, Robert Reguly, *Toronto Star*, March 05, 1965, P. 1.
24. Tumultuous Years, p. 234.

Chapter 19: The Flag Debate

1. "No Time for Flags," *Globe and Mail*, Toronto, Ont.. 29 Sep 1962: 6.
2. Tumultuous Years, 233.
3. Lester Pearson speech to the Royal Canadian Legion, May 17, 1964, Winnipeg, Manitoba.
4. "Diefenbaker: This Flag Hurts Unity," *Toronto Star*, June 16, 1964, P. 1.
5. "Canada's maple leaf flag born amid bitter debate," Paul Hunter, *Toronto Star*, Feb. 14, 2015.
6. "Balcer Invites Closure to End Flag Filibuster: Flag Vote Possible Today," *Globe and Mail*, Toronto, Ont.. 10 Dec 1964:
7. "Flag Rift Among Issues: Baker To Quit PCs, Sit As Independent Electors' Views Sought on Plan," *Globe and Mail*, Toronto, Ont. 21 Dec 1964:
8. Interview with the author, 2024.
9. "Neither Clique Nor Claque: Diefenbaker Calls Tory Rebels Goldwater Reactionaries, Insists He Won't Be Pushed Around," *Globe and Mail*, Toronto, Ont. 18 Feb 1965: 1

Chapter 20: 1965: One Last Shot

1. Tumultuous Years, p. 239.
2. Tumultuous Years, p. 242.
3. Tumultuous Years, p. 244
4. Tumultuous Years, p. 248.

5. Tumultuous Years, p. 249
6. Tumultuous Years, p. 251
7. Distemper of our Times, Peter C. Newman, McGill-Queen's University Press, January 15, 1968, p. 323.
8. The Elections: 1963 and 1965, Craig Baird, <https://canadaehx.com/2021/09/06/the-elections-1963-1965/>, accessed June 1, 2024
9. Distemper, p. 360.
10. Tumultuous Years, p. 260.
11. Tumultuous Years, p. 264.

Chapter 21: A Very Tory Sex Scandal

1. Ibbitson, John, "Diefenbaker and Pearson gave us the Canada that polarization could tear down," *Globe and Mail*, October 7, 2003.
2. "Dief ruled for Sevigny before national Security – Judge," Ottawa Bureau, *Toronto Star*, September 23, 1966, p. 1.
3. Tumultuous Years, p. 269.

Chapter 22: 1966: The Leadership Review

1. Tumultuous Years, p. 274
2. Tumultuous Years, p. 275.
3. Mulroney Memoirs, p. 117.
4. Tumultuous Years, p. 280.
5. "Praise Heaped on the Chief," *Toronto Star*, September 8, 1967, P. 8.
6. Tumultuous years, p. 282.

Chapter 23: A Troublesome Backbencher

1. Spencer, p. 130.
2. Lynch, p. 149.
3. Official Languages Act becomes law in Canada; Bilingualism a divisive issue at the time; bill aimed to promote national unity," Kevin Griffin, The Vancouver Sun, 07 Sep 2019: A.2.
4. House of Commons – May 25, 1961
5. *Globe and Mail*, March 6, 1971.
6. Spencer, p. 148.
7. Spencer, p. 151.
8. Toronto Star, December 8, 2008.
9. Spencer, p. 170.
10. Spencer, p. vii.
11. Rogue Tory, p. 552.
12. "A night for the Chief," Wayne Cheveldayoff, *Globe and Mail*, 20 Feb 1976: 1.
13. "Report of his views on Mulroney too favorable: ex-PM," *Globe and Mail* Toronto, Ont.. 17 Feb 1976: 8
14. Spencer, p. 175.
15. Spencer, p. 205.
16. "Greatness eluded him, historians say," Helen Worthington, *Toronto Star*, August 17, 179, P. 9.

Chapter 24: True North, Strong and Free

1. Spencer, p. 24.
2. There are various studies and approaches in use in evaluating prime ministers. One of the more rigorous is, "Evaluating Prime Ministerial Leadership in Canada: The Results of an Expert Survey," Stephen Azzii and Norman Hillmer, Canadian Political Science Review, Vol. 7, No. 1, 2013, 13-23, p. 13.
3. "Examining Federal Debt in Canada by Prime Ministers Since Confederation," Jake Fuss and Evin Ryan, Fraser Institute, July 2022.
4. Government of Canada, Canada Year Book (1964), p. 915.
5. "Six Stewards of Canada's Economy History by the numbers favours Mulroney and Chrétien, while Trudeau leaves a legacy of deficits and debt," Michael Hartt, Policy Options, June 1, 2003..
6. J.A. Munro, ed., The Wit and Wisdom of John Diefenbaker (Edmonton: Hurtig, 1982), p. 99.
7. "History of Parole in Canada," Government of Canada website accessed July 16, 2024, https://www.canada.ca/en/parole-board/corporate/history-of-parole-in-canada.html#p4
8. "Pierre Juneau doesn't deserve reputation as a savior of CBC," William Fox, The Windsor Star; 08 Aug 1989: A7.
9. "Static from Ottawa interferes with CBC," Thomas Walkom, *Toronto Star*, 14 Nov 1998: 1.
10. "Diefenbaker's vision had merit," Geoffrey Johnston, Kingston Whig - Standard; Kingston, Ont.. 21 Mar 2014: B.5.
11. The Crusading Years, p. 282.
12. Dutil, p. 205.
13. Janice Cavell and Ryan M. Touhey (eds), Reassessing the Rogue Tory: Canadian Foreign Relations in the Diefenbaker Era, Asa McKercher, UBC Press: Vancouver; Toronto, 2018, P. 169.
14. Janice Cavell and Ryan M. Touhey (eds), Reassessing the Rogue Tory: Canadian Foreign Relations in the Diefenbaker Era, Stephen Azzi, UBC Press: Vancouver; Toronto, 2018, P. 104.
15. Spencer, p. 91.
16. CBC (1956) "Leadership at last for John Diefenbaker" <https://www.cbc.ca/player/play/video/1.3593853>, accessed July 17, 2024.

Chapter 25: The Chief's Leadership Qualities: Vision, Courage, Contrarian

1. "Help Government Win War Prairie Conservative Urges," The *Toronto Star*, November 23, 1940, P 17.
2. Spencer, p. 195.

Postscript: Contrasting Conservative Prime Ministers

1. Based on expert polls conducted by *Maclean's* in 1997, 20011 and 2016. For an aggregation of the polls see <https://en.wikipedia.org/wiki/Historical_rankings_of_prime_ministers_of_Canada>, accessed August 28, 2024.
2. Sir Robert Borden won two majorities, the second of which was not under the Conservative banner as he had formed a Union coalition that included Liberals for the election in 1917.
3. Caroline Mulroney Eulogy to the Rt. Hon. Brian Mulroney, March 23, 2024, <https://www.youtube.com/watch?v=XJgUIpKh1Lw&ab_channel=CTVNews>, accessed October 4, 2024.

INDEX

BOOKS BY BOB PLAMONDON

The Shawinigan Fox: How Jean Chrétien Defied the Elites and Reshaped Canada

The Truth About Trudeau

Blue Thunder: The Truth About Conservatives from Macdonald to Harper

Full Circle: Death and Resurrection in Canadian Conservative Politics

Hay West: A Story of Canadians Helping Canadians

ABOUT THE ARISTOTLE FOUNDATION FOR PUBLIC POLICY

The Aristotle Foundation for Public Policy is a new educational and public policy think tank that aims to renew a common-sense approach to public discourse and public policy in Canada. The Aristotle Foundation is a federally registered Not for Profit Corporation and a registered charity under the federal Income Tax Act. Donations are eligible for a charitable tax receipt.

www.aristotlefoundation.org